I AM
THE
OTHER

I AM THE OTHER

Debating the Role of Islam in a Divided America

IMAM AZHAR SUBEDAR
ROBERT GARY

LIMINAL SPACE PUBLICATIONS

I am the Other

Published by Liminal Space Publications

ISBN (paperback): 9781662956201
eISBN: 9781662956218

Contents

Preface

I Am the Other is a book that aims to provide a fair hearing for both sides of one of the most hotly debated issues in contemporary culture: Is Islam an outdated, dangerous religion that is largely out of touch with modern society? Or does it, through the words of Allah in the Quran, offer a guide for living that *everyone* can benefit from, Muslim or not? These distinctly different viewpoints are set forth by authors Imam Azhar Subedar, a devout Muslim scholar, and Robert (Bob) Gary, an identified but secular Reform Jew. Like many who live in non-Muslim countries, Bob has spent decades questioning Islam's compatibility with the West.

Since 9/11, Muslims in the West have been stigmatized and often ostracized due to the actions of a handful of criminal extremists who, in the view of Imam Subedar, in no way represent the true tenets of Islam. For proof, Imam Subedar delves into the Quran, addressing what he sees as his coauthor's fears and misperceptions, as well as, in his view, the misguided thinking of Islamic extremists. He also goes further, explaining how the Quran can provide workable solutions for how all people should conduct their lives, wherever they live. Given the state of divisiveness and the failure of civil laws in the West, the guidelines provided in the Quran, he believes, would be better viewed not as a dangerous problem but as part of the solution.

Bob Gary details the ways in which he believes Islam is incompatible with Western values, citing portions of the Quran that he maintains illustrate its misogynistic, violent, and intolerant bent. He also acknowledges that, without this book, he would have had no concept of what life was like for an American Muslim. Yet despite these fundamentally opposite views, the thread running through the book is the coauthors' mutual respect and their hope that dialogue is the only way for individuals—and society as a whole—to rise above tribal divisions and prejudice inflamed by ignorance. In essence, they believe that the results of the 2024 election have changed America and not only impacted the role of Muslims and Jews in America but potentially necessitated a realignment of the relationship between the two groups. *I Am the Other* is neither a debate nor a conversation. It aspires to muster the deeply rooted arguments against Islam and confront and challenge them with an Islamic scholar's view of the true Islam. The authors have attempted to accurately represent Islam's and the West's disparate theological and cultural differences and contemporary life solutions. If they have each done their job, the arguments have been marshaled, the critical facts and information assembled, and the question is ripe for determination. For the West, is Islam the problem or the solution? You, the readers, are the judges. You are about to take a vital step toward examining the information necessary for an informed decision.

A Note from the Authors

Regardless of your own faith or beliefs, we promise that when you finish this book, Islam will no longer be the mystery it might have been when you began. If you are not a Muslim, know that what is in these pages is not meant to encourage you to adopt the faith, but rather to explain what it means to truly follow Islam, from the mouth of a scholar who is deeply knowledgeable about the subject. If you are Muslim, you will very likely learn something about your faith that you didn't know before.

Tribalism is further fracturing an already polarized human race, leading to war, economic inequality, and a world in which more and more humans are struggling to survive in deteriorating conditions while only a sliver of the population thrives. From our respective corners, we aim to break this cycle, though our proposed means of getting there are very different: One believes the path is through the democratic and constitutional political process; the other, that the way is through religion. More specifically, Bob Gary believes that rejecting authoritarianism, divisiveness, and misinformation and embracing democracy and a fact-based, scientifically rooted society is the only way to ensure the peaceful coexistence of Muslims and Jews. Imam Subedar, in contrast, argues that restoring the true narrative of Islam and Shariah law is the key to human salvation and even to potentially saving democracy from imminent collapse. Throughout these pages, we discuss Shariah law, which is essentially a set of guidelines for those who follow the way of Islam. Imam Subedar believes that without Shariah, we will continue to see a rise in extremism and an attendant threat to citizens who cherish living in democratically run nations. Bob Gary contends that Shariah is at odds with Western mores and culture and that it increases divisiveness. Where the authors agree is that when Muslims and non-Muslims face off against one another, the extremists win at the expense of the rest of us.

Some portions of this book may make you uncomfortable or upset. If you aren't Muslim or familiar with Islam, you will learn that Muslims subscribe to attitudes about women, criminal justice, warfare, and other religions that may seem antithetical to your idea of humane and civilized conduct. If you are Muslim, you will discover that the level of fear and distrust of Muslims by non-Muslims is pervasive and often based on Islamophobic stereotypes. Contrary to the popular assumption that finding how much we are all alike is the path to peaceful coexistence, we choose not to paper over the often stark differences between Muslims and non-Muslims in addressing societal problems. Instead, we embrace the reality that true acceptance of the other depends upon informed knowledge and understanding of the other. Well-intentioned but superficial efforts to find common ground inevitably collapse for their absence of intellectual honesty. We are aiming to present an honest and unfiltered expression of the belief systems and prejudices of two very different men from two very different backgrounds. But rather than confirming your worst fears, we hope the unvarnished truth will lead to a realization that honest dialogue, forged on a bedrock of reality, can indeed result in an enduring coexistence. Whatever your point of view, we ask that you strive to keep a curious, open mind and heart, along with a willingness to gain a better understanding of a subject that is too often clouded by emotion. We also hope you'll find inspiration in the hard-hitting and yet civil discourse between us that flows through these pages. Over the years, we two authors have often disagreed but have always listened to each other with respect and a desire to learn.

In 2013, Rabbi Marc Schneier and Imam Shamsi's *Sons of Abraham* hit bookstores, with a foreword by former president Bill Clinton. The book, like ours, billed itself as a candid conversation between a Muslim and a Jew about the issues that separated them. Yet in the more than 10 years since the publication of *Sons of Abraham*, the growing acceptance of authoritarianism and rise in the ideology of white supremacy in this country and around the world have created an urgent need for Muslims and Jews to talk to one another. Unlike *Sons of Abraham*, which set out to identify common ground between Muslims and Jews despite very real differences, our book illuminates our significant differences in an attempt to understand them, without the sometimes tortured objective of forging agreement.

As the United States experiences a resurgence of nativism in which "others" are seen as somehow less than true Americans, moderate points of view, not to mention respect and a desire to listen, are increasingly in short supply. When those in power do not explicitly reject these nativist views, the individuals who hold them, both in and out of government, grow ever bolder. That's why it is increasingly urgent that all of us speak from our respective platforms to unambiguously denounce the tactics of militias and hate groups, making it clear that what they do and say is outside the confines of acceptable behavior.

It is the authors' wish that you will add your voice to what we hope and pray will be a growing chorus demanding civility and mutual tolerance, and that you will always resist the urge to condemn the other.

CHAPTER 1

Setting the Foundation

Robert Gary's Statement

In my career as a lawyer and a prosecutor, I've learned how to separate facts from distortions and untruths whether intentional or otherwise. And it is in pursuit of the facts that I have traveled the globe attempting to get to the source of the white-hot rage that often seems to consume the Muslim world. That, too, is my goal with this book and my investigation of Islam. I take on this task with what I hope is great humility and respect.

I acknowledge that I started out on this journey wary of Islam. Like many non-Muslims in this country, I still am. After reading the Quran, I concluded that its precepts were intolerant, that they undermined the independence of women, and, of greatest concern to me, that they appeared to be calling for violence against non-Muslims. What I read fueled me to not only learn what I could about this religion but to spread the word that Islam presented a clear and present danger to the world.

As a non-Muslim, I have highlighted beliefs and practices of

Muslims that I see as problematic, while also subjecting those beliefs and practices to the kind of skeptical scrutiny I once used in the courtroom. As someone outside the Muslim faith and, admittedly, an often harsh critic of Islam, my purpose is to provide a lens on how the Muslim community is often viewed by non-Muslims, many of whom hold negative opinions of Islam supported by very little solid knowledge. Exploring whether such views are justified or not is, in part, the mission of this book. Attempting to be open-minded and to recognize my own biases does not make me a Jewish apologist for Muslims. Our book has been reviewed by several rabbis, and common complaints were that the Jewish perspective is not explained, nor is Imam Subedar addressing the long-standing animus of Muslims toward Jews. My response: I am not qualified to represent the Jewish faith. I am not a rabbi or even particularly knowledgeable about my own religion. My role in this dialogue is that of a non-Muslim who happens to be Jewish. Jews and anti-Semitism will have to be the subject of another book.

Still, as a secular Jew born in a generation for whom the horrors of Nazi Germany are, for many, top of mind, I am ever conscious of the fragility of democracy and the urgent need to preserve it. Autocracy, populism, and rigid dogma in all its forms, including religious extremism, are potential threats to democracy in general, to the Jewish people, and, indeed, to anyone who identifies as "other" in our society. But while I focused on the perceived threat of Islam, I failed to adequately recognize the growing menace of extremism, white supremacy, Christian nationalism, and neo-Nazism. These threats were not festering in Syria, Iraq, or Afghanistan, but in my backyard—Sarasota County, Florida. Democracy is the firewall that protects us, and my passion is to protect the rule of law, without which democracy cannot exist.

Which brings me back to Muslims and Jews in America, both of whom are facing common foes on the far right and the far left. Further, many Jews have a bias against Muslims, seeing them as adversarial and hostile. Many Muslims, it is safe to say, feel the same way about Jews. Yet it is the extremists in our society who seek to destroy the stability necessary for a peaceful and prosperous society. That's why it's necessary for American Muslims and Jews (and Christians and others) to know one another, understand our differences, and work together to protect our increasingly fragile social fabric from being torn to pieces.

Peaceful coexistence and mutual tolerance are the cornerstones of democracy, necessary to keep people of all lifestyles and faiths free and secure. But that cannot be achieved by denying what may seem like unpleasant truths; it requires that we recognize and accept that differences are part of the human condition. And so my coauthor Imam Subedar and I invite you to join our "grand experiment." We posit that it is possible for groups who have commonly viewed one another as enemies—and our focus in these pages is primarily Muslims and Jews—to fully disclose their beliefs and still stand together. For my part, that means pointing out worrisome details I have accumulated about Muslims and their beliefs. Imam Subedar, in turn, will offer his scholarly perspective on the Quran and Islam, defining Islam honestly, without accommodating the reactions of extremists or the hatred of Islamophobes.

Imam Subedar and I come to our tasks from two very different vantage points. Imam Subedar is a man of deep faith who is firm and unshakable in his belief that Allah speaks through the Quran and that the Quran provides guidelines for living today and in the future. In contrast, I see myself as the sole determiner of my fate, living life mostly without an instruction book.

I must also make it clear, again, that I am not purporting to speak on behalf of all Jews. Like Islam, Judaism is not a monolith. Reform Jews see Judaism very differently than Orthodox Jews or Conservative or Reconstructionist Jews. My sole aim is to express the post-9/11 concerns and fears that I believe many non-Muslim Americans, regardless of their attitude toward religion, may have about Islam. These are fears that I have grappled with myself. With that in mind, I ask my coauthor the questions that any non-Muslim reading this book might ask him if given the chance.

Today, politics is increasingly emulating religion and requiring "faith" and acceptance of dogma in place of examination and critical analysis. When political figures are bent on supplanting the democratic process and the rule of law with authoritarianism, they often falsely lay claim to an infallibility that is more commonly seen in the domain of religion. One dramatic example of the merger of politics and religion in America is a video titled "God made Trump." This video seems at the very least to suggest that Donald Trump and his political ambitions are God-inspired. I believe in separating religion and politics, and when I question Islam, my litmus test of acceptability is whether a particular theological belief or practice infringes on democratic values.

The traditional strongholds of Islam are in primarily nondemocratic countries such as Iran, Egypt, and Saudi Arabia. The U.S. has complicated and often mutually beneficial relationships with many of these nations, despite their being theocracies, monarchies, or even dictatorships. American Muslims, on the other hand, live under a different type of government. One of the questions

I ask in these pages is whether American Muslims are to be defined solely by Islam or whether they are also significantly shaped by the society in which they live. (Indeed, the same question might be asked of Orthodox Jews, but that, too, is another book.)

What I hope will become clear is that however we choose to define ourselves, we can't let the haters define us. That is one reason that I, as skeptical as I've been about Islam, have chosen to partner with Imam Subedar. Too often, the voices of moderation on both sides are drowned out by Muslims who see all nonbelievers as infidels and non-Muslims who see all Muslims as terrorists. What's missing are the voices of Muslim citizens who want to practice their religion, obey the laws of their country, and live peacefully with their neighbors as fellow citizens.

Beyond politics and religion, *I Am the Other* is about the bond between two very different men who live in very different worlds. Our goal is not to change the other's mind but to gain clarity and insight into our respective belief systems, without judgment or condemnation. I admit the task has not always been easy, but it is worthwhile—and necessary.

One thing I've learned along the way is that it's possible for one culture to view a practice as a violation of human rights while another sees it as a time-honored ritual. I have also learned that the biggest obstacles to understanding can be the unconscious biases we bring to the table, no matter how open-minded we believe ourselves to be. While it's nearly impossible to put these biases entirely aside, we can all strive to keep them in mind when we read something that makes us uncomfortable.

Imam Azhar Subedar's Statement

Since 2002, I have devoted my career to serving as an *imam* (Islamic religious leader). From the get-go, my primary goal has been to combat the constant hatred against Islam by trying to restore its true message, a message that is in danger of being lost completely. That danger emanates from two opposing powers that continue to gain momentum in our world. I am speaking about the terrorists who steal the name of Islam for their own purposes, and the Islamophobes who, often out of ignorance, foment hatred of Islam. Ironically, they share a common link: Shariah.

Shariah is a term widely used today to describe the law that Muslims must follow. It is important to note that the terms "Shariah," "Shariah law," and the "penal law of Shariah" each have a distinct meaning. Shariah is a divinely prescribed system of life. Shariah law is one aspect of that lifestyle and is not whole in itself. The penal law of Shariah is part of a broader system of the law that also includes family law and personal devotional law—all pieces that come together to form the entirety of Shariah law. Think of it like the world, a country in the world, and states within that country. This rudimentary understanding is essential.

In my observation, Muslims seem to fall into three categories when it comes to living by Shariah. There are those who are widely identified as extremist, such as members of ISIS or Al Qaeda whose understanding of Shariah justifies, in their minds, enforcing every aspect of it on Muslims and imposing it on the world at any cost, even bloodshed. On the opposite end of the spectrum are those who live by Shariah but have reservations about certain aspects of it, such as the messages surrounding jihad, polygamy, or marrying someone deemed underage. They see these teachings as a hindrance or even a barrier to the continued growth and perpetuation of Islam. Exhausted by being shackled to the neverending stereotype of terrorist, jihadist, polygamist, and pedophile, some go as far as to suggest the removal of certain parts of the scripture that result in their being painted as such. Between these two extremes are those who, while embracing Shariah as their guide in life, understand that living in a Western non-Muslim-majority country requires that they follow the civil laws of their home country even when those laws conflict with the penal laws of Shariah. They understand that even when certain laws are in conflict, their other obligations in faith under Shariah (such as prayer, fasting, and being a good human) aren't hindered or restricted in any way. And they acknowledge the clear line between practicing what they profess and imposing what they believe on others.

Among non-Muslims, there are some who reject the presence of Muslims in their personal space or country altogether simply because of what they think Muslims believe and what our holy text allows. Some of these individuals hold significant political power or societal influence. How I, as a Muslim, feel when a state legislature views the precepts of my religion as a threat to the general population fuels my ambition to explain Shariah precisely and accurately, so it can be understood as a positive force and a comprehensive framework that allows its followers to lead a successful life in this world and beyond.

In doing so, I am committed to challenging the ideas of both Islamic extremists and Islamophobes, both of whom continue to misrepresent and misinterpret Shariah. In the process, they further their agendas of hate. To counter those agendas, I aim to restore the true message of Shariah, not for myself but for the benefit of all of humanity. Like my coauthor, I want to bridge the gap that separates us into tribes and thereby others us, normalizing labels that stoke fear, rob us of dignity, and deny our common humanity.

How did I get here?

In November of 2000, I was a fresh graduate from an Islamic institution in England with the lofty title of Scholar of Islamic Sciences and Arabic Literature. As I left the cloistered world I had been in for more than a decade, I had great aspirations and ambitions for my life and career. I dreamed of being an informative voice of moderation in a world unaware of Islam's religious beliefs and practices. I also aspired to stay open and to strive to listen to others without fear, preconceived notions, or resentment.

Then came 9/11. As it did for so many others, that event shook me to the core, exposing the danger of extremism. It seemed to me that the world had changed, perhaps forever, and in my sorrow, I believed that my dreams of being a source of information about the true nature of Islam would never come to pass. Instead, I was forced to go into a constant defensive mode for my faith and my calling as an imam. I had spent years studying to understand every aspect of my Islam, a religion that now seemed to be discredited throughout the world. After all, the attackers claimed that their cause—and their anger—was rooted in Islam. This claim is false, but it had lasting repercussions for the fate of Muslims around the world, and on how we Muslims relate to one another.

People born after 9/11, and even those too young to remember the attacks, are likely to have inherited a hatred or at least a suspicion of Islam and of Muslims. In the minds of many Americans, all Muslims are terrorists. This bias extends to Shariah law as well as to the religion of Islam itself, which, for many, is perceived as terrorism's dark source. This conscious or subconscious association between terrorism and Islam is not only wrong; it is also dangerous.

There *are* terrorists who claim to represent Islam, but they do not represent all Muslims, nor do they represent me. The same holds true for ISIS and Al Qaeda and all other nongovernmental/rogue terror organizations. As for ISIS and Al Qaeda, the first is a radical terror group that emerged in Iraq in 2013, then took hold in Syria from the remnants of Al Qaeda in that region. Al Qaeda, in contrast, consists of self-proclaimed jihadists spearheading an Islamist revolution calling for Muslims the world over to unite under a Caliphate, or Islamic ruler.

What may surprise you is that neither of these groups follow the dictates of the Quran. In truth, their adherents are part of a cult of death and destruction.

And here's the rub: How can anyone not suspect that all Muslims are terrorists when Islamophobes and others remain willing to capitalize on the prevailing hatred of Muslims to rake in both money and attract followers? Just as troubling, as long as the U.S. is being torn apart by political problems on its own soil, it cannot refocus on the potential resurgence of ISIS or Al Qaeda–inspired terrorists abroad. That means another attack at the level of 9/11 remains a threat.

Among the domestic and political problems in the U.S. I refer to is the storming of the Capitol Building on January 6, 2021, which many Americans viewed as a shocking assault on one of our country's greatest symbols of democracy. That event, like 9/11 before it, also altered many people's perceptions of the world we live in, exposing the turmoil and divisions rending the United States in two. On one side are those who believe that the nativist policies of the far right along with the precepts of Christian teachings must be defended from "others" who, they believe, are determined to compromise what it means to be American. On the other side are liberals and, to the far left, ultraliberals, who claim to believe in inclusion and love but too often exclude any voices that don't align with theirs, inadvertently mirroring the "othering" they fervently condemn. As evidence, look to the fact that at the time of this writing, ultraliberals and the far right are now spouting the same anti-Semitic and Islamophobic tropes. Add to this the aftereffects of the global pandemic, including deepening inequities and societal problems, and it's clear that America needs a solution for all its people, and fast.

Although democracy in its various forms can be traced back to the ancient Greeks, in current-day America it is wavering, as theocracies, autocracies, and authoritarianism around the world are once again on the rise. As Americans, we must prevent democracy from failing altogether. What I believe—and this may surprise Western readers—is that Shariah law, the Islamic method of governing one's actions and ethics, could be helpful in warding off the political chaos that threatens to engulf us.

The truth is, America is a land of "others," including a growing and vibrant Muslim population of 3.5 million people, many of whom are dedicated to Shariah. Yet the question of whether Shariah might ever be integrated into America the way Judeo-Christian values have been absorbed into the fabric of our society is not even on the table for discussion. As an Islamic scholar and an imam, I believe the first step to putting our fears of the other (in this case, Muslims) to rest is to gain a true understanding of just who the other is. To do that, a true understanding of Shariah mainly focusing on its laws is essential. By illuminating Shariah law in these pages, I hope to reduce the fearmongering spread by Islamophobes about Muslims and expose "Islamic" extremists for the hollow charlatans they are.

First, though, it's important to clarify that when I talk about Shariah law, I am referring to two things: Islamic ways and mores *and* guidelines for living in a broader sense. You may be surprised to discover that I don't see the latter as necessarily confined to Islam or any one religion. Rather, I define Shariah as following the ideals and precepts of *any* faith, whatever it may be. Given that definition, Shariah law is already present in America. Indeed, part of the reason I cowrote this book is to make it clear why Shariah law is already embedded in American values—and why Americans shouldn't feel it's encroaching on their shores.

Like so many others in the West, my coauthor has expressed fear and mistrust of Shariah. But as I see it, neither Islam nor Shariah law need be a disruptive force in the lives of American citizens. As an imam with a formal Islamic education, my goal is to make it clear how Islam wants Muslims to see the issues of our time. I'm not trying to change minds or even asking for widespread acceptance of who we are and what we believe. My goal is simply to *define* who we are and what we believe, not from the perspective of a specific culture or of fringe extremists on any side, but from my wealth of experience and training.

The terrorists of 9/11 may have broken my dreams by ruining the name of Islam. But neither they nor the Islamophobes who fan the flames of hatred against Islam and Muslims have broken my willpower. To roughly paraphrase astronaut Neil Armstrong, this book may be just one small step for me, but I see it as a potential giant leap for humanity toward solving the never-ending problem that links terrorism, fear, and Islam. And while there are plenty of books out there that condemn Islam and decry the violence perpetrated in its name, it is extremely rare to find a book that unapologetically states what Muslims actually believe, that is aimed at both non-Muslims and Muslims and is written by coauthors with polar opposite views. Without question, the beliefs and practices of Islam are different from those of other religions. However, those differences do not mean that we cannot live together and unite against the common enemy—extremism—just as my coauthor and I have done.

Before we go any further, you may want to first take a look at the glossary of key terms used throughout the book. You'll find it at the end of the book and on our website (which also includes an appendix listing all the sources referenced in this book) at IAmTheOther.org.

CHAPTER 2

An Imam's Spiritual Journey

By Imam Azhar Subedar

The Making of an Islamic Scholar

My brother and I were anomalies from the start, two of just a handful of brown children in our mostly white Canadian elementary school in the early 1980s. Our parents—my mother from Africa, my father from Asia—met and married in England, then emigrated to Ontario, Canada. Religion wasn't a big part of our lives. My parents enjoyed going to the theater, parties, and the movies. My mom loved to dress up, and she had a '60s beehive hairstyle in the '70s, followed by a pixie cut in the '80s that made her stand out at crowded family functions. But when our family moved from the town of Malton to Brampton in the late '80s, things changed.

It was around then that my father's mother came from India to stay with us, rotating among her four sons, all of whom lived nearby. My grandmother was a simple lady who, for the most part, kept to herself and engaged in worship—of what type, I wasn't sure, since I didn't ask too many questions. It didn't help that she didn't speak English and that my older brother and I didn't speak Gujarati. If any of us needed to convey something important, we used our dad as a translator. But during one of her visits, I somehow picked up on the idea that my grandmother was urging my father to encourage my brother and me to take up religion—not just as a guide for living, but as a formal commitment. Specifically, she wanted one or both of us to start memorizing the Quran, though no one else from either side of my parents' families seemed to have a commitment to Islam. Memorizing the Quran from cover to cover is a tradition that stems from the Prophet Muhammad. It takes about three years on average, and once you do it, you become a *hafiz*, an honor that is highly prized in practicing Muslim families.

> *"A person who recites the Quran and masters it by heart,*
> *will be with the noble righteous scribes [in Heaven]."*
> (Hadith, Bukhari 4937)

My impression then was that my father never took her request seriously.

But my grandmother never gave up; I believe, deep down, that she continued to pray to Allah for this to happen. Looking back, it's clear her prayers influenced the course of our lives.

Another influence came from the teenage son of one of my father's childhood friends, a boy we'd all known and liked for years. Suddenly, or so it seemed to us, he decided to leave Canada and go off to England to an Islamic institution to memorize the Quran. And one day soon after, my brother, who was around the same age as this boy, came home and informed my parents that he'd also decided to leave school and focus on memorizing the Quran. My parents were taken aback. I was intrigued.

My brother's foray marked a shift in our family. In 1990, my father traveled with my brother to England and enrolled him in an Islamic institute to study. When my father returned after two months away, he had a full beard, a first in our extended family. Not too long after that, my mother began covering her hair, trading her Western dresses for the *burqa* and *niqab*, a cultural Islamic dress that covers the entire body and face. She stopped going out to the theater and movies and parties and even grew reluctant to do things like grocery-shop or mingle with family and friends. Eventually, she would decline an invitation to any gathering where men were present, even if they were relatives.

For me, a typically self-conscious teenager, this was difficult to bear. Our family had once blended easily into Canadian society. Now, with the change in our lifestyle, we stood out, and I didn't like it. Wherever we went with our mother, people would stare. Our annual trips to Canada's Wonderland theme park in Ontario were cut short, but instead of being disappointed, I was relieved. I didn't want to be seen with my parents. Over time, all of us would miss out on family weddings and important life milestones, and relatives began avoiding our home, once vibrant with family gatherings. To me, it seemed like one senseless change after another, all in the name of a religion I didn't understand.

My parents had traded our extended family for a religion-centric circle of people who looked like them and thought along the same lines they did. The men gathered in the mosque while the women gathered elsewhere, usually in someone's house in which no men were present. On Sundays, from 1 to 2 pm, our own basement became a venue for weekly women's gatherings. Over time, this created an everlasting wedge between our nuclear family and our other relatives.

As I observed all of this, I realized I had no choice but to fit in. Whatever I believed, my once-beloved cousins now considered us—including me—outsiders. Perhaps it's not surprising, then, that when my father casually asked me, one afternoon in 1991, "What do you want to become in life?" I instinctively replied, "I want to become *hafiz* like my brother." My words surprised me as I said them. My childhood dream had always been to be a doctor, a firefighter, or a pilot, and to this day, I dream of flying planes around the world, connecting families and friends with one another. But though he didn't say anything specific at the time, my dad took my statement seriously. In a matter of weeks, he knocked on the door of my sixth-grade classroom and announced to my teacher that he was pulling me out, suddenly, with no time to formally say farewell to my classmates. I told myself I would return in a few years and reunite with the friends I'd known since elementary school and those I'd now made in middle school. My friend circle was my life, even more so after my brother left home.

The following week, I was sent off to Arabi—no, not in the Middle East, but a small town in the U.S. state of Louisiana, where I began my studies. Soon after I arrived, I met the head of the Islamic school, who was visiting from the U.K.; he was also in charge of the institute where my brother was enrolled.

"What are you here to become?" he asked.

"I am here to become a *hafiz*," I replied.

Abruptly, he said, "No. You will become an *alim*. You can become a *hafiz* later."

Alim, an Arabic title for "scholar of the faith," is someone who has studied and mastered the 15 sciences necessary to accurately understand and interpret the Quran and the Hadith. This title—scholar of the faith—may be new to you, since the Muslim talking heads featured in the media don't typically attach their scholarly credentials to their names and work. That's because most of the time, they don't have any. When self-proclaimed and uneducated representatives of any religion gain access to the pulpit, the results can be detrimental to any faith, but Muslims in particular have witnessed the disastrous effects of this firsthand. The edicts and threats from the likes of Osama bin Laden and Abu Bakr al-Baghdadi lacked legitimacy because they were not based on correct interpretations of Islamic text. These men never studied the faith as true Islamic scholars, nor learned under teachers educated in principles that can be traced back to the Prophet Muhammad—teachers who were fully able to explain the Quran and the Hadith. Yet their messages of hate streamed across the globe, which gave them the air of legitimacy.

Before even touching the Quran and Hadith, I was required to master many subjects, including:

- Arabic Grammar
- Islamic/Quranic Jurisprudence and its Principles
- Logic
- Pronunciation, Intonation, and Caesura Pertaining to Quran Recitation
- Prophetic and General Islamic History
- Principles of Hadith
- Principles of Quranic Exegesis

The course would take 10 years, which meant that my dream of reuniting with my friends would never happen. The decision, one that was made for me, broke my heart. Yet I was also hopeful that my new life would ultimately prove worthwhile. For in Islam, we are taught that Allah has good in store for us all; we just need to find it where we are. That belief gave me solace.

At my new school, we students were confined to either the mosque or another building where we studied, slept, and lived. I had a fixed weekly allowance of $5, which I could use to buy cereal, chocolate, or cookies. I learned to use a washing machine and iron my clothes. Once a week, we were treated to a doughnut and allowed to go to a nearby park to play outside. In other words, it was a tough change for a kid who was used to Western ways. Indeed, after a year, I asked to return to Canada to be with my family.

Back in Canada, I began studying under my local imam before transferring to a new Islamic institution outside of Toronto; I was the very first student there. Then, in late 1993, when I was 14, I was granted admission to the institute my brother attended in England, as if I had been on course to follow in his footsteps from that first conversation with my father. And, in a sense, I had. Unbeknownst to me, the day I told my father I wanted to be a hafiz, he had called the British school and had me added to the waiting list. Going to Arabi and studying in Canada were just a means to get the ball rolling so that, when I arrived in England, I wouldn't have to start from the beginning, either with my studies or in getting used to living independently.

With the help of soccer, I adapted to my new life in England. From 1994 to 2000, I studied in Dewsbury, West Yorkshire, where I became obsessed with the sport. I loved playing it, especially five on five on a concrete court where I did well as a striker, or, on the pitch, as a goalkeeper. I soon became a die-hard Manchester United fan, and I still recall when they won the treble in 1999, nabbing the Premier League, the FA Cup, and the Champions League. (Just for the record, I am now a Liverpool fan.) There were no TVs, computers, or cell phones at the institute, but some students had gotten hold of portable radios, despite their being prohibited. I was one of them, and I used it to listen to games. When Man U secured its cup title, I was outside in the school parking lot, jumping for joy. I made sure to get a copy of the newspaper the next morning as a keepsake.

Those kinds of moments, however, were rare. For seven years, my weekly schedule entailed six days of classes and studying, with one day of rest each week. Every morning, I got up before sunrise for prayer and breakfast, then, at 8 am, dove into the set Islamic curriculum, rotating among different classes until noon.

Our morning classes were followed by lunch and a quick break, after which we tackled academic subjects from 1 to 4 pm. Even for students in private institutions, it was mandatory to complete British O-level studies—a qualification examination taken at the end of secondary school, around age 16. At 4 pm, there was a break for snacks, table tennis, soccer, laundry, or going shopping in town, if permission was granted by the head teacher. Because of the location of our mosque and institution, Muslims were a common sight in town, so going out dressed in Islamic garb— traditional Pakistani or Arabic cultural dress—didn't draw stares. At 6 pm, we gathered in one of the two main halls to complete our homework, followed by dinner at 8. Some of the higher-up students had night classes after dinner, usually until 10 pm or later. Our classes increased in intensity each year until we delved into Quranic interpretation followed by Hadith literature in our final three years.

From 4 o'clock on Saturday until 6 o'clock on Sunday, we could rest and relax, in a manner of speaking. With such a rigorous schedule, we were consumed by our studies. But maybe because my brother was also there, I didn't feel lonely as I had in Arabi. Or maybe it was just that I was getting older and feeling more comfortable with my position in life.

I graduated in 2000, the class of the millennium, as an Islamic scholar with a master's in Islamic Sciences and Arabic Literature. I was 21 years old and eager for some real-world experience. After spending the holy month of Ramadan with my parents in Saudi Arabia—my third visit to that country—where we worshiped and fasted the entire month, I traveled on to India, my father's home country, for the first time. There, I set out to do a one-year training in community service, learning how to work in a community as an imam, an experience highly encouraged by the leaders of our institute. For me, this was an opportunity to see the world and make decisions for myself after close to a decade of others making decisions for me. I didn't need to be in class at a specific time or ask for permission to go outside. Instead, my peers and I traveled by bus or train, visiting different mosques and engaging with different communities to learn how to speak, listen, and understand how a community functions, and how to effectively engage with people firsthand. I learned early on from the advice of senior scholars and from my own experiences that there is an art to interacting with people. It takes patience to hear someone through, and empathy to place yourself in their shoes. If I wanted to make a difference, I had to acquire those skills. I thought that time would be the key, but I couldn't have foreseen what happened next.

I'd anticipated staying in India for the greater part of that year, but on January 26, 2001, there was an earthquake in Gujarat, in the west of the country, which I felt all the way in Allahabad (known as Prayagraj), a little over 1,400 kilometers away. The shaking was so powerful, I couldn't walk; I couldn't even move. I can only describe the terror as debilitating. When the earthquake subsided, I looked up to see the crescent moon attached to the top of the minaret of the old mosque we were staying in tilted to one side. Shocked by what had happened, I instinctively wanted to leave for Pakistan immediately. But the earthquake also had an upside: My classmates and I became closer. We were all together in a foreign country, and adjusting to our new life wasn't easy. Now, it felt as if our willingness to stay on was being tested. As we supported one another, we learned to find comfort and value in the time we spent together. I ended up staying in India until June of that year, when I decided to travel to Pakistan and, I hoped, on to Bangladesh to immerse myself in different cultures and gain more hands-on experience. Ironically, it was on the morning of September 11, 2001, that I left Pakistan to make my way to New Delhi via the Wagah border, en route to Bangladesh. But I never got there. And it was only that night, when I arrived in Delhi, that I came to understand why the penultimate leg of my journey had been so peculiar.

I was traveling by bus, and when I stepped into the vehicle, the driver instructed me to sit directly behind him, presumably because I was a solo traveler on a bus full of families. The seat next to me happened to be reserved for the police officer, and when we crossed into the next state, he got off and another one got on, seating himself beside me. That happened every time we crossed from one state into another, until finally, as we approached New Delhi, our bus was stopped by a military vehicle. The police officer sitting next to me disembarked and spoke with one of the officers outside, then returned holding his gun, which he had kept between his legs while he snoozed, the tip of the pistol sometimes pointing toward me. At one point in the journey, I'd asked him, "*Kya huwa?*" (What happened?) but he didn't respond. By the time we entered the outskirts of New Delhi, there were multiple military vehicles in front of us and behind us, and as we entered the city, every traffic light leading to the bus station was green, manned by a police officer who waved us through, while cross traffic was halted altogether. Aside from our bus and the military escort, there were no other vehicles in sight. When we entered the empty bus station, all the passengers were pulled off by police officers and directed to different corners of the otherwise deserted station. I immediately showed them my Canadian passport and said, "I'm Canadian," and the officers moved on from interrogating me as they searched the other Pakistani passengers and their belongings. After a prolonged wait, we were allowed to leave, but there were no taxis or rickshaws. And so I dragged my two large suitcases for a few blocks until I found a taxi, which I took to the main mosque in New Delhi, where I was staying before heading to Pakistan. It was only there that I heard the TV from a barbershop across the street announcing that America was under attack. When I spoke with my mother over the phone about what had happened, she told me I needed to come home to Canada immediately. My one-year tour was cut short by three months.

The world had changed and so had my plans.

On my way back home, I flew first to England via Kuwait to meet with my former teachers at the institute for several days. I was only in Kuwait for a few hours, but the display of American military might at the airport made me realize how serious the response to the 9/11 attack would be.

Living as a Muslim Leader in a Post-9/11 World

I will never forget my flight from London back to Toronto. As a 22-year-old Muslim in Islamic attire with a long beard, I received dirty looks from everyone, including the flight attendants, from the moment I stepped onto the plane. To make things worse, I wasn't feeling well, due to fatigue, stress, or a bug I had picked up during my travels, and I vomited a few times during the flight. When we landed, as we filed toward the exit, the passenger in front of me turned to the flight attendant and said, "Have a good day." Looking at me pointedly, she responded, "I can *now,* knowing that we've landed safely." I disembarked with tears in my eyes, stopping at the Air Canada counter to share what had happened. I was given a phone number, which I called the following day. Letters were exchanged, but I never received a formal apology from either the airline or the flight attendant for her unprofessional conduct. For me, the post-9/11 nightmare had just begun.

At that moment, I realized I had three options: Ditch the spiritual life that had been laid out for me and instead go to college and get a secular degree; take some low-paying job at a local factory and bide my time; or continue with my plans to serve Islam as an imam, a teacher, and a lecturer. To me, the only thing that made sense was the third option. I knew my religion had just been hijacked by terrorists, and I could not stand aside and do nothing. I needed to become a leader in my community, and I set about looking for a position.

To better understand how an imam and a mosque are related, it's important to know that each mosque is an independent entity that hires and fires its leaders according to its own needs. The vast majority of the time, there are no links between mosques in different communities, cities, or states, just as there is no link between mosques in this country and those overseas (which is where the bulk of mosques are located). As with any other job, prospective imams write up a résumé and send it to potential employers when an opening is posted. At that time, I looked for openings in the back of Islamic magazines or on public notice boards in mosques; later, I looked online. If chosen, I would then go through an interview and vetting process with all the back-and-forth and contractual negotiations that ensue.

In February of 2002, I flew to Florida from my parents' home in Brampton, Ontario, where I'd been living. I was going to check out an opportunity in Tampa, Florida, at what was then considered to be one of the 10 most prominent mosques in America. Their imam was on his way out, and I was the first candidate interviewing for the position. I did a week of voluntary service there, leading prayers, delivering short lectures in the evening, and interacting with the community on a personal level, including officiating my first funeral service. I answered questions about Islam, spoke with congregants' children and with the sisters, our women members, to show that I was prepared to serve everyone, not just boys and men. I also delivered the Friday *Khutbah*, the sermon typically delivered by an imam on Fridays before the important midday prayer, to a packed audience. Ultimately, though, I decided not to take the job. The president of the mosque arrived an hour late for our dinner appointment, then wrote my contract on a napkin. When I asked what the arrangements would be for my accommodations, he told me I would need to "figure it out myself," despite the salary not being enough to live on. I knew that being born and raised in the West, being a native English speaker, and being young gave me a great advantage over other potential candidates, so I walked away.

This was a time when, I believe, the majority of imams serving in North America were still from North Africa or Asia. But there was just starting to be a shift toward mosques hiring imams born or raised in the West, and I would end up being at the forefront of that change. Several mosques, positions, and interviews later, I ended up saying yes to a mosque in Fort Myers, Florida, and I began my service in October of that year. It was a much smaller community than in Tampa, but I would be their first imam, which meant I would be setting the tone for how things would go rather than filling someone else's shoes. I would be leading prayers five times a day and teaching children how to read the Quran on weeknights, along with leading an Islamic school for kids on Friday nights. I would also be teaching a few other weekly evening classes for adult congregants; delivering the Friday sermons; leading special services for celebrations such as Eid; conducting funeral services, and attending various community events. I worked six days a week, sometimes more, my role evolving before my eyes. As a newlywed with my first child on the way, I found life itself evolving even faster. Learning how to juggle was my first priority.

One morning, only a few weeks into my career, I was woken up by a phone call from the local news station. The police had just apprehended "the D.C. sniper," who, in fact, turned out to be two men, John Allen Muhammad and Lee Boyd Malvo. In October of 2002, the two had gone on a shooting spree in Maryland, Virginia, and Washington, D.C., killing 10 people and injuring many others. Apparently, one of these men was a Muslim. My first response was happiness and relief at their capture. "Did you know that one of the suspects lives in Fort Myers?" the journalist asked. I told him I was new to the area. He went on to state that the suspect lived on the same street as our mosque, on Broadway Avenue. "Did he attend your mosque?" he asked. I was not only surprised but offended, so I said goodbye, cutting our conversation short. Later that afternoon, I walked outside to the parking lot and was confronted with two news media vehicles and another one arriving. For a few minutes, I watched them set up, unsure of what to say or do. All I knew is that I wasn't prepared to engage with the media. I hadn't been trained for that. However, I got a reprieve. George, a loyal neighbor of the mosque, came out of his house and demanded that the media vacate the property, so off they went. I assumed they complied only because he was wielding his gun at the time. It was only later that the board and congregation confirmed that the felon had never attended our mosque.

After that incident, it dawned on me, as it was dawning on all imams in the West, that our jobs were no longer confined to serving our own Muslim congregants. Now, after 9/11, it was vital for imams and spiritual leaders of the Muslim faith in America to engage with the greater community: clergy of different religions, city leaders, national leaders, the media, and everyone in between, something none of us had been prepared for.

I didn't let that stop me from stepping into the new role. During my five years in Fort Myers, I was invited to become a member of the White House's Faith-Based and Community Initiatives Committee under President George W. Bush, and, among other things, I delivered a national prayer alongside Florida's Governor Jeb Bush after Hurricane Charley in August of 2004. I also began serving as the only Muslim religious advisor to the Florida Department of Education's Faith-Based and Community-Based Outreach advisory board, a position I held for close to 13 years. Those broader duties continued once my family and I moved about

30 miles north to serve the Muslim community in Punta Gorda and Port Charlotte, where I became the first Muslim to deliver the opening prayer at the Florida Capitol to the Florida Senate and, the next year, to the Florida House of Representatives. Among these duties was giving a prayer at the 2021 presidential inauguration. The Quran seeks to speak to all people regardless of their political party.

Prayers were only part of what I was now called on to do. I was also responsible for educating the community on topics I had never imagined needing to discuss, including the true meaning of jihad and how killing is not the message of Islam. To repel the hate-filled rhetoric and fearmongering, I engaged non-Muslims, meeting with and building bridges with neighbors, clergy, reporters, and local officials. I also participated alongside my congregants in the building of an "interfaith house" in the community for Habitat for Humanity, as part of a project in which the three Abrahamic faiths participated together. I met regularly with law enforcement officials, who often had questions about the role of terrorism in Islam. I learned to speak less and listen more as I worked toward what I hoped was a common goal of peace and understanding for all people in my state and in the nation.

I also encountered unexpected challenges within my own community, struggling with the divide between the various Islamic texts I had studied during my formal education and the reality on the ground. Early in my service in Fort Myers, for instance, during late afternoon prayer, I noticed an unfamiliar light blue Ford Taurus with a rainbow bumper sticker in our parking lot. The mosque was usually empty for that prayer, and afterward, I went outside and waved to the driver, who waved back with a smile. He was there again the following day at the same time, only this time, he left his car and asked if he could come into the mosque. "I'm Jerry," he said, holding out his hand. He was tall and older than I was. After inviting him in and showing him around, I then performed the prayer as he observed. Every day after that, he arrived at the same time to pray alongside me. When I finished, I would answer a few of his questions, and he'd often give me a big hug once we'd finished talking. One day, however, he solemnly told me that he was interested in becoming a Muslim, adding, "Except I'm gay." He was trying to reconcile his desire to follow Islam yet continue to live life the way he wanted to live it.

At first, scouring through all I had learned, I was taken aback: I had no idea what to say about his concern. But after reflecting on his hope to convert, I said, "Allah brought you here to His house. As you strive to gain closeness to Him, you are not just His guest anymore, you are His servant. Pray to Allah to continue guiding your path in life, and He will help you each step of the way." Jerry must have been satisfied, because he converted to Islam and attended the mosque frequently. Although the Quran does not permit homosexuality, I had to learn to consider the difference between what is written in the text and the reality of a person's life as they try to merge into the faith. These were the kinds of lessons I was encountering almost every day, in real time.

I stayed at the mosque in Port Charlotte for eight years and settled into a routine. Every night, after teaching classes, I'd come home from work around 10 pm and watch the news while eating dinner. Often, it felt as if what I was watching was "open season on Islam," with every Tom, Dick, and Harry talking about what Islam meant as if they were experts. This frustrated me—and made me realize that I couldn't simply confine my duties to the four walls of a mosque in a small town. Why shouldn't experienced Islamic scholars speak for themselves and their faith? Who was to say that I couldn't share my understanding of Islam with the wider public? So, at the end of 2015, when my contract expired, I decided to step down from Port Charlotte to explore solutions for a more than decade-old problem: terrorism.

Before I elaborate on the risks of speaking out against terrorists (and there are many), I want to give you a sense of what it is like to be Muslim in America post-9/11. As you read about my journey in the pages that follow, all I ask is that you try to put yourself in my shoes.

In June of 2016, in the early days of Ramadan, the fasting month for Muslims around the world, the news broke that boxing great Muhammad Ali had died at home in Arizona. At the time, I was freelancing as a consultant while helping a friend build his nonprofit, and as Muslims and non-Muslims began mourning the loss of a great human and athlete, I mourned along with them. Though I'd never seen one of his fights on TV, I'd idolized him for being a true ambassador of Islam and for speaking the truth without ever sugarcoating it or dodging a question. I decided that I needed to be at his funeral service for his Janazah prayer, the final rite for a Muslim before burial.

The service would take place in his hometown of Louisville, Kentucky, and tickets for the service would be available at a certain time on a specific website. As soon as the link opened for the (free) tickets to the arena, which happened to be the site of Ali's final boxing match in 1981, I clicked.

According to Imam Zaid Shakir, who led the service, Muhammad Ali planned his funeral services long before his demise. "Ali wanted the Muslim prayer service . . . to be a teaching moment," said Imam Zaid Shakir. "And truly, it was just that."

News reports said there were more than 14,000 attendees, with thousands of people arriving on chartered buses. Cameramen were everywhere. Reporters continually stopped the streams of people heading into the venue, asking visitors where they were from, why they were there, and if they had known Ali personally. Like me, most people said they simply had to be there.

As I walked through the crowd, I noticed there were many notable people present, including former and current athletes, well-known Muslim figures, renowned professors, and, to my surprise, Recep Tayyip Erdoğan, the president of Türkiye, who had crossed the ocean to pay his respects. When the time for the funeral prayer arrived, Ali's coffin was brought forth. There was some silence followed by distinct sounds of crying, the pain in the crowd evident. For all of us, it felt as if we had lost a member of our own family.

After the service, a local imam offered to take me and a few other imams to his mosque for the afternoon prayer, then to his house to rest while he arranged for us to be dropped off at the airport before our flights. On the way, we passed through downtown, where we saw the digital billboards, LED screens on the front of buses (in place of the usual route numbers), and even people on the side of the road holding up signs, all with a similar message: *RIP Champ.*

Later, going through security at the airport, the TSA agent told me that he had seen Muhammad Ali come through the airport before, and although he had never spoken to him, he knew in his heart that he was a good man.

That evening, I flew back to Orlando. Instead of driving home to Tampa, I decided to stay in Orlando for a few days to capitalize on this rare moment of seeming unity between Muslims and non-Muslims, and to take the opportunity to explain how Islam was a great part of Ali's success. With Disney World and Universal

Studios attracting millions of tourists each year, I figured that Orlando would be an ideal place to engage with people from around the world. The next day, a Friday, I put together a questionnaire consisting of five simple questions, the first one being: "Did you know Muhammad Ali was a Muslim?" I intended to go out into the street that weekend and do some canvassing, as well as educate people on how Islam was a peaceful religion and how those who practiced could not only be good people, but humanitarians.

Except that night in Orlando, the singer Christina Grimmie, a former contestant on the TV show *The Voice*, was killed as she signed autographs after her concert. As a result, the next day, I decided to lie low, as the time was not right for me to go out asking questions about Islam. Instead, I fasted for Ramadan, then went for the nightly prayers at Jama Masjid, a nearby mosque.

During Ramadan, Muslims are instructed to wake right before dawn for the pre-fasting meal. I couldn't sleep that night, so I ended up eating my meal at 4 am, then turning on the TV to more breaking news, this time about a shooting in a downtown Orlando nightclub. I fell asleep assuming this was in retaliation for what had happened the night before, then woke up around noon to find numerous missed calls on my phone. Among them was one from my friend Omar, who happened to live in Orlando and who knew I was in town. I called him back, and when he picked up, he demanded to know where I was. "I'm at a hotel," I told him. "Don't you know what happened?" he asked, sounding exasperated. I didn't. "There was a shooting downtown in a nightclub. The shooter was Muslim."

The night before, Omar Mateen, a 29-year-old man from Fort Pierce, Florida, had killed 49 people and wounded 53 more in a mass murder at Pulse, a gay nightclub in Orlando. As I gripped my phone, I found myself trembling, the emotional high I'd experienced because of the shared sympathy and grief over the passing of Muhammad Ali ending abruptly.

My friend instructed me to get downtown as fast as I could to the scene of the crime, where he and others were gathered. As I drove, I saw media helicopters hovering above, and when I arrived, a reporter, noticing my Islamic garb and beard, asked for my thoughts on what had happened. "I'm here to help in any way I can," I said, then made a small prayer, which they streamed for their audience.

At the site, I met my friend Omar and other fellow Muslims, and we commiserated about the loss and what this incident might mean for the Muslim community. Then Omar got a phone call from a clergy member who worked for the Orlando Regional Medical Center. They were putting together a clergy response team and needed an imam to go down to the hotel adjacent to the hospital and meet with the other clergy members gathered there. "They need you," Omar said. A kind member of one of the media crews offered to drop us off as close as he could so we didn't have to navigate the traffic (and find parking) ourselves.

As we walked toward the front entrance of the hotel, which was barricaded by ambulances, I gripped my prayer beads so tightly that I broke them. Watching them drop to the sidewalk and roll onto the grass, it struck me that I'd lost the one thing I really needed for solace and strength.

Inside the hotel lobby, there was a crowd of anxious, desperate families waiting to learn about the fate of loved ones who had been at the nightclub and never returned home. Many were crying or consoling one another, clearly in a state of anguish. What I witnessed pained me deeply, but I also felt fearful of what these mourners might think of me, of what they might do or say. As I reflected on these conflicting emotions, a member of that community came up to me and hugged me.

"I'm so sorry," they said.

"Sorry? Why are you sorry? This was done by someone who took people's lives in the name of my faith. *I'm* sorry."

Their reply: "We are all in this together."

This gave me the strength to face whatever reactions I might get from the crowd, a few of whom seemed startled by my presence. I was ushered upstairs to join the other clergy, then escorted with my Muslim friends beyond a group of non-Muslim clergy to the end of a long hall, about 10 feet from a room we soon learned was being used by the police to show photos of victims to families for purposes of identification. As we stood outside, we could see and hear the entire tragic procession: individuals filled with dread emerging from the elevator, entering that room, then, within a few minutes, screaming and crying as they identified a loved one. Why they chose only me, a Muslim imam, to stand within earshot, and not the other clergy members as well, is a question that continues to haunt me.

Around 5 pm, in the lobby of the hotel, the police read out the names of those (few) people who were alive and in the hospital; anyone not named could either be presumed missing or dead. Screams of anguish greeted this news; some in the crowd became physically ill; others fainted, and others sobbed, their worst fears realized. I was also having difficulty maintaining my composure. Beyond my tears and distress, and the fact that I was also fasting for Ramadan, I felt viscerally uncomfortable. I remember thinking, *I am a Muslim standing with people who have lost a loved one to a shooting committed by a Muslim. What am I even doing here? What should I be doing?*

To make myself useful, I began grabbing bottles of water from a nearby stack and handing them out to mourners while offering what consolation and comfort I could—whether a hug or a few words. At one point, I noticed an elderly woman by the entrance of the hotel in a wheelchair who was in so much distress that she kept slipping down off her chair. She was flanked by two priests, but her eyes locked with mine and she sat up and gestured for me to come toward her. As I nervously approached, she slowly stood, opened her arms, and hugged me as we cried together. At that moment, our pain united us.

The next day, family members of the victims gathered at the Beardall Senior Center, and again, I went over to see what I could do. I found my area of service in the kitchen, preparing sandwiches that arrived from outside caterers, putting them on plates, and serving them while again offering words of consolation with the help of a Muslim interpreter who knew Spanish (many of the victims were Latinx). Florida Governor Rick Scott also dropped by along with Florida Attorney General Pam Bondi, but for the most part, they were met with a cold shoulder by family members.

Altogether, I served for nine days in the city, three of those as the only imam on the official clergy response team and, for the rest of the time, as an imam to many members of the community. There were vigils and press conferences attended by other local imams and community leaders, but my focus was meeting leaders of various faiths and attending their places of worship, always behind the scenes as a congregant to ensure this act of violence did not spill over into violence against Muslims or Islamic centers. I knew I needed to make myself available for people to ask questions, vent frustration, and clarify that Islam denounced this crime.

After the Pulse nightclub shootings, where Mr. Mateen had

pledged allegiance to ISIS before carrying out the attack, it was clear that radicalism was now present in Florida. But terrorism was not only a threat to non-Muslims; it was also endangering the lives of ordinary Muslims. I needed to do something. Ultimately, I decided that something was to counter the now- widespread belief that all acts of terrorism committed in the name of Islam were born out of the faith itself.

Fast-forward to 2017, when I set out to give a series of lectures on Shariah law. I felt the need to explain Islam from the roots up if I wanted to help people successfully differentiate between my religion, Islam, and the violent cult mentality that was besmirching its name. My first engagement was at Washington State University in Pullman. My goal was to show how Shariah—the one that was central to my existence—was very different from the religion most non-Muslims thought they knew. I had prepared notes, but not a PowerPoint presentation or handouts, and about halfway through, I sensed I'd lost my audience. From then on, I worked to put together more engaging presentations, something audiences consisting of Muslims and non-Muslims could relate to, designed to encourage listeners to question what they thought they knew about Islam.

I gave a dozen lectures on college campuses and at places of worship, attended clergy meetings, and had many discussions over coffee (for me, hot chocolate), with the goal of taking terrorism by the horns. Afterward, I settled down to work closer to home, which was now in Plano, Texas, with my growing family. From September of 2018 to February of 2024, I served as imam and spiritual leader of a mosque with more than 5,000 congregants.

As time-consuming as those duties were, my mission to explain Shariah outside the walls of the mosque were increasingly important to me. I also wondered, as you might, why there weren't more scholars willing to use their knowledge to bluntly and openly counter propaganda by terrorists.

The reason, I now suspect, is that anyone who does so puts their personal safety at risk. The sad fact is, there are people in our world who are prepared to destroy anyone daring to speak the truth if it interferes with their agenda. As someone who makes a practice of calling out violent extremists and others who use Islam to control their followers, I live with the ever-present possibility of becoming a target of terrorists.

Terrorists are not confined to one place but are spread across the globe, networking secretly, often living among us, well camouflaged, looking as different from a young, bearded man wielding an AK-47 as you can imagine. Terror networks are diverse; their members come in all shapes, colors, and genders. But whatever these criminals look like, they do not represent Islam, and they do not understand the Quran. They are the last people who should lecture or teach others about Shariah.

I believe that it's essential for all of us to be able to distinguish between the practices of a true Muslim and those of a terrorist, whether or not we are Muslim. Terrorism won't go away until our society is able to separate what is a legitimate religion from the illegitimate actions of a few Islamic extremists or even "Christians" who call for white supremacy. All religions, including Judaism, have people within their ranks who wreak havoc in the name of their faith, and these people are a problem for all of us. Since I am an authority on matters relating to Islam, my goal is to help people gain a clearer understanding of Islam, despite the potential risk to my well-being.

All faithful Muslims believe that the Quran is the word of Allah, but not all Muslims speak with one voice—there are many different views about what Islam is. That's because Islam is a global religion with no central authority or Pope-like figure. I do not intend to debate these views *or even present my own*. What I will do is lay out Shariah as it is, not as I feel it should be.

I will also say that there are differing opinions on the correct way of *practicing* certain commands in Islam while following Shariah, such as how certain movements in prayer are done. Here, too, I will not dispute or challenge those opinions but remain focused on stripping away all kinds of misconceptions that have become attached to Shariah and attempt instead to present it as a clear whole.

You will also hear my coauthor Bob Gary's views on Shariah. He does not read or speak Arabic. He is not a Muslim, he has no formal education in Islamic studies, but, as you will see, he is not shy about expressing his views on Islam. Should he falter in his explanation of my faith, I assure you, I will not be shy about correcting him in the chapters that follow.

Our world has made real progress in racial and religious tolerance, but it remains a dangerous place, especially now. My work, presented here before you in collaboration with my coauthor, may be criticized (and worse) by some in my world and perhaps beyond. But for me, the necessity of getting out the truth is paramount. We are all learning what can happen when the voices of truth and reason are silenced. That's why we cannot afford to succumb to fear and abandon the pursuit of tolerance, decency, and truth in pursuit of a better world.

CHAPTER 3

A Non-Muslim's Crusade to Expose Islam—and Lessons Learned

By Robert Gary

As my coauthor just pointed out, I am not a Muslim, I can't read Arabic, and I am most certainly not an Islamic scholar. I do, however, have strong opinions about Muslims and Islam, many of which Imam Subedar takes issue with (and some that might even be called Islamophobic). What I can promise is that I will offer my honest views on Islam without filtering for political correctness, while making every effort to remain aware of any conscious biases I may hold.

My first contact with Islam goes back to 1995, courtesy of former United States District Court Judge Ann Aldrich. Judge Aldrich asked me to take on pro bono representation of a group of African American incarcerated individuals who had converted to Islam while in prison. These individuals were suing the prison system, demanding that the guards stop calling them by their given names, which they considered their former "slave names," and instead use their new Muslim names. They were also suing for the right to use natural toothbrushes, or *miswaks* (a traditional teeth-cleaning twig recommended by Muhammed) and to pray in groups (because in Islam, group prayer is considered powerful). They claimed that the prison system was denying their First Amendment rights to practice their religion.

Prior to this, the only thing I knew about Islam was that a Jewish member of my childhood synagogue, who also happened to be our family plumber, had moved to Saudi Arabia and converted to Islam. In our Jewish community in Lorain, Ohio, this was considered an unusual if not shocking move. In other words, when I took on this suit, Islam was a total mystery to me, as it was for most Americans prior to 9/11.

If I was going to represent my new clients effectively, I was clearly in desperate need of a crash course in the religion. After doing some research, I discovered that there was a sizable mosque in Parma, Ohio, so I arranged to visit there with my law partner, Jori Naegele.

We were greeted warmly by Imam Fawaz Damrah, who, before becoming the spiritual leader of what was now the largest mosque in Ohio, had also served as an imam at the al-Farooq mosque in Brooklyn, New York. Damrah was born in the West Bank, and during our meeting, I found him engaging and helpful. We wanted to learn, and he was happy to speak with us. My law partner and I tried to approach this "new" and unfamiliar religion with openness and curiosity, and Jori even invited Damrah's associate to her Passover Seder.

As I dove into the lawsuit against the prison system, I learned that one of the State's defenses was that Islam was anti-Semitic, and so the incarcerated individuals' requests should not be allowed.

As I prepared for the trial, I asked Imam Damrah if this was true, assuming he'd vehemently deny it. Instead, he was noncommittal. When I eventually read the Quran myself, I understood his seeming ambivalence. The Quran does in fact contain many explicit and harsh criticisms of Jews.

Though we lost the case, Imam Damrah asked if I could represent imams who sought better access to incarcerated Muslims, many of whom were recent converts, asserting that unlike rabbis, priests, and pastors, Muslim religious leaders were being unfairly excluded from serving the prison population. For a variety of reasons, that project never came to be, but I later learned that these prison conversions were problematic because most of the imams doing the conversions had been trained in an extreme form of Islam.

I lost track of Imam Damrah until after 9/11, when he turned up as a guest at my daughter's school to explain Islam to the student body. I then arranged for him to be part of a panel discussion at Oberlin College, near my hometown in Lorain, at an on-campus event sponsored by the Hillel, an organization for Jewish college students. I envisioned an enlightening conversation between Imam Damrah and our local rabbi, but unfortunately, their back-and-forth deteriorated into a tense discussion about AK-47s. Incidentally, it was our rabbi, not Imam Damrah, who became confrontational during what was intended to be a peaceful example of interfaith harmony.

Shortly afterward, a videotape surfaced that showed Imam Damrah calling Jews "the sons of monkeys and pigs." As you will learn, this phrase plays an interesting role in my first encounter with Imam Subedar.

Perhaps spurred on by the video, the U.S. government accused Fawaz Damrah of entering the United States illegally, claiming that he had not disclosed his ties to the Islamic Jihad Movement and its offshoot, the Islamic Committee for Palestine. It was also alleged that he was connected to terrorist organizations that advocated violence against Jews and others, and that he had concealed these connections when he applied for U.S. citizenship in 1990. Ultimately, he was indicted for failing to make these disclosures and was deported back to the West Bank, where he was arrested by the Israeli government upon his return.

The press also reported that Fawaz Damrah was a disciple of "the blind Sheikh" Omar Abdel-Rahman, who was convicted in 1995 of playing a direct role in the February 1993 truck bombing at the World Trade Center that killed 6 people and injured more than 1,000. The government also alleged that Damrah had connections to conspirators who were planning attacks on the George Washington Bridge, the Lincoln Tunnel, and even the United Nations in 1995.

And then came the attack that changed everything. I first heard about the planes crashing into the World Trade Center from the radio shock jock Howard Stern, who I was listening to on my morning commute to the office. Both of my daughters lived in Manhattan, and when I arrived at work, I watched in horror on the tiny television in my office as the South Tower collapsed.

For the next several hours, my wife and I made frantic calls to our daughters, trying desperately to find them. Wendy, our eldest, was an attorney whose office was near the Twin Towers. When we finally got in touch with her, we learned that she had been on her way to work and very close to the Towers when they collapsed, and had ended up taking refuge in an office lobby, using her gym shorts as a filter against the thick, dense dust and smoke all around her. Her law partner and former husband was also close by and later recounted seeing people throwing themselves out of the windows of the Towers, then hearing the unbearable thud of bodies striking pavement.

Our other daughter, Tracy, was employed in the communications department at the headquarters of the American Red Cross at 520 West 49th Street and was directed to go down to Lower Manhattan to help survivors of what was initially believed to be an accident—a small plane accidentally striking one of the towers.

In the following days, Tracy, who was now the newly minted communication manager of the Red Cross 9/11 Recovery Program, made her way to the smoldering pit daily to hold press conferences. Funds were pouring into the Red Cross for injured survivors, of which there weren't very many, and people wanted to know how the Red Cross was going to use the money.

Shortly after 9/11, I flew down to New York City myself. Over a period of years, I had written a series of long essays about Israel and the intifada for our local newspaper, *The Lorain Journal*, and my editor asked me to go to Manhattan and write a story about the attacks. Tracy agreed to let me accompany her to the still-smoking site. I still remember one of her colleagues pointing to me, an older guy standing off to the side, and asking, "Who's that?" to which Tracy muttered an embarrassed "That's my dad." I spent most of that trip roaming the city and attending special memorial services. I heard a speech by Rudy Giuliani, who was then the hero of the hour, and I vividly remember the mood that prevailed—somber but united against this unseen and mostly unknown enemy.

Not surprisingly, it was during that visit that I first felt driven to learn what I could about a religion whose followers had reached across a vast ocean to wreak destruction on our country. I began by reading English versions of the Quran, comparing several different translations to make sure they corresponded to one another. (For the most part, if the translations were by Muslim scholars, they tended to be very similar.) I also read books on the life of Muhammed and, later, began traveling to Islamic countries with the express purpose of visiting mosques and engaging their English-speaking spiritual leaders. What I learned (or thought I learned) about Islam so concerned me that I was motivated to start speaking out in public about "the dangers" that Islam presented to the West.

One of those speaking engagements was at a private tennis club in Cleveland, Ohio, in the summer of 2014, where I wound up insulting a group of Muslims in the audience who took strong exception to my quoting verses from the Quran and describing them as promoting violence. This was the first time I had addressed an audience with Muslims in attendance, and as I look back on that experience, I cringe. This was not long after 9/11, and I had intentionally selected the most inflammatory verses in the Quran to discuss because, frankly, this was what non-Muslim audiences were interested in. Except my audience happened to include a number of highly educated professionals originally from Muslim countries. I gave no thought to how these people might practice their religion day-to-day, and after my talk, several Muslim audience members came up to say that I had misrepresented Islam, that Islam was a religion of peace. During the dinner that followed, it was clear that I had divided the room. The Muslims were understandably chilly while the non-Muslims and Jewish members of the club, many of whom I knew, were appreciative that I had "educated" them as to the threat presented by Islam.

I may have been naive, but I hadn't intended to offend anyone (though ignorance often does). As far as I was concerned, what I'd said reflected what I had learned from reading the Quran. Looking back, if I had truly sought to understand Islam, I would have sought out a practicing Muslim to guide me. That was before I met Imam Subedar.

Still, I continued to garner more speaking gigs, parlaying the public speaking experience I'd gained from my courtroom days into a lecture circuit on cruise lines, including, on one occasion, a cruise going to the Holy Land. My first lecture of what was to be a series of seven on that trip focused on the fact that for Muslims, reading the Quran is the equivalent to speaking to Allah or God directly. My quotations from the Quran sorely insulted my audience of Christian congregations and their pastors. After reading Quranic passages such as chapter 5, verse 17 (Quran 5:17)—*"In blasphemy indeed are those who say, 'God is Christ the son of Mary'"*—it's no wonder that I created a furor. Again, that's not what I had intended, particularly since I would be sharing a relatively small space at sea with these folks for several weeks. I've since learned that it is always a good thing to learn what other people believe before you speak to them. What I realized too late was that to a Christian audience, my words were heresy. One guest even stood up and said, "What makes *you* an expert?" Usually cool under fire, I am not proud to say that I retorted, "Because I know more than you do," which certainly did not help the situation.

For a few minutes, I feared being cast overboard like Jonah. Worse, I was summoned to the cruise director's office after complaints that I was promoting Islam and preaching from the Quran. What I learned: As a ship lecturer, your primary responsibility is to be entertaining. Being informative is a plus, but not if you agitate or provoke cruisers with facts that might intrude on their idyllic and expensive holiday.

Just to prove that I am an equal opportunity offender, in April of 2016, on a different cruise, I managed to alienate every Jewish member of my audience when I stated that Iran would never attack Israel except by a proxy force such as Hezbollah. I'd formed this impression after visiting Iran, where I observed wide highways, beautiful hotels, and well-developed infrastructure. It was my belief that Iran would not risk a retaliatory attack from Israel, but would use Hezbollah, a terrorist organization they controlled, to carry out any attack so that they could have plausible deniability. Subsequent events proved my opinion dead wrong when, on April 13, 2024, Iran launched hundreds of missiles and drones into Israel. Fortunately, all but a small handful were intercepted and destroyed.

For good reason, many American Jews were and are convinced that it is the goal of Iran to destroy Israel. As a speaker seeking to win over an audience, my offering a contrary view was a lose-lose strategy, even back then. I managed to alienate virtually every Jewish person on the ship, which was obvious from the glares I received from my fellow passengers over the next few days. I served penance by going to services led by the ship's rabbi and purposefully engaging those I had alienated, trying to explain the basis for what was, after all, merely my opinion, as I had no inside information on Iran's plans. As my wife, Karen, likes to say, "If it's your opinion, it can never be wrong"—not that I mentioned that to the passengers.

Since then, I have managed to offend Muslims by reading troublesome verses from the Quran and non-Muslims by reading the very same verses, though for very different reasons. When it comes to religion and politics, I, like others, am too often a prisoner of my own convictions and closed off to any information that conflicts with those views.

The fact that the Quran and Islam are inseparable has also made the actual physical book a magnet for hostility. In 2013, there were widespread stories in the press about a man named Terry Jones, an obscure evangelical pastor in Florida who announced his intention to burn 2,998 Qurans, one for each person who died in the World Trade Center attack. News of this caused rioting in Pakistan and Afghanistan, and he was soon identified as Al Qaeda's public enemy number one. CBS News reported that Al Qaeda placed a $2.4 million bounty on his head.

Ultimately, Pastor Jones was asked to abandon his quest by General David Petraeus. He was also roundly condemned by President Obama, and I made it my quest to meet the guy who had caused such a stir around the world. Jones also happened to own Fry Guys, a french fry stand in Bradenton, Florida, which is how I found myself in a food court in a nondescript mall, standing before an unimposing man with a mustache, muttonchops, and a sickly pallor.

Flattered by my interest in his crusade against Islam, Jones explained that when he'd first gotten the idea to burn the Quran, he wasn't sure if his idea was a message from God or the Devil. Soon, though, he came to realize that it was a message from God, but he was nonetheless stymied in his efforts because he wasn't able to raise enough money to buy the Qurans to burn. I'm not sure if he intended to buy English translations or Qurans in Arabic, but the distinction is crucial, since the former are not considered "true" Qurans. Chapter 41, verse 3, of the Quran (Quran 41:3) makes that clear—"*Quran is in Arabic*"—and Quran 41:44 specifically asks, "*Why would the messenger be an Arab and the language other than Arabic?*" Still, translations or not, the reaction to Pastor Jones across the Islamic world was an indicator of the respect and love Muslims have for the Quran—and demonstrated how one small-minded person can poke the giant and create an international stir.

I didn't want to be a Terry Jones, and so, as part of my self-education, I enlisted a few friends and neighbors to form a Quran study group with me, to be held in my home in Longboat Key, Florida. (Incidentally, nearby Venice, Florida, was where the 9/11 terrorists learned how to fly planes but not land them—and Sarasota was where President Bush happened to be reading a story to some local elementary school students when he learned of the attack.) The members of our study group included a rabbi and several retired Jewish men but no Muslims. However, I'd invited a new neighbor, Mohamed, an urbane man from Egypt who claimed to be a Coptic Christian. Mohamed was an unusual name for a Coptic Christian—this I knew—and he eventually revealed that he was Muslim but hiding it for fear of prejudice. I assured him of our open minds and prevailed upon him to be the first and only Muslim member of our group. The plan was to pick a particular *surah* (chapter of the Quran) to discuss, and we typically made a habit of picking surahs that were either critical of the Jews or that focused on war and jihad. Not surprisingly, on most days, our discussion would devolve into a debate over whether Islam was a religion of violence, with most of us concluding that it was.

Understandably, these discussions made Mohamed uncomfortable, and he begged off, explaining that he was neither religious nor particularly knowledgeable about the Quran. Plus, our choice of passages distressed him. He was unable, as Imam Subedar does so ably in these pages, to put the text into context for us.

The next step in my self-education was to engage with ordinary practicing Muslims and religious leaders on their home turf to begin to understand how Islam was practiced in Muslim countries.

I traveled to Jordan, Oman, Qatar, Bahrain, Turkey, United Arab Emirates (UAE), and Indonesia, going to the main mosque in each city, when possible, to talk with any English-speaking imam available. I was surprised that, as a Jew who didn't hide my religion, I never felt threatened, unsafe, or even unwelcome.

One of my most meaningful trips was to Iran in 2013. Iran is a Shiite Muslim country (as opposed to Sunni countries, such as Saudi Arabia). I came across an ad for a tour to Iran and, eager to glean the different approaches to Islam by Shiites (as opposed to Sunnis) I knew I had to go. My family wasn't pleased. When they heard about my plans, my son-in-law, Jeff, called for a family council to decide how everyone would react in the event that my reckless behavior resulted in my being kidnapped. My wife and daughters agreed with Jeff that this seemed more probable than not. They also agreed that since I was going voluntarily, it would be unfair for my wife to be forced into financial distress by my rash decision to put myself in danger—in other words, if ransom was demanded, no ransom would be paid. Aside from some personal distress over my family's theoretical lack of commitment to my rescue from my hypothetical kidnappers, I was not especially worried about my safety.

I will admit that risk-taking is in my DNA, but I was also confident that I would be safe, a confidence that stemmed from my acquired knowledge of the distinction between Sunni and Shiite terrorism. Sunni terrorism, inspired by Al Qaeda or ISIS, works from the bottom up. A single knife-wielding fanatic can wreak random havoc, inspired by something he has seen on the Internet. In Iran, Shiite terrorism is of the top-down kind. If the government wants to cause mischief, they enlist Hezbollah to do it. There is no random (unauthorized) terrorism in Iran, nor did there appear to be much street crime. So unless the Iranian government had some reason to grab me, I assumed I'd be pretty safe. Plus, President Obama was negotiating the nuclear deal at the time, making it a doubly bad moment for Iran to kidnap or frame an American visitor with some trumped-up accusation.

And the trip did unfold smoothly and safely, which is just about the only outcome that met my expectations.

Iranians are often portrayed by the Western press as religious fanatics shouting, *"Death to America!"* What I found were very young pro-Western people chafing under the religious oppression of the clerics who ran their country. Iran, and now Afghanistan, are among the rare examples of true theocracies in which the government is run by religious leaders in conformity with religious law. In my blue jeans and baseball cap, I was obviously an American tourist—a rarity there—and ordinary people often approached me to talk. When the piano player in the lobby of my hotel in Isfahan, in central Iran, spotted me, he stopped playing and approached. "Everything I know about America I have learned from the movies," he said, engagingly. He wanted to know if what he had learned was accurate.

"What movies have you seen?" I asked.

"Animal House," he replied.

"Um, not exactly," I said, smiling, and told him that he might want to see a few more American films.

As diverting as these encounters with ordinary Iranians were, I stayed focused on my quest to understand Islam, meeting with Shiite clerics in mosques in a number of large Iranian cities. In Shiite Islam, the religious leader is referred to as a cleric, not an imam. The distinction goes beyond the name. Shiites (or Shia), as opposed to Sunnis, consider their spiritual leaders to be endowed with special metaphysical qualities. An imam, on the other hand, is more like a rabbi; he is hired by a mosque primarily to be a leader of that mosque as well as a teacher, and is not considered to be selected by Allah or possessed of any more influence with Allah than any other Muslim. The Shia structure is centralized under the leadership of mullahs who are much more powerful than the Sunni imams, and the most powerful Shia spiritual leaders are the ayatollahs, who, in Iran, run the government.

One afternoon, our tour group went to a mosque in Shiraz, a city in southwest Iran, where we met with two clerics who talked to us about Islam. As an aside, this was no ordinary tour group: One of our fellow travelers managed war crime tribunals, including the trial of Charles Taylor, former president of Liberia; another woman was an expert on atomic energy.

As usual, I was the most outspoken, asking the cleric of the Shiraz mosque, "Is it true that Muslims should not make friends with the Jews because Jews are friends with the Christians?" The origin of this question came directly from my reading of the Quran: chapter 5, verse 51, which says, per numerous translations, *"O you who believe, do not take the Jews and the Christians for intimate friends. They are friends with each other. Whoever takes them as intimate friends is one of them. Surely, Allah does not take the unjust people to the right path."*

The cleric's response was not what I expected. "You do not fully understand the passage," he said. "It's fine to take Christians as your friends, but you should not be friends with the Jews because they are evil." Instead of being offended, I felt like an anthropologist who had stumbled across a new insight, one that was valuable to understanding the larger puzzle. The cleric didn't mean to insult me; he assumed our group consisted of all Christians and he wanted us to view Islam in a positive light.

Later on, that same cleric invited me to come to his office for a private meeting and offered me a pamphlet on the Quran and the Virgin Mary. At that point, I thought I should make it clear to the cleric that I was Jewish. He was clearly surprised but offered me an out. "You may be Jewish," he said, "but do you support Israel?" When I said I saw Israel as the one place where Jews would always be welcome, he determined that we had little left to discuss, and our previously cordial meeting was somewhat abruptly terminated.

I tell this story to illustrate a long-running point of contention between myself and Imam Subedar, who often contends that the Quran is not biased against Jews. My response is that any reader of the Quran (with the possible exception of someone with Imam Subedar's learned background) would likely come to a different conclusion, since a number of passages do seem to disparage Jews in the harshest manner. And I can only conclude that since the passages are in the Quran, any Muslim would assume that it was Allah himself doing the disparaging. By way of example, in chapter 2, verse 65, of an English translation of the Quran given to me by a cleric in Qom, Iran, there is a passage that, referring to the Jews, says: *"Be as apes despised."*

The power of the Quran's messages was dramatically illustrated to me in Qom, one of the Shiites' holiest cities and the location of an important mosque where Ayatollah Khomeini was trained. There, I met an English-speaking cleric in an office specifically designated for travelers. The cleric was impressed that I showed some knowledge of the Quran and, furthermore, that I had read the full text (albeit in English). He told me he was going to arrange a special tour for me and my traveling buddy and close friend, Rick Taft, who also happens to be the great-grandson of former president and Supreme Court Justice William Howard Taft.

Rick and I met when we both served in the Ohio State government in the 1970s, when he was an advisor to the attorney general and I was on the governor's staff. But whenever I mentioned Rick's unique pedigree to various Iranians we met in our travels, rather than seeming interested, they were strangely cool in their response. Later, I came to realize that they must have feared the consequences of engaging with any Westerner perceived as having influence. The danger in the ayatollah's Iran was saying the wrong thing to the wrong person. On this occasion in Qom, Rick and I were taken to the courtyard at the Azam Mosque, where the Grand Ayatollah Khomeini, the first supreme leader of the Islamic Republic of Iran, had lectured. Non-Muslims were not permitted to enter, but to my surprise, our escort turned to me and said he would like to take me inside, "since you've read the Quran." When I asked why he was making an exception, he made it clear that he assumed I wished to convert.

That isn't as far-fetched as it might seem. Unlike converting to Judaism, which requires extensive study with a rabbi over a period of months, converting to Islam is known to be easy. All one needs to do is to proclaim with belief the few lines of the Shahada, or Declaration of Faith: *Ash hadu an La ilaha illa Allah, Wa Ash hadu anna Muhammadan Rasool ul Allah,* or "I bear witness that there is no true god except God (Allah), and I bear witness that Muhammed is the (final) Messenger of God." Given his position, the Qom cleric was perhaps reasonable in assuming that, having read the Quran, I would not only see that it presented the truth of how I should live my life but would, of course, want to convert.

I didn't want to mislead the man, so I asked, "What happens if I change my mind after I convert?" Our guide cut in at this point, responding, "If you convert, it's assumed that you are old enough to make such a decision." This was his way of saying that I couldn't take the conversion back. As curious as I was to see the interior of the mosque, I declined the invitation.

In the end, what I found in my travels from mosque to mosque is that my interest in and basic understanding of Islam were always met with appreciation. At the famous Sultan Ahmed, or Blue Mosque, in Istanbul, I met with the imam who, at first, explained he did not have much time because he had to pick up his son. Once he realized that my questions to him were informed and that I read the Quran, however, he somehow found time for our discussion.

We all want to interact with those who share an interest in and respect for what we view as important, and though I didn't know it then, this story illustrates why my coauthor and I believe that acquiring a basic understanding of Islam is a critical first step Westerners must take in connecting with their Muslim neighbors.

In March of 2015, my future coauthor was invited to speak at All Angels by the Sea Episcopal Church, which happened to be located right next to my synagogue. He had come to talk about the all-inclusive and peaceful nature of Islam, and my first impression was of an imposing-looking man with a striking beard who was warmly received by the non-Muslim audience. I'm sure that for many listeners, it was their first exposure to the theology of Islam.

During the Q&A afterward, I raised my hand and asked, "Is it true that Allah turned some Jews into pigs and monkeys?" I heard gasps as many heads swiveled in my direction. My fellow audience members must have considered my question to be, at best, provocative; at worst, rude and disrespectful. But I knew that the Quran clearly stated that Allah had transformed some Jews into apes and swine (Quran 5:60): "*Shall I tell you who will receive a worse penalty from God? Those whom God has rejected and with whom He has been angry. They were condemned as apes and swine and those who worship evil. These are in the worst plight and farthest astray from the right path.*" (Since the previous verse was referring to "the people of the book," Jews were without doubt the subject of this transformation.)

My intention was to see if Imam Subedar would acknowledge or disavow this passage. As I look back, perhaps I also wanted to demonstrate my knowledge of the Quran and signal to the speaker that he could not sweet-talk everyone into believing that Islam was a religion of peace.

To the shock of the gathered audience, Imam Subedar answered, "Yes, this did happen, but they [the apes and swine] did not live long enough to have children." I took this to be his way of defusing the Muslim slur that "Jews are the sons of apes and swine," because if none of the apes and swine lived long enough to have children, this couldn't be the case. The distinction may seem subtle, but Imam Subedar's answer had a profound impact on me. Here was a learned and devout Muslim who was not going to turn away from his beliefs because they might sound bizarre or threatening or racist to his audience. His answer suggested to me that this person was a man of faith and integrity. He would not come up with something more palatable simply because it would be easier for his non-Muslim audience to digest. I would contrast this with my experience with the clerics in Iran who, assuming their audience was Christian, were concerned about not portraying Islam in a negative light.

At the time, I believed that Imam Subedar could have chosen to answer my question in a less controversial way, even if his answer wasn't strictly true. From my reading about Islam, I had come to understand, perhaps incorrectly, that under certain circumstances, Muslims were not prohibited from lying. The support for this is in

Quran 3:28, explained by Muhammad ibn Jarir al-Tabari (d. 923), author of a standard and authoritative Quran commentary: *"If you [Muslims] are under their [non-Muslims'] authority, fearing for yourselves, behave loyally to them with your tongue while harboring inner animosity for them . . ."* This concept is known as *taqiyya*, and I assumed it meant that Muslims were allowed to lie if they had to, to avoid presenting Islam in an unfavorable light to non-Muslims. Yet Imam Subedar explained his view of these potentially offensive verses in a straightforward, unvarnished manner.

After the lecture, I introduced myself and told Imam Subedar that I had been reading and lecturing and teaching adult education courses on Islam. Rather than being put off, he seemed intrigued by my interest, and, later, after we had talked more, he agreed to be a guest lecturer at some of my courses. Whenever we spent time talking about these presentations, I found him to be open-minded and deeply concerned that Islam was being distorted not only by Islamic extremists but also by those seeking to blame the religion for provoking violence in certain individuals.

Unbeknownst to Imam Subedar, I fit into the latter category quite comfortably. I kept my views to myself (at least until writing this book) as Imam Subedar and I joined together on a number of other projects, including a public debate on whether the language of the Quran was intolerant and encouraged violence. When he was invited to speak at the international headquarters of Scientology in Clearwater, Florida, he wrangled me an invitation, despite Scientology being notoriously secretive and normally closed to outsiders.

After Imam Subedar finished his speech to the Scientologists, which garnered a standing ovation, the two of us were given a tour of The Flag—the mysterious inner sanctum of Scientology. We were shown a magnificent building filled with art and were even permitted to watch (from a respectful distance) as Scientology adherents were monitored by a so-called E-meter that measured their response to stress. At some point, I agreed to be hooked up to the E-meter and was asked to think of an emotional experience; when I did, the dial registered my distress. I imagine this is similar to how a lie detector test might work.

I tell this story because while I had difficulty suppressing my own skepticism about this religion, I noticed that Imam Subedar was not only unfazed by what we were seeing and hearing, but respectful and poised throughout. All of this is part of why I eventually proposed the idea of our doing a book together. His answer took me aback at first. "If we do this book," he said, "it has to portray the true Islam—that's the only way we can create mutual understanding between Muslims and non-Muslims. That has to be your purpose, too."

I absorbed that, silently. To be honest, at that point, my motivation for doing a book was to expose Islam for the threat I sincerely believed it to be. At the time, I wondered how Imam Subedar could justify some of the violent and controversial verses found in the Quran. Passage 2:190, for instance, commands adherents to fight in the cause of Allah; 9:5 to slay the pagans; 22:39–40 gives permission to take up arms if attacked.

"It's all about context," is what he told me. "Before passing judgment, it's necessary to understand the context and situation." It became a phrase I'd hear over and over, to which I'd often reply that I doubted that the terrorists and thugs who belonged to Al Qaeda and ISIS were Islamic scholars or took context into consideration. "When they read the Quran," I'd argue, "they read the same words I do, but believe that what they are reading are Allah's words spoken directly to them. You're a just and decent man of faith, but these troubling verses do not come with an instruction book. There's nothing in there to temper the passions of newly radicalized extremists."

To my admittedly uneducated ear, the Quran, with its violent passages throughout, sends a very different message than the one Imam Subedar is hearing. Granted, that message is likely influenced by listening to years of anti-Muslim rhetoric that has inundated the media and Internet—the gruesome depictions of ISIS beheadings; the movies portraying Muslims as a violent and barbaric enemy. Who could remain unaffected by this messaging? Not me. The undeniable reality is that these extremists exist, and they often quote the Quran to justify their heinous crimes, carrying out their barbaric acts in the name of Islam—or at least that's what the average person in the West believes.

As I've learned more, however, my views have evolved. At the beginning of this project, I saw this book we were writing as a zero-sum game with a winner and a loser—and I was certain that I would be the winner. I now know that most Muslims—including those I have met face-to-face—are not secretly bent on carrying out the disturbing commands in the Quran. The threat posed by Islam is not the same as the threat from radicalized "Muslims." Knowledge, tolerance, and respect are always worthy goals, and I have become more tolerant of Islam without endorsing or adopting Sharia, the Quran, or any of the theology myself.

Part of that likely has to do with the relationship I've developed with Imam Subedar over the years. Perhaps the greatest gift you can receive from a person of faith is having their beliefs directed powerfully toward you in times of distress. Whether or not you share those beliefs does not diminish the value of this gesture, one that has the capacity to end the cycle of hate fomented by those who seek power for their own benefit. I'm thinking of one particular weekend in July of 2021, when I was going into the hospital for a valve transplant in which my heart would be stopped and my breathing and heartbeat functions transferred to a heart-lung machine outside my body.

I had access to some very fine doctors, but I was not at all certain what the future would bring. And as I was wheeled into an enormous, brightly lit operating room filled with gleaming technology, where 10 to 15 people were carrying out various critical assignments, I was suddenly struck by the momentousness of the procedure I was about to undergo. I also understood why surgeons are so often accused of having God complexes. What ordinary human could command the intricate choreography of people, computers, medical devices, wires, and tubes with the goal of stopping a heart, operating on it, and inserting a valve from another species?

Yet I was also intrigued and energized by the knowledge that while I was under the knife at the Cleveland Clinic in Ohio, a group of Muslims in Plano, Texas, led by Imam Subedar, would be saying a prayer for my speedy recovery. In today's polarized world, Republicans and Democrats can barely speak to one another (at least over social media), but in that mosque, a group of Muslims would be praying for the health of an unknown Jew in a distant city. To me, in our tribal society, that was its own miracle.

As it happened, just a week after my surgery, I was out of the hospital and pain-free, my new cow valve doing its part. The lesson, to my mind, is not whether this act of far-off faith and kindness made a difference in my recovery, but whether such acts can change the world, transforming hate into tolerance and alienation to acceptance.

Coincidentally, Imam Subedar was scheduled for surgery himself one week after my ordeal. After I returned home from the hospital, I asked three rabbis at Temple Beth Israel in Longboat Key, Florida, to pray for Imam Subedar. I am not a religious man, but Imam Subedar is a devout Muslim, and I understood that Muslims viewed the power of prayer to be magnified by the number of people praying.

The morning before his surgery, when it was still dark, I sent Imam Subedar the Jewish prayer that is recited before surgery, and he responded by saying that he would pray using this prayer. I am happy to say that at the time, all of our prayers for his good health matched the result.

CHAPTER 4

My Understanding of Islam

By Robert Gary

I n this chapter, I offer my understanding of Islam through the lens of an American, a lawyer, and a Jew. I aspire to provide to our non-Muslim readers a rudimentary understanding of the origins and basic theology of Islam. I believe this is the bare minimum required to see Islam as a religion and not a political entity hell-bent on world domination by violent means.

Over the years I have read books, prepared talks from random notes, traveled to Islamic countries, and interacted with imams, clerics, and everyday Muslims, all in an effort to understand Islam. Of course, any study of Islam begins with the Quran. However, the Quran is not like the TaNaKh—the Hebrew Bible— or the Christian Bible. These Bibles contain important life stories and insights about the origins of Judaism and about Jesus and the origins of Christianity. The Quran, by comparison, does not contain the sayings of Muhammed, details of his life, or a comprehensive narrative and history of the origins of Islam. Thus I have had to acquire this information from secondary sources over an extended period of time beginning in 1983. To be transparent, there are more than a few instances in these pages where I am not certain of my source. Thus I must beg your indulgence if, in this exposition of my understanding of Islam, I have, heaven forbid, inadvertently lifted information intact from another book or article. This is unlikely but possible. What I do know is that most of my knowledge of Islam comes from conversations with Muslim spiritual leaders and Islamic scholars. I also know that if I get it wrong, Imam Subedar will, in his chapters, correct what I have misstated.

The Origins of Islam

Muslims consider Muhammed to be God's final prophet. Born in 570 CE in Mecca, he was orphaned at an early age and raised by his grandfather for a couple of years and then by his paternal uncle, Abu Talib. As an adult, he worked as a trader leading caravans and eventually married a woman he met through his work, a widow named Khadija, who was a wealthy trader. The couple had four daughters, as well as two sons who died in infancy, over their 25 years together.

Then, in the year 610, Muslims believe, while alone in a cave outside Mecca, Muhammed began receiving revelations from Allah through the angel Gabriel. These revelations continued until Muhammed's death in 632 CE. According to Islamic tradition, Muhammed was illiterate and had to memorize the revelations. He repeated them to his associates, who in turn recorded them. It was not until 20 years or so after the death of Muhammed that scribes assembled these writings and compiled what became the Quran.

The initial revelations to Muhammed tended to be more peaceful than those that followed, and less likely to overtly call for fighting or aggressive responses to criticism of Islam. The tone of the revelations changed when Muhammed moved from Mecca to Medina in 622. By that time, he had gained many followers and was the leader of a rapidly expanding religion. The verses Muhammed received while he was in Medina are less tolerant of non-Muslims, and some are clearly a call to violent action. It is these later verses that often serve as justification for radicals and fundamentalists to carry out their terrorist agenda.

The Importance of the Quran to Muslims

It is not hyperbole to say that the Quran is integral to the lives of all observant Muslims. It is recited at birth and at death as well as on a daily basis; it is the foundation that anchors all that Muslims do and believe. Appreciating and understanding its unique role in Islam is indispensable to understanding Islam itself. The Quran guides the conduct of 2 billion Muslims across the globe, whether Shiite or Sunni. At the risk of repeating myself, it is universally accepted by Muslims that the Quran is the actual word of God and that Allah speaks to them directly through the Quran. Because of this, there is no need for any imam to serve as an intermediary, which makes Islam somewhat unique among religions. Although other sacred books such as the Hebrew and Christian Bibles are considered by the faithful to be the word of God, neither Christianity nor Judaism make the claim that reading these sacred texts is synonymous with God actually speaking at that moment. It becomes easier to grasp how Muslims think about the Quran if you think of the book as a time machine capable of putting the faithful in the presence of Allah.

As I studied, I kept this concept uppermost in my mind. I suggest you do the same as you read this book. To reiterate, the Quran in the Muslim faith is more than a sacred book authored by God; it is the speech of Allah, uncreated and always in existence. As you read the Quran, it transports you before Allah as he speaks to you through the words on the page. This idea is unique to Islam and may be difficult for non-Muslims to fully absorb. It is not possible to add or subtract a word from the Quran without corrupting its intention and meaning. Quran 6:115 says: *"The Word of your Lord is perfect in truthfulness and justice; no one can change His words. He is the All-Hearing, the All-Knowing."*

Muslims recite the Quran in a state of reverence, usually while facing in the direction of the Ka'bah, which is located on the grounds of Masjid al-Haram, the Great Mosque of Mecca, in Mecca, Saudi Arabia, as they do when in prayer. Quran 2:144 says: *". . . during prayer, turn your face towards the Sacred Mosque."*

Hearing or reciting the Quran in its original Arabic is thought to confer a blessing, and Muslims believe that the verses of the Quran can heal both the body and soul. Many Muslims carry small copies of the Quran (or digital apps of the Quran in their phones/tablets) with them at all times. The Quran sets out very specific rules as to who can handle it and how it is to be touched and stored. Verses 77, 78, and 79 of chapter 56 (Quran 56:77-79): *"Indeed, it is a noble Quran. In a Register well-protected; which none can touch except the purified."*

To touch the Quran, Muslims must be clean and pure. In order to meet that requirement, Muslims must wash their hands, face, mouth, nose, arms, and feet with clean water. Muslims must perform that same purification process before each prayer as well. This process is called *wudu*. After menstrual bleeding or intercourse, a Muslim is required to bathe before touching the Quran. Many Islamic scholars say that non-Muslims should not touch or handle the Quran because they are "unclean," though they may listen to recordings. Non-Muslims may also touch translations, which are not considered actual Qurans but "interpretations." Complicating matters, many scholars believe the Quran cannot be accurately translated from Arabic to another language.

Reading the Quran As a Non-Muslim

Because the Quran is the (immutable) word of Allah, it is an unimpeachable and uniquely transparent source for learning what Muslims believe and how they are to conduct themselves. You might say that in prosecutorial legal terms, the Quran is the equivalent of a deposition of Allah that in turn makes Islam accessible to non-Muslims. However, there are some significant caveats. To be a true Quran, it must be in Arabic, and some scholars say the Quran cannot be accurately translated. Thus I, like many others, can only read a "translation," which is not considered a true Quran. In addition, the structure of the Quran is unique.

When I delved into my first English translation of the Quran, I was surprised to find that it didn't read like any book I had ever encountered; indeed, it was almost impossible to comprehend. For one thing, the Quran isn't organized by topic or chronology. Instead, it is loosely structured by chapter length, with the longest chapter first and the shortest chapter last. The topics like women's rights or warfare are woven throughout the text in what some would consider a random fashion and others would describe as a tapestry. Muslims believe that the perfection of the Quran is itself proof that it could only be created by Allah. As a non-Muslim, I found it to be a daunting read, perhaps even more so because I did not begin my studies with an open mind. I encourage all of you to make an effort to read the Quran in order to form your own opinion. You can, for now, put that task aside for another day.

The Quran and Sharia

The Quran is not the only source of Sharia law. It is my understanding that Sharia law is made up of not just the Quran but also the Hadith and Sunnah—the words and actions of the prophet Muhammed. Both are subject to interpretation and even debate as to their authenticity. Both are meant to be resources for students of Islam and learned scholars, primarily to help explain the text of the Quran. Sharia is also partly based on fatwas, or declarations by respected and influential religious leaders. And unlike the Quran, the laws of Sharia do have some flexibility.

Yet for the average Muslim or non-Muslim, the Quran is the foundation of Islam. What the average Muslim understands about Islam is that the Quran is to be obeyed as the word of God.

Is the Quran a Book of Peace?

Prior to Islam in Arabia, the laws of one tribe did not apply to another. Technically, that meant that it was not considered wrong or immoral to steal from or kill someone who was not a member of your tribe. If they were powerful enough, the victimized tribe could enact revenge and retribution, which made for a chaotic way of living. Islam and the Quran helped bind often-warring tribes under the banner of one religion, but the Quran still reflects this tribal us-versus-them mentality, offering up two sets of rules—one for dealing with those inside the larger Islamic tribe and another for dealing with those outside of it. Other sacred books such as the TaNaKh and the Christian Bible may make similar us-versus-them statements, but Islam, in my opinion, is most intent on actually maintaining those beliefs in practice. The Quran is often described by Muslims as a book of peace. For non-Muslims, or "infidels," however, a very different set of rules and standards apply, standards that leave me questioning whether non-Muslims living in an Islamic society governed by Sharia law are truly secure. You may already be guessing how I would answer that question.

The Quran in Our Complex and Often Hostile Contemporary World

I have hammered away at the reverence Muslims have for the Quran and the many rules regarding its use in order to help non-Muslim readers understand why threatening to defile, or actually defiling, the Quran causes so much distress and disruption in the Muslim world. Once I understood that the Quran is the voice of Allah, it became central to my perception of the Quran and of Islam itself, leading me to the logical but perhaps incorrect conclusion that Muslims would under no circumstances not strictly obey its mandates. For this reason it surprises me that any Muslim would consider reinterpreting or de-emphasizing any verse of the Quran for political expediency or to present Islam as more acceptable to non-Muslims. Personally, I view such flexibility as hopeful and necessary if Muslims hope to thrive in the West and coexist with the other Abrahamic religions.

Still, just as in other religions (or in the U.S. Constitution, for that matter), there are those who argue that you have to consider the context and adjust to the circumstances. It is my opinion that my coauthor holds such views while remaining a devout Muslim whose faith is his internal compass. That being said, at times I believe he uses context as an escape hatch of sorts, to explain away certain troubling, harsh, or violent passages or to soften their meaning. For example, when I direct Imam Subedar to verses that clearly identify the Jews as "cursed by Allah" for rejecting "clear proofs" sent by Allah, or verses that mention them dying as disbelievers (Quran 2:159,161), he says, "Consider the context." I can accept that Muhammed and the Jews in Muhammed's day might have had a rocky relationship, but the Quran is considered eternal, and nowhere in the Quran is there a qualification to consider the circumstances and that modern-day Jews should get a break.

When it comes to the U.S. Constitution, I am not an originalist; I also believe context matters. But by definition, the words of the Quran are considered immutable since they come directly from Allah. Does a Muslim's adherence to Allah's commands in the Quran supersede that individual's independent intellectual and moral authority—qualities that might lead them to disagree with a particular passage in the Quran? It would seem so, because to reject the Quran would be a rejection of the faith. What is right or wrong, good or bad, stems from the words of the Quran, which are the words of Allah. That's why it makes sense to ask if, for Muslims, the words of the Quran override the civil laws of their home country. As I've indicated here, I believe that to be the case.

For me, and for many in the West, that's a problem. Take the Quran's stated punishment for stealing, in 5:38: "*And for the thief, male or female, cut off his or her hands . . .*" Or 2:282: "*. . . And get* *two witnesses out of your own men, and if two men are not there then a man and two women . . ."* meaning the testimony of one woman is not equal to that of one man. As a trial attorney, I assure you that no such distinction exists in any American courtroom. Imam Subedar is not troubled by such passages; he is clear that Muslims are expected to obey the laws of the country in which they reside. Yet it is also clear that the preferred law for devout Muslims is Sharia. We need only look at Saudi Arabia, Iran, and now Afghanistan to see what life is like under Sharia law. In Iran, women are facing down the "morality police" and, at grave risk to their lives, attempting to throw off the requirements of having to cover their hair, just to give one example.

That black-and-white perspective can be a double-edged sword. For a non-Muslim like me, taking the Quran—the words of Allah—at face value makes it easier to gain insights, however superficial, into what Muslims believe. So what are we to assume a suicide bomber or members of Iran's morality police believe? Are the words of the Quran the source of Islamic extremism? This question troubles me.

And yet Islam has many iterations and many followers, from those in Al Qaeda or ISIS who believe everyone on the planet should adhere to the edicts of the Quran, to those who are more moderate. Obviously, there is no room for alliances with the Taliban or the Iranian regime. Indeed, any alliance between Muslims, Jews, and other groups may have its best chance of success in the United States, simply because the American Muslim population is generally more moderate than Muslims in other countries. In today's America, the old canard "the enemy of my enemy is my friend" is increasingly relevant. Did the mass pardoning of the Proud Boys and Oath Keepers for their actions on January 6th also send a signal that

America is for white Christians and others are fair game? Time will tell, but the threat to Muslims and Jews from Christian nationalists is a reality. However, it is not this common threat, but the plight of the Palestinians that defines the relationship between America's Jews and Muslims.

Nevertheless, across the world signs of improbable alliances are emerging, such as business ties between the UAE and Israel, as well as Saudi Arabia seeking to attract American travelers to create a thriving tourist industry. That is why I remain hopeful that the goal of a Jewish-Muslim partnership will one day be possible, despite efforts by terrorist groups such as Hamas to disrupt any attempt at détente.

CHAPTER 5

What Is Shariah?

By Imam Azhar Subedar

In March of 2015, nearly 15 years after 9/11 and amid the pervasive Islamophobia in the West since those attacks, I was invited to give two talks on Islam by the All Angels by the Sea Episcopal Church in Longboat Key, Florida. The first would be an introduction to Islam, and the second an in-depth look at the practices of the faith. That in itself was a tall order because of the complexity of the topic. Even more daunting was the knowledge that the crowd would consist of mostly retirees. Throughout my years of giving presentations to a variety of audiences, I've found that seniors in America may be the most informed demographic. Their lives are rooted in knowledge, service, careers, experiences, interactions, travels, and a wealth of history, and I knew the group would have a lot of questions. I also knew that, despite my training, I was only in my mid-30s, and I still had much to learn from this group and their world.

So when Bob posed his potentially provocative question about pigs and monkeys that day, I was actually grateful to be reminded of the fears held by many about Islam—including that Islam might be anti-Semitic. I was grateful to be taken out of my world, which can sometimes feel like a protected bubble. The truth is, every extremist terrorist attack intensifies the perception that all Muslims are a threat to the West and the world beyond. And it made sense that Bob would see certain phrases in the Quran as substantiating that threat.

I recall that first exchange with my now coauthor as vividly as he does, but what really lingers in my mind is the common ground we found in our conversations that followed that first meeting. One thing that concerned both of us from the very beginning was the fact that when the average non-Muslim hears the word *Islam*, they are likely to think "terrorism."

This mutual concern grew into a partnership, one I sometimes liken to two competitors who are ready to go all out to make their point heard above all others. That's how it started, anyway. Bob invited me to lecture on Islam as a guest at several of his classes. On another occasion, we did a joint presentation on the Quran and its compatibility with the West, our views often diametrically opposed. But even as we disagreed, we had a common goal (one we still share): to challenge our audience (including you, our reader) to keep an open mind between two very different perspectives. Bob has read translations of the Quran, traveled the Islamic world, and met with imams and clerics in many countries. Yet his view of Islam is still (understandably) shaped by the actions of a few who have carried out heinous acts in the name of Islam. My view, on the other hand, has been shaped by what I've learned through my studies, as a religious leader, and as a devout follower of the Quran and Shariah law.

As my coauthor rightly emphasizes, no Muslim is in a position to deny or reject what the Quran says, for it is the word of Allah to us all. But it is also true that every Muslim must strive to understand the word of Allah in its correct context, including its relevance to the present time and situation. For my coauthor, the Quran reads, in part, as a book of commands and laws to be obeyed, literally. To me, it is so much more. I see the Quran as a beautiful conversation that the Lord Almighty is having with me, in which I reciprocate by standing in prayer and conversing with Him while reciting those very same verses.

Beyond prayer, I strive to live by the Quran in my everyday life, using it as a tool to rectify my character, maximize goodness in my life, and nourish my soul. As a Muslim, I don't see the Quran as consisting of commands from Allah but as guidance or directions given by Allah, my creator and master, who knows what can harm me and what is truly best for me.

When Allah speaks in the Quran of Good and Evil, He is giving me direction on how to live. When He brings up stories of past nations, like Moses and the Jews wandering the desert and receiving food from heaven, or Jonah's repentance in the belly of the whale, He is teaching me lessons from history. When He rebukes past nations for their actions, such as those who went fishing on the Sabbath, or the once powerful pharaoh who, after claiming to be God and torturing the Children of Israel, met his fate at the Red Sea, He is sharing concerns and tenets for living: to obey rather than be disobedient; to be humble and not arrogant; to not disrupt His perfect creation. When He talks about categories of people, including believers, disbelievers, and hypocrites, He is illuminating the paths that lie before all Muslims as we navigate life through Islam. It is through that lens and a perspective on Islam shaped by years of studying under Islamic scholars that

I intend to present the true nature of Islam. Read what I have to say with an open mind, jot down your concerns and questions, and feel free to engage with us after reading this book. If time permits, perhaps we can even meet up. As is evident from my first and succeeding encounters with my coauthor, I'm no stranger to contentious conversation.

An Introduction to Shariah

If you've heard of Shariah, even vaguely, chances are you have a strong opinion about it. State legislators have tried to ban it; extremists have gone to war over it; others, like me, see it as a guide to living. Whatever your opinion, in the pages that follow, my aim is to essentially provide a primer on Shariah, since knowledge, as we've said, is the basis of understanding. Shariah is the path or legislation that Allah set forth for His followers. That path is the *deen* (practice), or way of life, for those who believe in Him. For Muslims, that is the religion of Islam. Shariah is not a particular book or a manual found in a particular chapter of the Quran or elsewhere. Rather, it is a complete life code disseminated through the Quran and the Hadith. Scholars of the faith, through their education and expertise, have the duty and religious obligation to educate and exemplify the lifestyle of Shariah for their congregants and followers and the Muslim community at large. But instruction from experts is not always required; every aspect of daily life—including how to worship, dress, eat, and live with integrity—is found within the Quran and Hadith, accessible to all.

Every Muslim who adheres to the teachings of the faith is a follower of Shariah.

(Quran 42:13)

شَرَعَ لَكُم مِّنَ ٱلدِّينِ مَا وَصَّىٰ بِهِ نُوحًا وَٱلَّذِىٓ أَوْحَيْنَآ إِلَيْكَ وَمَا وَصَّيْنَا
بِهِۦٓ إِبْرُٰهِيمَ وَمُوسَىٰ وَعِيسَىٰٓ أَنْ أَقِيمُوا۟ ٱلدِّينَ وَلَا تَتَفَرَّقُوا۟ فِيهِ كَبُرَ عَلَى
ٱلْمُشْرِكِينَ مَا تَدْعُوهُمْ إِلَيْهِ ٱللَّهُ يَجْتَبِىٓ إِلَيْهِ مَن يَشَآءُ وَيَهْدِىٓ إِلَيْهِ مَن يُنِيبُ

He [Allah] has ordained for you the same religion which
He ordained for Noah (the first Messenger), and that which
We have revealed to you [O Muhammad—the last Messenger],
and that which We ordained for Abraham (the father of the
Abrahamic faiths), Moses (the Messenger of the Jews), and
Jesus (the Messenger of the Christians) saying you should
establish religion and make no divisions in it.

Muslims believe that all messengers (prophets) taught their people the path set forth by Allah, but that in some cases, the specifics of the laws differed. Often, the laws of Islam also differ from the tenets of Christianity and Judaism. The goal of Islam, the path of life for all Muslims, along with the overarching goal of all the laws of Shariah, is to ensure that every human being who follows Islam—i.e., Muslims—embodies the highest level of character, morality, and goodness. Kindness, mercy, empathy, love, and forgiveness are just a few of the many good human characteristics, and all Muslims are expected to live by these values. The Prophet Muhammad was sent for the perfection of moral conduct.

Remembering that is the key to understanding why the laws in Shariah were established: to prevent followers from falling short of the level of character and morals that define a Muslim.

To help make Islam and Shariah accessible to non-Muslim readers, I'll be turning to some tools I created when I was studying in England in the '90s, in my fifth year of Islamic scholarship. Back then, I was introduced to a textbook entitled *The Principles of Shariah* by Ash-Shashi. That book, dry as it was, ignited my passion for Shariah, and I decided to write much simpler chapter summaries to help my classmates and myself prepare for the final exam.

Two decades later, when I visited my institute in England in 2016 to mourn the loss of the principal there, a man I considered to be my spiritual father, I was surprised to find that students there were still making copies of those chapter summaries and using them to study. I'll be using a version of those notes in this section.

The Pillars of Shariah

Shariah is established on four foundational sources or pillars. Like the four wheels of a car, each pillar is essential to the whole—the beauty is in that balance. It is also important to note that the Shariah of Islam is fluid, evolving over time and adapting to circumstances in modern life. It is not set in stone.

The four pillars of Shariah are:

1. The Quran
2. The Hadith
3. The Consensus of Scholars
4. Juristic Analogy

The first two pillars are from divine sources: The Quran is the word of Allah, and the Hadith are the words and actions of the Prophet Muhammad (peace be upon him). Note that Hadith literature, which comprises the sayings of the Prophet Muhammad and/or descriptions of his actions, is considered secondary to the

Quran, which is the word of God (verbatim), in which Allah Himself promises to preserve the word from any type of alteration.

(Quran 15:9)

إِنَّا نَحْنُ نَزَّلْنَا الذِّكْرَ وَإِنَّا لَهُ لَحَافِظُونَ

Indeed, it is We who sent down the Quran, and indeed,
We will be its guardian.

Over the past 1,400 years, many attempts have been made to alter and even manipulate the text of the Quran. Yet it remains in its original form, the sanctity of the words preserved, in part, by the hundreds of thousands of individuals who have memorized the Quran from cover to cover and continue to teach it to the next generation of Muslims.

As for *Hadith*, it, too, is the word of Allah, as the Prophet Muhammad never spoke on his own accord but only through Allah's direction. The Quran confirms that.

(Quran 53:3,4)

وَمَا يَنطِقُ عَنِ الْهَوَى إِنْ هُوَ إِلَّا وَحْيٌ يُوحَى

Nor does he [Muhammad] speak from [his own] inclination.
It is not but a revelation revealed.

This might seem confusing, but the meaning is relatively simple: The Quran, which is the direct word of Allah, is protected by the promise of Allah, as stated in 15:9 above. In addition, merely reciting the Quran is considered to be an act of worship. The Hadith, on the other hand, is a compilation of not just the words but also the actions of Muhammad. Another difference: Unlike the Quran, the Hadith is not read as an act of worship and is not protected against alteration by Allah, despite the fact that its words, too, were divinely guided. The reason for the difference is that rather than being the direct word of Allah, the Hadith is a compilation of traditions established by companions of Muhammad—individuals who observed him, passing along what they saw and heard orally and eventually writing them down.

It's important to keep in mind that unlike the Quran, the contents of Hadith have been transmitted over time by a rigorous but not infallible method that started with oral teachings that then became written. As a result, certain Hadith are considered less reputable than others, depending on how well the initial words were preserved and how they were transmitted. Worse, some Hadith have been specifically manipulated, with words intentionally altered, fabricated, or translated incorrectly. This primarily affects those who can't read or understand the Arabic text and so are reading in translation. There is actually an entire branch of study focused on how to vet Hadith, which is not the case for the Quran, since it is protected by the Divine.

I remember once, back in the '90s, on a visit from England to a mosque in America, I was sharing a meal with a fellow Muslim brother, both of us seated on the floor and eating from the same plate, as is customary.

Midbite, I observed that this man was looking at me in an odd way, his expression reflecting the discomfort I was feeling about him. The reason behind that exchange of looks, we discovered, is that I was eating with my right hand while he was eating with his left hand. "Why are you eating with your left hand?" I burst out.

"I was about to ask you the same thing about your right hand," he responded.

When I told him that eating with the right hand was the prophetic way, as documented in the Hadith, he disagreed, citing the same source. I told him that the Hadith states that Muslims should eat with their right hand.

"The devil does!" was his retort, and he repeated that the Hadith clearly directed Muslims to eat with their left hand.

Later that evening, he brought his book to the mosque, which was an English translation, and I saw that his version did indeed command Muslims to eat with their left hand. The Arabic text, however, directed the opposite, which I promptly showed him, explaining that in Arabic, *yameen* means "right" and *shimaal* means "left." After more explanation on my part, he agreed that his version likely contained a translation error.

The second two pillars of Shariah are considered to be from human sources. The first is Consensus, which is when recognized Islamic scholars mutually agree on the legality of an issue but no explicit ruling exists in either of the divine sources. This pertains mostly to contemporary issues that have no precedent—for instance, whether Islam allows the use of a cell phone or permits a Muslim to live in a non-Muslim country.

The final pillar is Juristic Analogy, which are logical deductions based on primary principles that are extracted from the Quran and Hadith, but that don't require the consensus of recognized Islamic scholars. When an immediate answer is needed for confounding issues such as whether it is permissible to pray on a plane if your seat does not face Makkah, or when to fast if you happen to be in a country or region when the sun doesn't set (such as Alaska in summer), a recognized Islamic scholar will come to a decision based on explicit guidance from the two divine sources.

It's important to note those words: "recognized Islamic scholar(s)." I use them intentionally. My point is that the two human sources doing the interpreting cannot be laypeople or anyone who deems themselves knowledgeable (whether due to their social media following or any other factor) but hasn't studied the subjects required for understanding and interpreting the Quran and Hadith. I feel this point must be highlighted because, as I explain aspects of Shariah in the coming pages, my words are based on this foundational knowledge and what I consider to be a stable interpretation.

While this may all seem abstract to the average reader, the objectives of Shariah are anything but. They include:

1. To reform society for the better, so that people contribute to their communities rather than harm them
2. To establish justice for all humans
3. To promote the well-being of all communities
4. To create a safe and secure society as well as a socially stable environment
5. To create an environment that fosters self-development, where everyone can thrive and reach their full potential

By following Shariah, humans increase the chances that they and their communities will meet the objectives noted above.

Who Follows Shariah?

Each of the Abrahamic faiths has its own Shariah (such as Jews, who have the Halakhah), but the *concept* of Shariah applies to anyone who subscribes to or follows any belief system. To be clear, if you follow a prescribed way of life, a religious teaching, or a divine revelation aside from Islam, that is your Shariah. Even the mere belief that you live according to a specific code for a particular purpose—say, to uphold individual values—may be considered your Shariah. Even if you don't believe in a prescribed faith, a divine code of life, or any religion, whatever code you live by is your Shariah.

Given how many Americans perceive the Shariah of Islam as an extremist ideology that was formulated in a cave by radicals harboring the sinister objective of dominating the world, my explanation may surprise you. Perhaps you're wondering: What about the imposition of rigid rules governing what all citizens can say or do in Iran and Saudi Arabia? What about brutal practices such as honor killings, public stonings, floggings, public beheadings, and amputation of limbs, not to mention child marriages, polygamy, spousal abuse, and a lack of rights for women? For all of these reasons, Shariah is often perceived as a threat to the free world. You may be even more surprised when I tell you that the true Islamic Shariah bears no resemblance to the description above.

My goal in laying all this out is to chip away at biases toward Islam that are based on ignorance and that may be resulting in baseless fears. In a survey taken in 2018, more than 2 in 5 Americans said that Islam was incompatible with American values. I have listened to those fears firsthand when traveling for speaking engagements or otherwise performing my duties as an imam. Back in 2015, for instance, in a small town in Florida I once called home, an anti-Muslim lobbying group known as Act for America brought a complaint to the Charlotte County Public School board that a particular history textbook assigned to high schoolers was "indoctrinating" children with Islam and had inadvertently made them Muslims without their knowing it. Incidentally, during the first Trump presidency, the founder of this group, a woman named Brigitte Gabriel, boasted about her access to the Trump administration and remains in close contact with Trump today.

Though their claim had no substance, a petition was created and enough signatures gathered that the county school board was compelled to assign a committee of individuals to look into this accusation. The committee included a Muslim woman, a member of Act for America, the school's history teacher, and a few community members. As the imam of that town and a concerned resident and parent, I, too, participated in most of those hearings.

During one specific meeting, some parents brought their children along and had them line up against the back wall of the conference room holding signs that made their parents' negative opinions about Islam quite clear. To me, it was heartbreaking to see them standing there as the proceedings dragged on, shifting their feet uncomfortably, almost as if they were stuck in after-school detention. The member on the panel representing Act for America made a point of bringing a copy of the Quran to each meeting and placing it on the floor in front of her. After she sat down, she would rest her feet on top of it.

The meetings occurred over the course of several weeks, and by the last one, the tension in the room was palpable: Would the history book in question continue to be used or not? Just as bad, would Act for America bring their hate-and-fear-filled agenda to towns and cities beyond our area?

Sitting next to me at one meeting was an elderly white woman who, I noticed, kept throwing me looks of disgust. I wore what

I always wore to those meetings—my Islamic garb, usually a one-piece long robe, known as a *thawb*, the traditional dress that clearly distinguished me in the crowd as a Muslim. Time and time again, she would look at me, pointedly scoff, then turn back toward the front of the room where the discussions were taking place.

There was a moment in that session when I pulled out my phone to take a picture of the committee members as they were deliberating, except I couldn't because this woman stuck her hand in front of my phone. To avoid an argument, I put my phone down until, absorbed by the discussion, I absentmindedly pulled out my phone to take a picture of the members again, and, once again, she put her hand up, this time tapping on the screen of my phone with her bright red nails. At that time, I became agitated and told her she didn't have the right to stop me from taking pictures. Luckily, a break was called a few minutes later, and I happened to notice that sitting next to her on the other side was one of our mosque's Christian interfaith partners, Sushila Cherian. I leaned over, and she and I began sharing our views of the ongoing process, of which we both disapproved. To my surprise, when we finished speaking, the elderly woman turned to Sushila and asked with amazement, "Do you know this person?" Sushila responded, "Sure, he is the local imam." The elderly lady seemed taken aback and, after a pause, turned to me and asked if I was indeed an imam. I nodded, and she then asked if there was a mosque nearby. When I nodded again, she grew quiet for a while, then asked, "Am I allowed to visit the mosque?" I responded, "Certainly." She then leaned close to my ear and whispered, "I won't get shot, will I?"

Trying to dispel her fear with a little levity, I responded, "No, you won't. At least not the first time. I can't guarantee what will happen in your follow-up visits." As the color drained from her face, I realized that maybe that wasn't the best response on my part.

Ultimately, the committee determined that the history book was acceptable. However, in retrospect, Act for America actually succeeded in their mission by sowing enough doubt about Islam in the hearts of those who attended the meetings that they met their objective of spreading baseless fear of Islam in a small town.

In addition to *Shariah*, the word *Caliphate* often strikes fear into the hearts of Westerners. The Caliphate (*Khilafah* in Arabic) was the Islamic system of governance that spanned three continents (parts of Africa, Asia, and Europe) for almost 1,300 years. Shariah law was practiced under this system.

Given the implications of the word today, it may surprise some that, historically, education was highly valued by the Caliphate, paving the way for constructive growth and innovation. As stated in a Hadith, Prophet Muhammad said, *"Seeking knowledge is an obligation upon every Muslim."* (Hadith, Ibn Majah 224). And in the first centuries after Muhammad, Muslims were indeed innovators. In the year 852, during the Abbasid Caliphate, which lasted from 750 to 1258, Abbas ibn Firnas jumped from the tower of the Great Mosque of Córdoba in Spain using the world's first parachute, which he fashioned from canvas. During that same era, the writings of Abdallah Ibn-Sina, born in 970 in Uzbekistan, formed the basis of medical instruction in European universities until the 17th century.

Given these advances and the inspirational Muslims behind them, how did Islam come to seem anti-education, as evidenced by the ongoing battles in Afghanistan and Pakistan, where women continue to fight for the right to be educated?

Take, for example, the situation in Afghanistan. When America withdrew from that country in August of 2021, a Taliban-led government took over, promising to govern with a better understanding of the needs of their people (at least compared with their rule prior to 9/11). Yet soon after they came to power, women were banned from pursuing a college education. In Afghanistan, the highest level of education most girls can now obtain is grade 6—the final year of primary school. Although the Taliban will claim they have their reasons for doing so, it is difficult to accept this decision as being in the best interest of the country and the people they govern. Nor is this ruling in alignment with the teachings of the Islamic faith.

Dictatorships, of course, are known for censoring information and preventing the dissemination of knowledge among their people, since information and education can be used against them. As I've mentioned, this is not the teaching of Islam, nor was this the case under Caliphates, where opportunities for education flourished. The oldest university in the world, for instance, was founded in 737 CE during the Umayyad Caliphate, and it is still operating in today's Tunisia as the Ez-Zitouna University. The House of Wisdom was also established in the 8th century by the Abbasid dynasty, in Baghdad, Iraq, attracting men and women of many faiths and ethnicities to learn from Muslim experts in mathematics and astronomy, medicine and zoology, and to do research in its renowned library of Islamic history. That this history and love of education has now reversed course in so many Islamic societies should be a matter of grave concern for all Muslims, for it serves as a testament that Muslims have veered far from their core principles. The Prophet Muhammad stated, *"Whoever travels a path in search of knowledge, Allah will make easy for him a path to Paradise"* (Hadith, Muslim 2699). This saying of his makes clear that the path to Paradise is connected to seeking knowledge, for only knowledge will provide the right tools to build actions that will make one worthy of Paradise. Life for a Muslim is better lived with rooted knowledge, and so is life's outcome. Those who devalue, discredit, or even deter people from acquiring knowledge are red flags under Islamic teachings. Whether they do so out of ignorance, fear, political expediency, a cultural drift toward suppression, or anything else is something I don't have a precise answer for. What I do know is that this path is not what Islam promoted nor what the Prophet endorsed. These are self-serving restrictions meant to suppress the masses for personal gain.

Equally disturbing is how alternative views or opinions can supplant stable and rooted knowledge passed down through generations from person to person in classroom settings and institutes of knowledge. When we uproot time-tested knowledge, humankind will flock to anything and everything else as if it were equally credible. No wonder there is an epidemic of ignorance fueled by apps and social media platforms that equate popularity with insight and wisdom. And as AI reshapes our world, the distinction between fact and fiction will become increasingly difficult to discern. Even more concerning is when fiction literally becomes fact, and facts are written off as false altogether—a shift we are already beginning to witness.

Many children in the West now see school attendance as a burden and something they shouldn't have to do. The result of this mindset is a lower regard not only for school, but for knowledge, textbooks, and teachers as well. In other parts of the world, compulsory school uniforms help create an environment that encourages respect for knowledge and prioritizes learning over personal style and fashion. In America, a child's day-to-day experience at school can be impacted by the clothing brands their parents can afford to buy them. At the same time, ironically, it has also become acceptable to show up to class in pajamas.

In 1848, Horace Mann, a pioneer of American education, famously declared "Education . . . is the great equalizer." Yet for that to be the case, we need to reform our current education model here at home. America is fighting its own battles in classrooms across the country, with our schools increasingly getting caught in the crossfire between competing political and religious ideologies as children and teachers watch from the sidelines.

This is in addition to the fact that the U.S., once a leader in education, now ranks 38th in math and 24th in science in terms of the knowledge of its high school students compared with other industrialized nations, according to a 2017 study.

The bitter cherry on top is the staggering cost of higher education in the U.S. While primary school through high school is free and accessible (which is not the case in many countries), in January 2021, 45 million Americans carried student loan debt worth a total of $1.7 trillion. In 2019, before the pandemic, 11.1% of aggregate student debt was either 90 or more days delinquent or in default. No wonder, given that from 2016 to 2020, student loan default rates were around 10% to 11.5%. Contrast that with 50 years ago, when going to college within the University of California system was virtually free, as was the case in many state university systems. To graduate with a respected degree, you were not required to drown in debt.

How can we expect our society to continue to grow and flourish when the young people who have our nation's future in their hands must take on this staggering burden just to equip themselves with the basic tools—i.e., a college degree—to stay afloat in a competitive world?

It is here where I believe that the teachings of Shariah can help turn this vicious cycle around. Under Shariah law, it is prohibited to charge interest and is considered to be a sin.

(Quran 3:130)

يَـٰٓأَيُّهَا ٱلَّذِينَ ءَامَنُوا۟ لَا تَأْكُلُوا۟ ٱلرِّبَوٰٓا۟ أَضْعَـٰفًا مُّضَـٰعَفَةًۖ وَٱتَّقُوا۟ ٱللَّهَ لَعَلَّكُمْ تُفْلِحُونَ

O you who have believed, do not consume usury, doubled and multiplied, but fear Allah that you may be successful.

Charging interest on loans for productive purposes (such as for education), much less loans that come with disproportionately high interest rates, is utterly disgraceful.

The less educated our nation, the more difficult it will be for young adults to take our economy to the next level, innovate for the future, and be the leaders of tomorrow. Just as bad, we will also be more vulnerable to lies and misinformation, which have no place in the leading nations of the world. And that is why Americans must work desperately to restore education as a top priority.

Islam mandates that everyone should have the opportunity to be educated. And since my contribution to the field of education is teaching about Shariah law, I will do my part.

Teaching a wide variety of people (including readers of this book) the fundamentals of Shariah law is the only way to truly understand Islam and end the demonization of Muslims that has taken hold in this country since September 11, 2001. One reason Shariah has become such a contentious topic is because it is so poorly understood, not just by non-Muslims but also by those who follow Islam. Even the vast majority of Muslims don't know where culture ends and where religion begins (or vice versa). And that is why Shariah, when presented freestanding and alone from all cultures, may come as a surprise to so many, whether Muslim or not.

I strongly believe that disseminating the basics of Shariah is one way to stem the tide of misinformation and the demonization of Muslims and lay down a basis for mutual acceptance and tolerance between Jews, Muslims, and beyond.

In the pages to come, we will be embarking on a journey that will feel unfamiliar, if not totally alien, to the majority of non-Muslims in the West. I'm speaking of the Quran, which is greatly misunderstood even by Muslims. The Quran is both the word of Allah and a guide for all those who adhere to it. From the outset, it's important for readers to understand that I find the rules presented by my Lord more credible than the man-made rules and laws in Western society. That doesn't mean that I accept one and reject the other. The law of the land is a trust I must uphold, one that doesn't devalue the law of Allah or the respect I hold for His words. Like any other Muslim in the United States, I must follow the laws of my country. The only way I could be guided exclusively by the dictates of the Quran is if I lived in a country under Shariah law. What may surprise you, though, is that while certain countries today lay claim to living by the Quran, all of them govern with a mix of Shariah as well as laws that are passed in the name of Islam, if not in its spirit.

If you are Muslim, expect the pages in this section to be informative. If you are not, you may find yourself rejecting my words out of hand, especially when it comes to my discussion of the treatment of women and the punishments meted out by the Quran for breaking the law. You may question who I am or conclude that I'm a misogynist, or barbaric. You may be tempted to put this book down. But I urge you to keep reading and not get distracted from the objective of learning about Islam. Instead of acting as a judge or jury, think of yourself as an archaeologist delving deeply into another religion, one that does not always propose the same solutions to society's problems as Christianity or Judaism or Western civil law. My task is not to convince you of anything but to provide you with sound information so that you can learn what Muslims believe. Only then will you be able to determine the legitimacy of a terrorist threat or the claims of an Islamophobe.

CHAPTER 6

The Imam Takes On Hot-Button Issues in Islam, part I: Honor Killings, Stoning, Flogging, and More

By Imam Azhar Subedar

The Shariah of Islam is, in fact, practiced by Muslims across the globe, including here in America. But it's important to distinguish between belief in what Allah says in the Quran (which includes the penal codes encompassed in Shariah law) and the belief that those laws should be imposed in every society at every time. Believing and enforcing are not the same thing. The objective of the laws of the Quran is to uphold peace in society, not to disrupt it. The Quran is too complex to cover adequately in these pages, but consider the following overview, which breaks down its content into categories and percentages.

Out of the 6,236 verses of the Quran, 22% speak about belief,

14% speak about community, and 13% about character. Stories, teachings, admonitions, and affirmations make up 11% each. In all, that makes up 93% of the Quran. The remaining 7% of the Quran, or 437 verses, address law or legal issues. Yet 65% of that 437, or 284 verses, are not "law" at all. Rather, they relate to personal custom and devotion. Another 30% (131 verses) relate to matters such as contracts and family law, and only 5% (or 22 verses) deal with state power issues such as criminal law. These 22 verses account for only 0.35% of the entire Quran.

My point in crunching these numbers is to highlight the prominence—or lack thereof—of the seemingly barbaric laws in the Quran. Relatively speaking, they are a very small part of the Quran indeed. But they do exist, so it's important that I address these verses and put them into context.

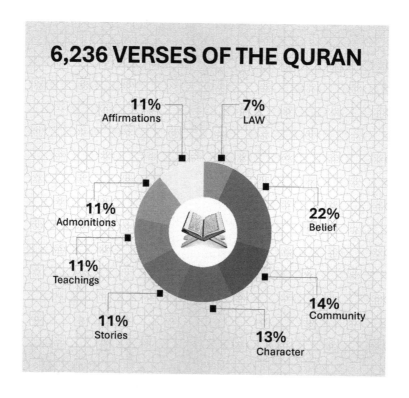

7% OF THE QURAN, OR 437 VERSES, ADDRESSES LAW OR LEGAL ISSUES.

65%
Personal Custom and Devotion

Non-Judicable Issues
(purity, prayer, fasting,pilgrimage, food and drink, oaths)

30%
Transactional and Family

Judicable Issues
(contracts, partnerships, endowments, probate, custody, marriage, and divorce)

5%
Criminal

adjudication, penal code, international relations

Criminal Justice and the Penal Code

One hot-button issue that tends to get the attention of non-Muslims like my coauthor is how Islamic countries enforce their criminal code. Many perceive Islamic laws and punishments such as honor killings, public stoning, flogging, amputation for theft, and the way capital punishment is imposed as barbaric and uncivilized. My goal is to review each of these punishments, not for the purpose of making them more acceptable or justifying them, but to explain the reasoning behind them and create understanding.

Honor Killings

To start, let's take honor killings, defined as the killing of a relative, often a female member of the family such as a daughter or a wife, who is accused of dishonoring the family with a premarital or extramarital sexual engagement. It is widely believed Muslims are obligated to carry out such a practice.

In reality, there is not one verse in the Quran that allows for this act. In fact, in Islam, so-called honor killing is considered to be murder. There are, however, four verses on how to deal with the claim of a wife's infidelity, which is usually the trigger point for such an act to take place.

(Quran 24:6-9)

وَٱلَّذِينَ يَرْمُونَ أَزْوَٰجَهُمْ وَلَمْ يَكُن لَّهُمْ شُهَدَآءُ إِلَّآ أَنفُسُهُمْ فَشَهَٰدَةُ أَحَدِهِمْ أَرْبَعُ شَهَٰدَٰتٍۭ بِٱللَّهِ ۙ إِنَّهُۥ لَمِنَ ٱلصَّٰدِقِينَ

And those who accuse their wives [of adultery] and have no witnesses except themselves—then the witness of one of them

[shall be] four testimonies [swearing] by Allah that indeed,
he is of the truthful.

وَٱلْخَٰمِسَةُ أَنَّ لَعْنَتَ ٱللَّهِ عَلَيْهِ إِن كَانَ مِنَ ٱلْكَٰذِبِينَ

And the fifth [oath will be] that the curse of Allah be upon him
if he should be among the liars.

وَيَدْرَؤُا۟ عَنْهَا ٱلْعَذَابَ أَن تَشْهَدَ أَرْبَعَ شَهَٰدَٰتٍ بِٱللَّهِ ۙ إِنَّهُۥ لَمِنَ ٱلْكَٰذِبِينَ

But it will prevent punishment from her if she gives four
testimonies [swearing] by Allah that, indeed, he is of the liars.

وَٱلْخَٰمِسَةَ أَنَّ غَضَبَ ٱللَّهِ عَلَيْهَآ إِن كَانَ مِنَ ٱلصَّٰدِقِينَ

And the fifth [oath will be] that the wrath of Allah be upon her
if he was of the truthful.

In Shariah, this is a process known as *Li'aan*, which means cursing
each other by praying for the wrath of Allah to fall on the other.
Why is this even a process for addressing infidelity? Let's unravel
these verses to better understand their meaning.

In Islam, to accuse someone of committing adultery, one must
back the claim with the corroboration of four witnesses.

(Quran 24:13)

لَّوْلَا جَآءُو عَلَيْهِ بِأَرْبَعَةِ شُهَدَآءَ ۚ فَإِذْ لَمْ يَأْتُوا۟ بِٱلشُّهَدَآءِ فَأُو۟لَٰٓئِكَ عِندَ ٱللَّهِ هُمُ
ٱلْكَٰذِبُونَ

Why did they [who slandered] not produce for it four
witnesses? And when they do not produce the witnesses, then it
is they, in the sight of Allah, who are the liars.

The reality is often quite different from what is described above. If a husband catches his wife committing adultery, the mere shock and utter shame might prevent him from obtaining witnesses to seek retribution. Shariah law offers a solution: In the absence of four witnesses, the aggrieved husband can go to a judge and claim that his wife committed adultery and that she should be punished for her actions. If she denies that claim, she, in turn, can demand that her husband be punished for his slander against her. (*Slander* is defined as the action or crime of making a false statement damaging a person's reputation.) The punishment for the crime of slander is 80 lashes. Other than Islam, I do not know of any other religion that protects the honor of women to the extent that it has a prescribed punishment for men making a false accusation against them.

(Quran 24:4)

وَٱلَّذِينَ يَرْمُونَ ٱلْمُحْصَنَٰتِ ثُمَّ لَمْ يَأْتُوا۟ بِأَرْبَعَةِ شُهَدَآءَ فَٱجْلِدُوهُمْ ثَمَٰنِينَ جَلْدَةً
وَلَا تَقْبَلُوا۟ لَهُمْ شَهَٰدَةً أَبَدًا ۚ وَأُو۟لَٰٓئِكَ هُمُ ٱلْفَٰسِقُونَ

And those who accuse chaste women and then do not produce
four witnesses—lash them with eighty lashes and do not
accept from them testimony ever after. And those are defiantly
disobedient.

In addition to the punishment meted out in the present, slanderers earn the curse of Allah today and His punishment in the afterlife.

(Quran 24:23)

إِنَّ الَّذِينَ يَرْمُونَ الْمُحْصَنَاتِ الْغَافِلَاتِ الْمُؤْمِنَاتِ لُعِنُوا فِي الدُّنْيَا وَالْآخِرَةِ
وَلَهُمْ عَذَابٌ عَظِيمٌ

*Indeed, those who [falsely] accuse chaste, unaware, and
believing women are cursed in this world and the Hereafter;
and they will have a great punishment.*

Why such a harsh punishment for a false accusation? To protect
innocent people from unjust accusations.

In this case, since neither party has substantial proof of the other's
wrongdoing, the two will enter the process of Li'aan.

According to the verses above (Quran 24:6-9), for the husband,
Li'aan would involve swearing in the name of Allah that his claim of
adultery against his wife is truthful. If he is not being truthful, Allah
will curse him for this accusation. If his wife responds by swearing
on Allah's name that her husband is lying, and that Allah's anger will
be on her if this isn't the case, his accusation will be declared baseless
and she will be absolved. In short, neither the husband nor a judge
can take action against her, and the wrong party will be punished
after death and resurrection on the Day of Judgment, when every
human being must account for their actions.

When it comes to right and wrong, the Day of Judgment is
always top of mind for Muslims: No one can hide from the truth
before their Lord. What, then, becomes of the estranged couple?
Speaking more practically, a judge appointed under the Caliphate
to overlook or execute judicial matters could rule for the marriage
to be terminated.

The bottom line, in less lofty language, is that the couple would
be subject to the governing laws of the country they reside in.
Shariah law cannot be substituted for secular law if it conflicts with
those laws. Which brings me back to honor killings and retribution:
Shariah law does not permit the public humiliation or physical
harm of the accused party—I'm referring to beating or throwing

acid in the accused's face, much less murdering them. These are the actions of barbaric folks who have no regard for religion or law. Under Shariah law, a system of due process exists. In Islam, as in the United States, leaving the law to vigilantes is detrimental to the stability of any society.

Public Stoning

Public stoning is widely perceived to be a punishment in Islam for adulterers, or for anyone who is married and has sex with someone other than their spouse. Just for historical context, the practice of stoning an adulterer was commanded in the Torah and was practiced in Madinah by the Jews who lived there. Leviticus 20:10–12 reads: "If a man commits adultery with another man's wife—with the wife of his neighbor—both the adulterer and the adulteress are to be put to death . . ." The punishment was carried out through stoning.

When Muslims first migrated to Madinah, they adopted the practice of stoning as a form of punishment due to a verse in the Quran: *"An old man and an old woman, if they commit adultery, stone them."* There is an understanding among Islamic scholars that though this verse was once revealed, it was subsequently abrogated. The process of abrogation, which means that a verse is removed from the Quran and replaced by another verse, occurred several times during the 23 years of the Quran's revelation and was done by Allah. And it may surprise many to know that there is not a single verse in the Quran that commands stoning for adultery.

Nevertheless, many Islamic scholars today still believe it is a valid punishment under Shariah law. In reality, the burden of proof is so high that it's next to impossible to prove it unless the person confesses to it themselves. And that confession would have to take place four separate times for the act of adultery to be proven and then punished. The ultimate decision, however, is in the hands of a judge living in a place governed by Shariah law. As for obtaining forgiveness for one's sin, in Islam, that is not only possible but encouraged: Muslims may seek and gain Allah's forgiveness for sins by asking Him directly, no mediator or even a confession required. However, forgiveness for a sin and punishment for a sin are two separate things. One can ask for Allah's forgiveness and thereby be absolved of the sin but still be punished according to the law set in the Quran. The public punishment meted out in this world would absolve the offender of punishment for that sin in the afterlife, while their private repentance and penance will help clear their conscience in this world and also clear their record of deeds when they are presented before God.

Flogging

Flogging is another punishment related to sex—this one for consensual sexual intercourse between two unmarried people. (When one or more of the partners having consensual sexual intercourse is married to a third person, it is called adultery; when both are unmarried it is called fornication.)

The punishment for fornication is 100 lashes, as ordered by a single verse in the Quran:

(Quran 24:2)

ٱلزَّانِيَةُ وَٱلزَّانِى فَٱجْلِدُواْ كُلَّ وَٰحِدٍ مِّنْهُمَا مِائَةَ جَلْدَةٍ ۖ وَلَا تَأْخُذْكُم بِهِمَا رَأْفَةٌ فِى دِينِ ٱللَّهِ إِن كُنتُمْ تُؤْمِنُونَ بِٱللَّهِ وَٱلْيَوْمِ ٱلْءَاخِرِ ۖ وَلْيَشْهَدْ عَذَابَهُمَا طَآئِفَةٌ مِّنَ ٱلْمُؤْمِنِينَ

*The fornicating woman or fornicating man found guilty of
sexual intercourse—lash each one of them with a hundred
lashes, and do not be taken by pity for them in the religion of
Allah, if you should believe in Allah and the Last Day. And let
a group of believers witness their punishment.*

The problem in Islam isn't two people having sex. Islam does not condemn relationships; it condemns sex outside of marriage. More to come on this shortly.

The most important question then becomes: How does one determine if fornication or adultery was committed and whether the punishment of stoning or lashing is valid?

Under Shariah law, one's private life in one's private space is just that: private. No one can invade that space to determine what is being done behind closed doors. That is considered spying, and in Islam, spying is prohibited.

(Quran 49:12)

يَـٰٓأَيُّهَا ٱلَّذِينَ ءَامَنُواْ ٱجْتَنِبُواْ كَثِيرًا مِّنَ ٱلظَّنِّ إِنَّ بَعْضَ ٱلظَّنِّ إِثْمٌ وَلَا تَجَسَّسُواْ
وَلَا يَغْتَب بَّعْضُكُم بَعْضًا

*O you who have believed, avoid much [negative] assumption.
Indeed, some assumption is sin. And do not spy or backbite
each other.*

Entering someone's residence without their consent and knowledge is prohibited.

(Quran 24:27)

يَـٰٓأَيُّهَا ٱلَّذِينَ ءَامَنُواْ لَا تَدْخُلُواْ بُيُوتًا غَيْرَ بُيُوتِكُمْ حَتَّىٰ تَسْتَأْنِسُواْ وَتُسَلِّمُواْ عَلَىٰٓ
أَهْلِهَا ۚ ذَٰلِكُمْ خَيْرٌ لَّكُمْ لَعَلَّكُمْ تَذَكَّرُونَ

O you who have believed, do not enter houses other than your own houses until you ascertain whether you welcome and greet their inhabitants.

Shariah law requires at least four mature, clear-minded adults to actually witness the act of fornication, with no variation in testimony. If those who testify are deemed liars (slanderers), they, in turn, will be punished.

Additionally, since spying isn't permitted under Shariah law, this could only mean that the couple committed the act publicly, in the presence of at least four witnesses. Keep in mind, holding hands, caressing, kissing, hugging, and so forth do not fit the criteria of fornication; the actual act of fornication must be witnessed.

Only then can a judge rule for a punishment of 100 lashes. The underlying goal behind such a law is to preserve morality in all public spaces.

The punishments described for fornication and adultery may seem harsh. Indeed, most people in today's world may find these prohibitions absurd. But the true reason behind this detailed description about punishments is to preserve the things that are truly precious to human society: love, trust, safety, honor, and dignity in our most intimate relationships.

Talk to any person who has ever been cheated on by a partner and you will see their mental and emotional pain. Infidelity destroys trust in relationships and, for the person who has been betrayed, can shake their confidence in themselves and their own judgment, hampering their ability to enjoy life and fully contribute to society. And when they tell the story of being betrayed to others, that in itself can sow distrust among their friend circle. In other words, the breakup of an intimate relationship is not only about the two people involved but can influence others as well.

Capital Punishment

It may surprise some readers to learn that there are no verses in the Quran that order capital punishment or the beheading of a murderer.

There is, however, one verse in the Quran that commands justice for someone who has been murdered:

(Quran 2:178)

يَٰٓأَيُّهَا ٱلَّذِينَ ءَامَنُوا۟ كُتِبَ عَلَيْكُمُ ٱلْقِصَاصُ فِى ٱلْقَتْلَى ۖ ٱلْحُرُّ بِٱلْحُرِّ وَٱلْعَبْدُ بِٱلْعَبْدِ وَٱلْأُنثَىٰ بِٱلْأُنثَىٰ ۚ فَمَنْ عُفِىَ لَهُۥ مِنْ أَخِيهِ شَىْءٌ فَٱتِّبَاعٌۢ بِٱلْمَعْرُوفِ وَأَدَآءٌ إِلَيْهِ بِإِحْسَٰنٍ ۗ ذَٰلِكَ تَخْفِيفٌ مِّن رَّبِّكُمْ وَرَحْمَةٌ ۗ فَمَنِ ٱعْتَدَىٰ بَعْدَ ذَٰلِكَ فَلَهُۥ عَذَابٌ أَلِيمٌ

O you who have believed, prescribed for you is legal retribution for those murdered—the free for the free, the slave for the slave, and the female for the female. But if the offender is pardoned by the victim's guardian, then blood-money should be decided fairly and payment should be made courteously. This is a concession and a mercy from your Lord. But whoever transgresses after that will suffer a painful punishment.

This verse doesn't talk about the crime of murder but about how to deal with the murderer. The key word used in this verse is *Qisas*, which is Arabic for legal retribution—i.e., a punishment imposed on a convicted criminal for purposes of repayment or revenge.

Who has the right to decide that punishment? The family of the one murdered, whom Allah addresses in this verse.

In Islam, a life for a life is permitted only if the victim's family demands it in court before a judge. However, the family can also choose to receive financial compensation and forgive the perpetrator, which is encouraged in the verse. The latter, obviously, is not permitted in America, where, to uphold the law, the government initiates a criminal case, the alleged perpetrator is tried by a jury of their peers, and a judge decides on a just punishment.

If the decision is to execute the murderer, the judge will determine the method based on how a specific region or country enforces the death penalty under Shariah. In countries where Shariah law isn't practiced, the law of the land will stipulate that punishment. Here, I'll just note again that a "judge" is someone who is both qualified in the field of law and has been appointed by the Caliph to make judgments on societal matters and disputes. The scope of a judge's authority is also determined by the Caliph. In the absence of the Caliphate or Shariah penal law, however, people must follow their governing laws to determine the penalty for these crimes.

In Shariah, the framing of law and punishment is meant to curb killings and enforce justice. Allah revealed divine instructions meant to help society evolve into one that respected and upheld the sanctity of life and to promote peace for all people.

Whether or not you agree with Shariah, it's clear that something is awry with our system in the West, where shootings have become a daily occurrence. The Pew Research Center found that in 2021, the most recent year for which complete data is available as of this writing, 48,830 people died from gun-related injuries in this country. If the frivolous debates in Congress are any indication, gun violence isn't going away anytime soon.

Which brings me back to the reason Islam stands behind legal retribution even if that retribution results in death:

(Quran 2:179)

وَلَكُمْ فِى ٱلْقِصَاصِ حَيَوٰةٌ يَـٰٓأُوْلِى ٱلْأَلْبَـٰبِ لَعَلَّكُمْ تَتَّقُونَ

And there is life for you in legal retribution, O men of
understanding, that you may guard yourselves.

How is there life in death?

Death in response to murder prevents the normalization of a culture of murder and killing. Yet in the U.S., where, as of this writing, Gun Violence Archive (GVA) recorded 656 mass shootings in 2023, we have become numb to the problem of gun violence, simply because mass shootings happen so often.

Theft

The Quran also takes what may seem like a harsh view in terms of punishment for lesser crimes, such as theft. There is one verse in the Quran that orders amputation for theft, which is defined as when a sane adult takes an item valued at 10 silver coins or more. One silver coin (known as a dirham in those days) is equal to about 82 cents today. Therefore, theft would be defined as the taking of anything valued at around $10, with the punishment being the amputation of the thief's hand. Although that punishment may seem unwarranted given the small amount of money at stake, this law is less about the value of what has been stolen than about the act of theft itself—specifically, *how* something was stolen.

For instance, if what was stolen was protected by being locked inside a safe in a house, the criminal will be tried and punished to the full extent of the law, meaning their hand will be amputated. In contrast, if something is stolen off the street due to an owner's negligence, such as leaving a bike unlocked on the sidewalk overnight, the criminal would be punished with a lesser penalty, such as a fine or imprisonment as determined by the judge.

Whether a theft consists of burglarizing a secure vault or stealing a bike from the sidewalk, normalizing the unlawful seizure of another's property or belongings can and does spread insecurity in any society.

(Quran 5:38)

وَٱلسَّارِقُ وَٱلسَّارِقَةُ فَٱقْطَعُوٓاْ أَيْدِيَهُمَا جَزَآءًۢ بِمَا كَسَبَا نَكَـٰلࣰا مِّنَ ٱللَّهِۗ وَٱللَّهُ عَزِيزٌ حَكِيمٌ

And [as for] the thief, the male, and the female, amputate their hands in recompense for what they committed as a deterrent [punishment] from Allah. And Allah is Exalted in Might, and Wise.

The underlying objective of Shariah is to preserve and uphold trust in society and prevent citizens from experiencing constant stress about their security and the safety of their belongings, while, at the same time, keeping thieves at bay. The goal, as I've said, is to prevent the normalization of theft, and, just as important, the normalization of robbery in society. Shariah, in other words, isn't only about enforcement. It is about remedying a problem that, if left unaddressed, can ultimately fester and damage society.

As we can see from the examples of crimes described in this chapter, there is a process by which punishment is determined and meted out. However, under Shariah, the guiding principle for all judges is that "penalties and punishments are averted by seeking out doubts," meaning that the slightest doubt will prevent a penalty from being applied, with the judge's job being to find any such doubt. As in the U.S., the idea is that the accused is innocent until proven guilty beyond a reasonable doubt.

The variation in how these laws are applied (even in today's world) comes down to how these verses and commands are interpreted, as I've said earlier. Which begs the question: How is it possible to interpret anything in a fair way when the implementation of these laws vary so widely among countries, places, and people?

To find common ground for all Muslims, the Prophet Muhammad taught a guiding principle:

> *"Verily, the religion is easy. And no one burdens himself in religion but that it overwhelms him. Follow the right course, seek closeness to Allah, give glad tidings, and seek help for worship in the morning and evening and a part of the night."*
> (Hadith, Bukhari 39)

This principle can serve as a gauge for interpretation, with the view that all the laws discussed here were prescribed through Shariah with one purpose: to serve as a deterrent to crime so punishments wouldn't ever be necessary. Another goal of these laws was to change the mindset of a people unused to living in a society that valued accountability. Without law and order, chaos and disruption are inevitable.

The penal code under Shariah law is also supposed to be straightforward and self-explanatory, easy for all Muslims and societies governing with Shariah to interpret. That clarity makes them more difficult to manipulate.

In the Quran, Allah commands strict adherence to the ultimate goal of laws, which is the pursuit of justice.

(Quran 4:135)

يَا أَيُّهَا الَّذِينَ آمَنُوا كُونُوا قَوَّامِينَ بِالْقِسْطِ شُهَدَاءَ لِلَّهِ وَلَوْ عَلَىٰ أَنفُسِكُمْ أَوِ الْوَالِدَيْنِ وَالْأَقْرَبِينَ ۚ إِن يَكُنْ غَنِيًّا أَوْ فَقِيرًا فَاللَّهُ أَوْلَىٰ بِهِمَا ۖ فَلَا تَتَّبِعُوا الْهَوَىٰ أَن تَعْدِلُوا ۚ وَإِن تَلْوُوا أَوْ تُعْرِضُوا فَإِنَّ اللَّهَ كَانَ بِمَا تَعْمَلُونَ خَبِيرًا

O you who have believed, be persistently standing firm in justice, witnesses for Allah, even if it be against yourselves or parents and relatives. Whether one is rich or poor, Allah is more worthy of both. So follow not [personal] inclination, lest you not be just. And if you distort [your testimony] or refuse [to give it], then indeed Allah is ever, with what you do, acquainted.

No one has the right under Shariah to bend the law for personal gain, including the Prophet Muhammad.

In a Hadith, it is stated that Muhammad said:

"If a reputable man amongst the children of Bani Israel [the Jews/Christians of the past] committed a theft, they used to forgive him, but if a poor man committed a theft, they would cut his hand. But I would cut even the hand of Fatimah [his own daughter] if she committed a theft."
(Hadith, Bukhari 3733)

In addition, when upholding Shariah law, no one should ever feel compelled to waver in the pursuit of justice, whatever pressure they may feel from society.

(Quran 5:8)

يَا أَيُّهَا الَّذِينَ آمَنُوا كُونُوا قَوَّامِينَ لِلَّهِ شُهَدَاءَ بِالْقِسْطِ ۖ وَلَا يَجْرِمَنَّكُمْ شَنَآنُ
قَوْمٍ عَلَىٰ أَلَّا تَعْدِلُوا ۚ اعْدِلُوا هُوَ أَقْرَبُ لِلتَّقْوَىٰ ۖ وَاتَّقُوا اللَّهَ ۚ إِنَّ اللَّهَ خَبِيرٌ بِمَا
تَعْمَلُونَ

O you who have believed, be persistently standing firm for
Allah, witnesses in justice, and do not let the hatred of a
people prevent you from being just. Be just; that is nearer to
righteousness [Taqwa]. And revere Allah; indeed,
Allah is acquainted with what you do.

Righteousness through the reverence of Allah, known in Arabic as *Taqwa*, is the gold standard pursued by Muslims in all they do. Our goal as Muslims is to attain that lofty status in the eyes of Allah, the creator of everything. As the creator of Humankind, He made within us the desire for power, and He tested us with bad traits such as greed.

Humans, as we know, all have their individual motives, desires, and reasons for what they do and why. As our Creator, Allah serves as a neutral voice and authority regardless of His knowledge of each human's nature and intention. That's why I see Shariah as a wholesome system—it isn't biased or one-sided. It doesn't serve some people and discard others. It is all-encompassing and just. Unlike human-made laws and systems, Shariah cannot be manipulated.

The Job of a Caliph

A governing Caliph is meant to govern by the laws of Allah and nothing more; to uphold Shariah without regard for any one individual's power or greed. If a society were to truly embrace

Shariah law as its system of governing, with all the correctly appointed governors, judges, and law officers, their processes and decisions would be effective because they would conform to what Allah called for in the Quran.

Instead, today, there are systems that have been manipulated and distorted in the name of Shariah law and Islam. In recent years, for instance, ISIS has claimed that their leader, al-Baghdadi, was a contemporary Caliph. But as someone who is advocating a false vision of Islam by deploying suicide attackers, roadside explosives, car bombs, and other forms of violence that have deepened the instability and insecurity in Iraq and then Syria, al-Baghdadi could never be a Caliph or serve as the foundation of a 21st-century Caliphate. Such a Caliphate has and would only hurt the image of Muslims and tarnish the value of Islam.

For true Shariah law to be instituted in its correct, pure form, it would have to be administered by a Caliphate focused on administering all aspects of society in accordance with the Quran.

CHAPTER 7

The Imam Takes On Hot-Button Issues in Islam, part II: Women, Marriage, Polygamy, and More

By Imam Azhar Subedar

Women Under Shariah Law

For non-Muslims unfamiliar with Islam, perhaps no issue provokes as emotional and even as volatile a response as Islam's perceived treatment of women, whether the subject is gender equality, child marriage, polygamy, or rules surrounding the wearing of the hijab. That's no surprise, given that there is a wealth of misinformation on the topic.

I've noticed that many people believe that a Muslim society is one in which men rule and women are enslaved; where women don't have an equal say; where a woman's property is never truly her own. In other words, a society where girls and women are forced into subjugation and even wedlock; where men are allowed multiple wives; where husbands are allowed to beat their wives with impunity; and where women can wear only what they are ordered to.

The reality is that life for Muslim women, at least in a society governed by Shariah, would look very different than the description above. And while there are verses in the Quran that drive misperceptions about the treatment of women, too often, they are poorly explained and understood by those who are responsible for interpreting them. That can lead to the text being manipulated and, ultimately, to Muslims approving behavior toward women that is not in compliance with Shariah.

It bears repeating that the Quran is the guide provided to Muslims by Allah as an instruction book for life; it's literally the word of Allah. Within this guide to life, however, certain verses are inevitably singled out by non-Muslims—typically, verses that provide societal solutions that differ from those found in the West. And too often, these verses lead to a zero-sum game—a black-and-white view of who is right and who is wrong. For instance, there are those who insist that the Quran's suggestion that women be covered violates women's rights. In this moral tug-of-war, we lose sight of the fact that there can be more than one solution, and that different people with different traditions need not agree on every matter involving women's rights, criminal justice, and a host of other matters. This doesn't make one side or the other more civilized or decent.

I will point out these differences for the sake of knowledge rather than attempting to persuade or "win." Let's go back to what the

Quran says regarding the treatment of women. Generations of non-Muslims (as well as Muslims) do not understand the true meaning of these verses. That's partly because current-day Islamic scholars have had a tendency to double down on Quranic interpretations made generations ago in a different time and place, insisting that only these interpretations are correct. It is indisputable that the Quran *does* contain verses about the treatment of women that seem incompatible with Western civil laws. These differences, however, can and do coexist with Western laws and attitudes; there is room for more than one point of view on this topic.

The #MeToo movement has placed women and women's rights front and center in our society. Yet too often, Islamic leaders stay silent about what the Quran says regarding women, perhaps because any honest discussion of women's rights in Islam will certainly be subject to fierce criticism and accusations that Islam is against women and must be reformed. Certain Muslims, meanwhile, may deem an Islamic leader who speaks up as deviant and misguided.

Getting to the truth about the meaning of certain verses in the Quran related to women's rights can be challenging. In an effort to appease Westerners, some Muslim leaders and groups offer interpretations of the Quran that, according to Islamic scholars, go against the teachings of Islam. I am not among those groups or leaders; I will not water down the intent or meaning of any Quranic verse to make it more palatable. What I aim to do is explain what these verses mean when viewed in their relevant context.

A Woman's Testimony and Equality

Let's take the example that according to Shariah, a woman's testimony is considered to be worth half that of a man's:

(Quran 2:282)

. . . وَٱسْتَشْهِدُواْ شَهِيدَيْنِ مِن رِّجَالِكُمْ ۖ فَإِن لَّمْ يَكُونَا رَجُلَيْنِ فَرَجُلٌ
وَٱمْرَأَتَانِ مِمَّن تَرْضَوْنَ مِنَ ٱلشُّهَدَآءِ أَن تَضِلَّ إِحْدَىٰهُمَا فَتُذَكِّرَ إِحْدَىٰهُمَا
ٱلْأُخْرَىٰ ۚ وَلَا يَأْبَ ٱلشُّهَدَآءُ إِذَا مَا دُعُواْ

. . . And bring to witness two witnesses from among your men.
And if there are not two men [available], then a man and two
women from those whom you accept as witnesses—so that if
one of the women errs, then the other can remind her. And let
not the witnesses refuse when they are called upon to testify.

According to the segment of the verse written above, it is clear that is the case. So let us understand it in its correct context.

In the beginning of the segment of the verse quoted above (which is the longest verse in the Quran), Allah states:

(Quran 2:282)

يَٰٓأَيُّهَا ٱلَّذِينَ ءَامَنُوٓاْ إِذَا تَدَايَنتُم بِدَيْنٍ إِلَىٰٓ أَجَلٍ مُّسَمًّى فَٱكْتُبُوهُ ۚ وَلْيَكْتُب بَّيْنَكُمْ
كَاتِبٌۢ بِٱلْعَدْلِ ۚ وَلَا يَأْبَ كَاتِبٌ أَن يَكْتُبَ كَمَا عَلَّمَهُ ٱللَّهُ ۚ فَلْيَكْتُبْ وَلْيُمْلِلِ ٱلَّذِى
عَلَيْهِ ٱلْحَقُّ وَلْيَتَّقِ ٱللَّهَ رَبَّهُ وَلَا يَبْخَسْ مِنْهُ شَيْـًٔا ۚ فَإِن كَانَ ٱلَّذِى عَلَيْهِ ٱلْحَقُّ
سَفِيهًا أَوْ ضَعِيفًا أَوْ لَا يَسْتَطِيعُ أَن يُمِلَّ هُوَ فَلْيُمْلِلْ وَلِيُّهُۥ بِٱلْعَدْلِ ۚ . . .

O you who have believed, when you contract a debt for
a specified term, write it down. And let a scribe write [it]
between you in justice. Let no scribe refuse to write as Allah

has taught him. So let him write and let the one who has the obligation dictate. And let him fear Allah, his Lord, and not leave anything out of it. But if the one who has the obligation is of limited understanding or weak or unable to dictate himself, then let his guardian dictate in justice . . .

This verse mandates that Muslims document all financial dealings with contracts, regardless of the amount at stake or the relationship between the two parties. The thinking is that following these principles will result in a business environment that is trusted, just, and can thrive. That, in turn, will enhance the beauty of Islam through business ethics that spur economic growth and prosperity in any and every business and financial transaction for the benefit of all parties involved, Muslim or not. This is the overarching premise of this verse: It is less about a woman's testimony and more about business ethics, which are integral for a flourishing society. Islam, as a faith, is only as good as the values upheld in the marketplace through honest dealings.

Under Shariah, it is mandatory that any contract is signed in the presence of witnesses, either two men, or one man and two women. To understand the reason for this, it's necessary to go back in history. During the time of Muhammad, Makkah thrived because of the various trade routes crossing through the area. Most businesses and caravans were run by men, while women were more likely to be customers. Women generally weren't involved with the ins and outs of merchant-to-caravan or merchant-to-merchant contracts, loans, and debts. If, by choice, a woman or a group of women happened to be witness to a contractual agreement and were later called to court to testify in the event of a contractual dispute, the Quran stipulates that two women are required, though the two are counted as only one witness. This mandate may have been for the purpose of providing comfort or stability for women, who, at that time, for the most part, were unaware of these dealings and thus more susceptible to confusion on the matter. (Not to say there weren't any women who ran their own businesses; the wife of Prophet Muhammad ran her own business, for one. But this edict leaves the door open for any woman who isn't well versed in business the opportunity to pair up with another woman if called on to give testimony.) In addition, the requirement of two women also made a lone woman in this space less vulnerable to witness intimidation.

Here, the Quran is also trying to prevent the consequences of false testimony. Keep in mind that giving false testimony results in harsh punishments (including in the afterlife). Knowing this, it might be easier to understand and accept that the two-witness rule was also meant to reduce women's responsibility and their risk of punishment, not because women were incapable of testifying, but to ensure that they would not be required to testify unless one man and two women were present when the disputed contract was formed.

In a Hadith, the Prophet Muhammad said:

> *"Shall I not tell you of the greatest of major sins?" We said, "Yes indeed, O Messenger of Allah." He said, "Associating others with Allah and disobedience towards parents." He was reclining, but then he sat up and said, "And false speech and false witness, and false speech and false witness." He kept on saying it until I thought he would never stop.*
> (Hadith, Bukhari 2654)

Any two parties who enter into a binding contract, male or female, must know what they are doing, and any two parties, male or female, pulled into witnessing their deal must feel comfortable in that role and with the fact that they may be called to be a witness in court at a later date. And those who were not familiar with financial contracts, which was the case for many women back then, should not be compelled to either witness any transactions or serve as a witness in court and held to the highest standard of the law.

I'd go further and say that upon reflecting on this verse from a positive angle, which people rarely do, the fact that women are mentioned here at all, despite their not being significant players in business, trade, or finances during the time of the revelation, is proof that Allah never wrote women off altogether, as some claim. If He had, they wouldn't have had the option to give testimony at all. Going a step further, you could also read this verse as an indication that women *should* be a part of the community of trade folks rather than being considered outsiders.

To get back to this case specifically, a woman's testimony is considered equal to a man's outside the realm of business and trade matters because nothing in the Quran or Hadith states otherwise. In fact, if a woman happens to be well versed in business and trade, in contracts, and in financial dealings, she will be considered an equivalent witness. And it's important to note that both women and men are subject to the same consequences if they give false testimony.

Yet the verse in discussion (in Quran 2:282) continues to be used by Muslims to prove that since a woman's testimony is worth only half the weight of a man's, women aren't as intelligent or reliable as men, never mind equal to men. Yet Allah clarifies that men and women are equal in their creation.

(Quran 33:35)

إِنَّ ٱلۡمُسۡلِمِينَ وَٱلۡمُسۡلِمَـٰتِ وَٱلۡمُؤۡمِنِينَ وَٱلۡمُؤۡمِنَـٰتِ وَٱلۡقَـٰنِتِينَ وَٱلۡقَـٰنِتَـٰتِ وَٱلصَّـٰدِقِينَ وَٱلصَّـٰدِقَـٰتِ وَٱلصَّـٰبِرِينَ وَٱلصَّـٰبِرَٰتِ وَٱلۡخَـٰشِعِينَ وَٱلۡخَـٰشِعَـٰتِ وَٱلۡمُتَصَدِّقِينَ وَٱلۡمُتَصَدِّقَـٰتِ وَٱلصَّـٰٓئِمِينَ وَٱلصَّـٰٓئِمَـٰتِ وَٱلۡحَـٰفِظِينَ فُرُوجَهُمۡ وَٱلۡحَـٰفِظَـٰتِ وَٱلذَّٰكِرِينَ ٱللَّهَ كَثِيرًا وَٱلذَّٰكِرَٰتِ أَعَدَّ ٱللَّهُ لَهُم مَّغۡفِرَةً وَأَجۡرًا عَظِيمًا

Indeed, the Muslim men and Muslim women, the believing men and believing women, the obedient men and obedient women, the truthful men and truthful women, the patient men and patient women, the humble men and humble women, the charitable men and charitable women, the fasting men and fasting women, the men who guard their private parts and the women who do so, and the men who remember Allah often and the women who do so—for them Allah has prepared forgiveness and a great reward.

(Quran 16:97)

مَنۡ عَمِلَ صَـٰلِحًا مِّن ذَكَرٍ أَوۡ أُنثَىٰ وَهُوَ مُؤۡمِنٌ فَلَنُحۡيِيَنَّهُۥ حَيَوٰةً طَيِّبَةً وَلَنَجۡزِيَنَّهُمۡ أَجۡرَهُم بِأَحۡسَنِ مَا كَانُواْ يَعۡمَلُونَ

Whoever does righteousness, whether male or female, while they are a believer—We will indeed cause them to live a good life, and We will surely give them their reward [in the Hereafter] according to the best of what they used to do.

Both genders will be equally rewarded in the afterlife for equal deeds done on earth. The roles men and women play while on earth, however, according to Islam, are different.

(Quran 92:3,4)

وَمَا خَلَقَ ٱلذَّكَرَ وَٱلْأُنثَىٰٓ إِنَّ سَعْيَكُمْ لَشَتَّىٰ

And [by] He who created them male and female, indeed, your efforts are diverse.

The fact that they have unique roles does not impinge on their equality or their common humanity. In Islam, men and women deserve fair treatment, respect, and acknowledgment for their individual efforts.

Another common misperception is that Muslim women are not permitted to go out and do things without a male companion, known as a *mahram*—often a spouse or a blood relative they cannot marry, such as a father or a brother. The Prophet Muhammad instructed:

"It is not permissible for a woman who believes in Allah and the last day [Day of Judgment] to make a journey of one day and night unless she is accompanied by a mahram." (Hadith, Riyad us Salihin 989)

This mandate was to ensure women's protection in what was then an unsafe society; it also applies today if an environment is unsafe.

Yet the Quran, in its description of an incident that occurred with Prophet Moses and two women he helped fetch water from a well, also reminds us that women can be independent in terms of going out and about. In the story, when the women returned home (without a male companion) and told their father that Moses had helped them, their father requested that Moses be their guest and sent one of his daughters to bring Moses back to her father's house.

(Quran 28:25)

فَجَاءَتْهُ إِحْدَىٰهُمَا تَمْشِى عَلَى ٱسْتِحْيَاءٍ قَالَتْ إِنَّ أَبِى يَدْعُوكَ لِيَجْزِيَكَ أَجْرَ مَا سَقَيْتَ لَنَا ۚ فَلَمَّا جَاءَهُ وَقَصَّ عَلَيْهِ ٱلْقَصَصَ قَالَ لَا تَخَفْ ۖ نَجَوْتَ مِنَ ٱلْقَوْمِ ٱلظَّٰلِمِينَ

Then one of the two women came to him, walking with shyness. She said, "Indeed, my father invites you so that he may reward you for providing water for us." So when he came to him and related to him the story [of him fleeing the pharaoh for killing a person accidently], the father said, "Fear not. You have escaped from the wrongdoers."

In the particular area where the incident occurred, during the time of Moses, women could go about life and conduct daily chores without a male companion by their side because it was safe for them to do so. In Saudi Arabia today, women are no longer required to be accompanied by men when going on a pilgrimage, since that situation is also considered safe. But while customs restricting women are easing up in several countries, in others, such as Afghanistan and Iran, the government is tightening those restrictions. I believe it is up to well-educated Islamic scholars in those areas to ensure that Islam is not being manipulated for political purposes or used to oppress others or to serve the interests of those in power.

Inheritance

There is also a common belief in Islam that a woman is entitled to only half the inheritance of a man, leading some to make the case that women aren't "worthy" of being treated equally.

And indeed, there is a verse in the Quran that describes women getting half the inheritance of a man:

(Quran 4:11)

يُوصِيكُمُ ٱللَّهُ فِىٓ أَوْلَـٰدِكُمْ ۖ لِلذَّكَرِ مِثْلُ حَظِّ ٱلْأُنثَيَيْنِ ۚ

*Allah instructs you concerning your children: for the male,
what is equal to the share of two females.*

What many tend to miss are the lines that follow in that same verse:

(Quran 4:11 continued)

فَإِن كُنَّ نِسَآءً فَوْقَ ٱثْنَتَيْنِ فَلَهُنَّ ثُلُثَا مَا تَرَكَ ۖ وَإِن كَانَتْ وَٰحِدَةً فَلَهَا ٱلنِّصْفُ ۚ
وَلِأَبَوَيْهِ لِكُلِّ وَٰحِدٍ مِّنْهُمَا ٱلسُّدُسُ مِمَّا تَرَكَ إِن كَانَ لَهُ وَلَدٌ ۚ فَإِن لَّمْ يَكُن لَّهُ وَلَدٌ
وَوَرِثَهُۥٓ أَبَوَاهُ فَلِأُمِّهِ ٱلثُّلُثُ ۚ فَإِن كَانَ لَهُۥٓ إِخْوَةٌ فَلِأُمِّهِ ٱلسُّدُسُ ۚ مِنۢ بَعْدِ وَصِيَّةٍ
يُوصِى بِهَآ أَوْ دَيْنٍ ۗ ءَابَآؤُكُمْ وَأَبْنَآؤُكُمْ لَا تَدْرُونَ أَيُّهُمْ أَقْرَبُ لَكُمْ نَفْعًا ۚ فَرِيضَةً
مِّنَ ٱللَّهِ ۗ إِنَّ ٱللَّهَ كَانَ عَلِيمًا حَكِيمًا

*But if there are [only] daughters, two or more, for them is
two-thirds of one's estate. And if there is only one, for her, it
is half. And for one's parents, to each one of them is a sixth
of his estate if he left children. But if he had no children and
the parents [alone] inherit from him, then for his mother is
one third. And if he had brothers [or sisters], for his mother is*

a sixth, after any bequest he [may have] made or debt. Your
parents or your children—you know not which of them are
nearest to you in benefit—[These shares are] an obligation
[imposed] by Allah. Indeed, Allah is ever Knowing and Wise.

The verse that follows the one above (Quran 4:12) also presents scenarios for who gets what and when, confirming that women are not allotted half of what men get in every case; sometimes they are entitled to equal or more. Under Shariah law, it is family structure and the lineup of heirs, not just gender, that determines inheritance. In addition, inheritance rights do not change based on a person's marital status or financial status.

In Islam, the family unit is central. Within it, a woman has no financial obligation to anyone in her family but is financially cared for by her parents and relatives before marriage and her spouse after. If she divorces, she will obtain the Islamic equivalent of alimony, for a set period of time, determined by a judge. If she becomes widowed, society will care for her well-being through general funds allocated in the *Bait ul-mal* (funds for general welfare of the Muslims, translated as "House of Wealth"), until she is able to support herself. In the early Islamic Caliphate, the Bait ul-mal administered taxes in Islamic states and also cared for the widowed, orphans, and those unable to care for themselves.

Child Marriages and Polygamy

Another common concern with Shariah is that child marriages are allowed. It's true that in Islam, there is no set minimum age for marriage. There are different ways of looking at this, including the fact that some people may be more mature than others and able to choose marriage when they feel ready. What is clear, though, is that to be able to marry, a woman's consent is required. I'll repeat: A woman must give her own consent, free and clear of any duress. Otherwise, the marriage is not legally valid under Islam. Moreover, there isn't a single verse in the Quran that promotes child marriage.

In Islam, the goal of marriage is for two people to obtain a life of peace by sharing affection and mercy with one another.

(Quran 30:21)

وَمِنْ ءَايَـٰتِهِۦٓ أَنْ خَلَقَ لَكُم مِّنْ أَنفُسِكُمْ أَزْوَٰجًا لِّتَسْكُنُوٓا۟ إِلَيْهَا وَجَعَلَ بَيْنَكُم مَّوَدَّةً
وَرَحْمَةً ۚ إِنَّ فِى ذَٰلِكَ لَـَٔايَـٰتٍ لِّقَوْمٍ يَتَفَكَّرُونَ

And of His [Allah's] signs is that He created for you from
yourselves mates that you may find tranquility in them; and
He placed between you affection and mercy. Indeed, there are
signs in it for a people who give thought.

In Islam, the rights and responsibilities of one human toward another is a common theme. The subjects of sex and marriage are no different.

The purpose of marriage in Islam is to clearly lay out responsibilities and expectations for both parties—before engaging in a physical relationship. Marriage is also designed to protect the legal rights of both parties for the various situations that arise during the course of a romantic partnership. Entering into a physical relationship with another person introduces feelings and emotions into the equation, which can create a power imbalance, among other things.

Marriage often results in children, whether intentional or not. And in Islam, procreation is only lawful for those who are married.

As for sex, it must be practiced only with someone who is of the age to potentially procreate (i.e., not a child).

On a side note, sex *is* encouraged in Islam—something some readers may find surprising. Sex is considered an act of worship, even during holy seasons of devotion, such as Ramadan. The term Allah uses to grant permission for sex is noteworthy:

(Quran 2:187)

أُحِلَّ لَكُمْ لَيْلَةَ الصِّيَامِ الرَّفَثُ إِلَىٰ نِسَائِكُمْ ۚ

*It is made lawful to you to go to your women [wives] on
the nights of the fast;*

Allah used the term "women" and not "girl" or "child." Why? Because Allah equated the purpose of having sex to farming and growing the seed from the earth, meaning the seed/egg of a woman through the sperm of a man—that is, sex, and therefore marriage—is only allowed between two people of reproductive age.

(Quran 2:223)

نِسَاؤُكُمْ حَرْثٌ لَّكُمْ فَأْتُوا حَرْثَكُمْ أَنَّىٰ شِئْتُمْ ۖ وَقَدِّمُوا لِأَنْفُسِكُمْ ۚ وَاتَّقُوا اللَّهَ
وَاعْلَمُوا أَنَّكُم مُّلَاقُوهُ ۗ وَبَشِّرِ الْمُؤْمِنِينَ

*Your women [wives] are a place of sowing of seed for you, so
come to your place of cultivation however you wish and put
forth for yourselves. And fear Allah and know that you will
meet Him. And give good tidings to the believers.*

Another indication that marriage is meant for women and not underage girls are the guidelines the Quran sets forth for a woman whose relationship fails. She is allowed to enter into another relationship, but only after three menstrual cycles pass between her last relationship and the next one.

(Quran 2:228)

وَالْمُطَلَّقَاتُ يَتَرَبَّصْنَ بِأَنفُسِهِنَّ ثَلَاثَةَ قُرُوءٍ

(Before marrying someone else) Divorced women will remain
in waiting for three periods [menstrual cycles].

The age of puberty, of course, differs, and research shows that for girls, it is coming on sooner and sooner. Shariah law does not set a fixed age for determining a woman's adulthood. In Islam, a girl becomes a woman from the time she reaches puberty, as do boys. Islam permits (but does not obligate) marriage only after puberty has been reached, but a woman can also marry at a much later phase in life. The choice is hers, which again may surprise some readers.

There are two traditions in the Hadith that support a woman's right to consent to marriage:

1. The Prophet Muhammad said, *"A matron should not be given in marriage except after consulting her, and a virgin should not be given in marriage except after her permission."* (Hadith, Bukhari 5136)

2. A companion of Prophet Muhammad, Khansa bint Khidam Al-Ansariya, said: *"Her father gave her in marriage when she was a matron, and she disliked that marriage. So she went to the Prophet, and he declared that marriage invalid."* (Hadith, Bukhari 5138)

My point is that to be married, a woman must be of reproductive age (past puberty) and able to comprehend what is happening so she can enter a relationship willingly.

Incidentally, the consensus of scholars across centuries is that pedophilia is prohibited under Shariah law, a conclusion drawn from the teachings presented from the Quran and the Hadith, above. Families may still betroth their children to one another, even at a young age. Yet these children can only come together under one roof as a couple when they are of reproductive age and they are of sound mind—that is, mature enough to be able to give their own consent willingly. The Prophet Muhammad's youngest wife, Aishah, was betrothed by her father many years before the actual consummation of the marriage.

So why these words by Aishah, where she states: *The Messenger of Allah married me when I was 6 years old and consummated the marriage with me when I was 9 years old.* (Athar, Bukhari 5134)

Some Muslims use these words as an excuse to marry underage girls. But a closer look by the Syrian scholar Salahuddin Idlibi at Aishah's life through the light of history and tradition finds that Aishah was born four years before Muhammad's prophethood began, and that she didn't marry Muhammad until the 10th year of his mission, which would make her 14 years old. She began living with him one year after the migration to Madinah, the 14th year of his mission, which would make her 18 at the time the marriage was consummated.

Another way of cross-referencing Aishah's age is that she was 10 years younger than her sister, Asma, who was 14 years old when Muhammad's mission began. That means Aishah would have been 4 years old at *that* time, not when she was married.

Perhaps it's time for Muslims to initiate a broader, more critical discussion of child marriages, which are still of concern in the Muslim world as well as a source of confusion. The same might be said for these unions in the U.S.: In 2017, while countries such as Zimbabwe, Malawi, and El Salvador banned child marriage, half of the states in the U.S. had no minimum cutoff point for marriage; that same year, marriage before age 18 was legal in all 50 states. Currently, marriage under age 18 is still legal in 43 states, and marriage at *any* age is legal in 20 states as long as parental consent is given. Between the years 2000 and 2015, more than 200,000 minors were married in the U.S.

In Florida, the location of my former mosques, the BBC reported that a girl named Sherry Johnson was forced by her mother to marry her rapist at the age of 11 and had six kids by the time she turned 16. Johnson went on to challenge the status quo to ensure that no one else went through what she did, and in 2018, various members of the Tallahassee, Florida, community came together in support of a bill to ban this practice and put limitations on underage marriage. However, according to a report in the *Orlando Sentinel*, there was an unexpected result: The Florida House of Representatives wasn't entirely willing to outlaw child marriages.

"The day after the Senate unanimously passed a bill to ban marriage for anyone under 18, a House committee approved exceptions for 16- and 17-year-olds who were pregnant if their partners were no more than two years older than they were." These were eventually overruled, and thanks to the efforts of Sherry Johnson, marriage in Florida is now prohibited for anyone under 17.

Islam does not consider a woman's body to be a political toy to be played with, abused, or misused. Her body has been entrusted to her by Allah, and she is accountable to Him alone for her ways and actions.

When the Supreme Court overturned Roe v. Wade in June of 2022, the legal battle over abortion shifted to the states, where anti-abortion forces, often for religious reasons, intend to continue the fight to ban all abortions. Islam itself does not categorically prohibit abortion, and many Islamic scholars agree that a woman's life should be prioritized over that of an unborn fetus. Scholars have also given a range of time during which they consider it appropriate for a Muslim to have an abortion—from a few weeks to a few months (specifically, up to 120 days). Additionally, abortion is allowed in cases of rape or if the parents are physically or mentally unable to raise a child. These decisions are based on the consensus of scholars.

Shariah is not static; its rulings have evolved over time in response to cultural, social, and political shifts to stay relevant to Muslims. From birth control to in vitro fertilization (IVF), scholars look first to the circumstances to decide on permissibility, rather than politicizing women and their bodies.

Let's move on to polygamy. Though less than 5% of Muslim marriages are polygamous worldwide, in Islam, a man is permitted to marry up to four women:

(Quran 4:3)

فَٱنكِحُواْ مَا طَابَ لَكُم مِّنَ ٱلنِّسَآءِ مَثْنَىٰ وَثُلَٰثَ وَرُبَٰعَ فَإِنْ خِفْتُمْ أَلَّا تَعْدِلُواْ
فَوَٰحِدَةً أَوْ مَا مَلَكَتْ أَيْمَٰنُكُمْ ذَٰلِكَ أَدْنَىٰٓ أَلَّا تَعُولُواْ

Then marry those that please you of [other] women,
two or three or four. But if you fear that you will not be just,
then [marry only] one or those your right hand possesses.
That is more suitable that you may not incline
[to injustice].

It's important to understand that this verse is not a mandate—it is a *limit* on the number of lawful sexual partners a man can have. It's also important to note that polygamy is not something that is practiced out of sheer frivolity and carnal desire. If a man chooses to have more than one wife at a time, he must adhere to certain conditions, treating each wife the same financially, spending time with each equally, and making sure the quality of their housing, standard of living, and rights of each wife's children are equitable. Each wife also has the right to leave the marriage. By the same token, if the husband divorces any one of the wives, her rights are the same as if she had been the only wife. If the husband passes away, the inheritance rights of her children are the same as that of any of his other children.

The Quranic verse referenced above cautions men that if they can't be just and fair with more than one wife, they should not marry more than one woman, or else risk answering before Allah for that injustice. And Muslim men do take their legal obligations toward their wives, and before Allah, seriously.

Again, it's important to consider context. In a world where promiscuous sex was the norm, the Quran put boundaries into place, offering guidelines as to who can have a sexual relationship with whom and under what circumstances (namely, marriage).

(Quran 4:23)

حُرِّمَتْ عَلَيْكُمْ أُمَّهَاتُكُمْ وَبَنَاتُكُمْ وَأَخَوَاتُكُمْ وَعَمَّاتُكُمْ وَخَالَاتُكُمْ وَبَنَاتُ الْأَخِ وَبَنَاتُ الْأُخْتِ وَأُمَّهَاتُكُمُ اللَّاتِي أَرْضَعْنَكُمْ وَأَخَوَاتُكُم مِّنَ الرَّضَاعَةِ وَأُمَّهَاتُ نِسَائِكُمْ وَرَبَائِبُكُمُ اللَّاتِي فِي حُجُورِكُم مِّن نِّسَائِكُمُ اللَّاتِي دَخَلْتُم بِهِنَّ فَإِن لَّمْ تَكُونُوا دَخَلْتُم بِهِنَّ فَلَا جُنَاحَ عَلَيْكُمْ وَحَلَائِلُ أَبْنَائِكُمُ الَّذِينَ مِنْ أَصْلَابِكُمْ وَأَن تَجْمَعُوا بَيْنَ الْأُخْتَيْنِ إِلَّا مَا قَدْ سَلَفَ ۗ إِنَّ اللَّهَ كَانَ غَفُورًا رَّحِيمًا

Prohibited to you [for marriage] are your mothers, your daughters, your sisters, your father's sisters, your mother's sisters, your brother's daughters, your sister's daughters, your [milk] mothers who nursed you, your sisters through nursing, your wives' mothers, and your step-daughters under your guardianship [born] of your wives unto whom you have gone in. But if you have not gone in unto them, there is no sin upon you. And [also prohibited are] the wives of your sons who are from your [own] loins, and that you take [in marriage] two sisters simultaneously, except for what has already occurred. Indeed, Allah is ever Forgiving and Merciful.

I'll add that in America today, surveys show that the average heterosexual man and woman (ages 18 to 60) have had between four and six opposite-sex partners in their lifetime.

So sex, clearly, is a human need. But without guiding principles, problems can occur. Infidelity is common, even among happily married couples. And though more than 90% of Americans consider infidelity to be immoral, around 30% to 40% of Americans admit to cheating on their partner.

One problem with infidelity is that it increases the chances of spreading a sexually transmitted disease to a partner. Indeed, the Centers for Disease Control and Prevention reported a record 2.6 million new cases of STDs in 2019.

Allah created in humans the need for a companion, which can be fulfilled through monogamy. However, polygamy is also a need, perhaps not for all, but for some, and Allah caps the number of intimate relationships allowed at one time at four, irrespective of outside circumstances, such as men dying because of war or a fluctuating ratio between men and women. And it is through marriage—not casual encounters—that Islam sees the possibility of commitment and loyalty. The bond of marriage preserves the honor of both partners, beyond their pleasure, with a promise of commitment to each other.

Within the family unit, however, the husband is defined as the one in charge, affirmed by this verse in the Quran:

(Quran 4:34)

ٱلرِّجَالُ قَوَّٰمُونَ عَلَى ٱلنِّسَآءِ بِمَا فَضَّلَ ٱللَّهُ بَعْضَهُمْ عَلَىٰ بَعْضٍ وَبِمَآ أَنفَقُواْ مِنْ أَمْوَٰلِهِمْ

Men are in charge of women by [right of] what Allah has given one over the other and what they spend [for maintenance] from their wealth

This means that the responsibility for the family's well-being and accountability, both in this world and in the next, rests on the husband/father rather than the wife/mother. That also means that according to Shariah law, the responsibility for decisions and the consequences of those decisions don't fall on the wife/mother.

People who equate the word *responsibility* with "authority" or "power" tend to use this same verse as carte blanche for abusing and controlling women.

(Quran 4:34)

ٱلرِّجَالُ قَوَّٰمُونَ عَلَى ٱلنِّسَآءِ بِمَا فَضَّلَ ٱللَّهُ بَعْضَهُمْ عَلَىٰ بَعْضٍ وَبِمَآ أَنفَقُواْ مِنْ أَمْوَٰلِهِمْ فَٱلصَّٰلِحَٰتُ قَٰنِتَٰتٌ حَٰفِظَٰتٌ لِّلْغَيْبِ بِمَا حَفِظَ ٱللَّهُ وَٱلَّٰتِى تَخَافُونَ نُشُوزَهُنَّ فَعِظُوهُنَّ وَٱهْجُرُوهُنَّ فِى ٱلْمَضَاجِعِ وَٱضْرِبُوهُنَّ فَإِنْ أَطَعْنَكُمْ فَلَا تَبْغُواْ عَلَيْهِنَّ سَبِيلًا إِنَّ ٱللَّهَ كَانَ عَلِيًّا كَبِيرًا

Men are in charge of women by [right of] what Allah has given
one over the other and what they spend [for maintenance]
from their wealth. So righteous women are devoutly obedient,
guarding in [the husband's] absence what Allah would
have them guard. But those [wives] from whom you fear
arrogance—[first] advise them; [then if they persist], forsake
them in bed; and [finally], **beat*** *them. But if they obey you*
[once more], seek no means against them. Indeed, Allah is ever
Exalted and Grand.

Let's look at the word *beat* in the above verse. In Arabic, the word
is *darb*. Like many Arabic words, this one has multiple meanings,
depending on the context. In each of the examples below, the bolded
words stand for darb:

(Quran 14:24)

أَلَمْ تَرَ كَيْفَ ضَرَبَ ٱللَّهُ مَثَلًا

Have you not considered how Allah **sets forth** *a parable*

or (Quran 47:4)

فَإِذَا لَقِيتُمُ ٱلَّذِينَ كَفَرُواْ فَضَرْبَ ٱلرِّقَابِ

So when you meet those who disbelieve [in battle], **chop off**
[their] necks

or (Quran 24:31)

وَلْيَضْرِبْنَ بِخُمُرِهِنَّ عَلَىٰ جُيُوبِهِنَّ

and to **wrap** *[a portion of] their head covers over their chests* or (Quran 3:156)

وَقَالُواْ لِإِخْوَٰنِهِمْ إِذَا ضَرَبُواْ فِى ٱلْأَرْضِ

*and said about their brothers when they **traveled** through the land . . .*

Getting back to Quran 4:34, the translation for darb is not necessarily "beat." On the contrary, I believe the command is more accurately translated as "shun."

> *But those [wives] from whom you fear arrogance—[first]
> advise them; [then if they persist], forsake them in bed; and
> [finally], **shun them**. But if they obey you [once more], seek
> no means against them. Indeed, Allah is ever Exalted
> and Grand.*

Choosing this meaning is not arbitrary; indeed, it coincides with the actions of the Prophet Muhammad himself.

Once, during the 8th year of migration (21 years into prophethood), the Prophet's wives asked for a bit more material comfort than they had. Muhammad was not pleased, so he swore to Allah that he would not come close to his wives for one month (i.e., shun them). What he didn't do was beat them, curse them, or fight with them—none of these are in his teachings. Rather, from the Hadith, we find it was quite the opposite.

The Prophet Muhammad said:

> *"The most complete of the believers in faith is the one with the
> best character among them. And the best of you are those who
> are best to your women."* (Hadith, Tirmidhi 1162)

He also stated:

"The best of you are the best to their families, and I am the best
to my family." (Hadith, Tirmidhi 3895)

In addition to Muhammad's advice is the testimony of Aishah,
his wife. She reports:

"He [Muhammad] never beat anyone with his hand, neither a
woman nor a servant." (Hadith, Muslim 2328)

The only treatment the Quran condones for one's wife is that of
kindness:

(Quran 4:19)

وَعَاشِرُوهُنَّ بِٱلْمَعْرُوفِ ۚ

And live with them in kindness.

Even if the relationship ends in a divorce, it, too, must be processed
in good character. In the chapter on divorce, Allah instructs:

(Quran 65:2)

فَإِذَا بَلَغْنَ أَجَلَهُنَّ فَأَمْسِكُوهُنَّ بِمَعْرُوفٍ أَوْ فَارِقُوهُنَّ بِمَعْرُوفٍ

So when they have reached their prescribed time, then retain
them with kindness or separate them with kindness.

We must all agree that everyone deserves to be treated fairly and
kindly, particularly within a family. More than 1 in 3 women and
1 in 4 men in the U.S. will experience rape, physical violence, or
stalking by an intimate partner—more than 12 million women and
men over a single year. I think we can agree that, right now, there is

no society—either in the Muslim or non-Muslim world—where the treatment and rights of women are as they should be. The undeniable ill treatment of women in today's Muslim world has nothing to do with Shariah. Instead, that treatment is frequently justified through ultraconservative policies that are unrelated to true Islam and that almost always result in oppression.

Then there is the other extreme of ultraliberalism, in which every check and balance is removed from the equation. Many Muslims are concerned about issues related to gender identity, homosexuality, excessive focus on sexual matters for commercial purposes, and rampant permissiveness. These concerns reflect the teachings of Islam. In Western countries, these matters have mostly remained in the family, setting children and more traditional parents against one another. The issue of modest dress exemplifies this conflict (e.g., "You're not leaving for school in that short dress, young lady!")

Women and the Hijab

Many in the West believe a Muslim woman in a *hijab* (headscarf) is being oppressed—forced to wear what she is told by her parents, husband, or community of faith. Women wearing long black dresses known as *abaya*, or face coverings known as *niqab*, reinforce this perception.

In the Quran, Allah refers to clothing as a gift from God to humankind:

(Quran 7:26)

يَا بَنِي آدَمَ قَدْ أَنزَلْنَا عَلَيْكُمْ لِبَاسًا يُوَارِي سَوْآتِكُمْ وَرِيشًا ۖ وَلِبَاسُ التَّقْوَىٰ ذَٰلِكَ خَيْرٌ ۚ ذَٰلِكَ مِنْ آيَاتِ اللَّهِ لَعَلَّهُمْ يَذَّكَّرُونَ

*O children of Adam, We have bestowed upon you clothing to
conceal your private parts and as adornment. But the clothing
of righteousness—that is best. That is from the signs of Allah
that perhaps they will remember.*

For men and women, clothing tends to serve two distinct
purposes: to cover one's nakedness and to look good. When Adam
and Eve were sent to earth from heaven, they came with bare bodies.

(Quran 7:22)

فَدَلَّاهُمَا بِغُرُورٍ ۚ فَلَمَّا ذَاقَا الشَّجَرَةَ بَدَتْ لَهُمَا سَوْآتُهُمَا وَطَفِقَا يَخْصِفَانِ عَلَيْهِمَا مِن وَرَقِ الْجَنَّةِ ۖ

*So he made them fall, through deception. And when they tasted
of the tree, their private parts became apparent to them, and
they began to fasten together over themselves from
the leaves of Paradise.*

Under Shariah law, men and women alike are required to dress
in a manner that portrays self-respect and dignity. Muslims believe
their bodies are entrusted to them by Allah and must be respected
in public and private. Contrary to many current Western cultures,
where exposing the skin and the shape of the body are compatible
with current values of the West, Shariah encourages modest dress.
That doesn't mean that one set of values should be imposed on
another.

I'll take this further and say that despite Shariah calling for
modest dress, this requirement should not be enforced in the
harsh, oppressive manner we see in some Muslim countries today,
where "morality police" beat and discipline women for not wearing
headscarves. This leads only to women turning against Islam.

Compliance can't come at the price of alienating women and young people who dress differently than what the Quran's "personal devotional law" requires but a given society wants to impose.

In the Quran, the Prophet Muhammad was instructed by Allah to command women to cover themselves:

(Quran 33:59)

يَا أَيُّهَا النَّبِيُّ قُل لِّأَزْوَاجِكَ وَبَنَاتِكَ وَنِسَاءِ الْمُؤْمِنِينَ يُدْنِينَ عَلَيْهِنَّ مِن جَلَابِيبِهِنَّ ۚ ذَٰلِكَ أَدْنَىٰ أَن يُعْرَفْنَ فَلَا يُؤْذَيْنَ ۗ وَكَانَ اللَّهُ غَفُورًا رَّحِيمًا

O Prophet, tell your wives and your daughters and the women
of the believers to bring down over themselves [part] of their
outer garments. That is more suitable that they will be known
and not be abused. And ever is Allah Forgiving and Merciful.

This also includes using the lower part of the headscarf (hijab) to cover their breasts.

(Quran 24:31)

وَلْيَضْرِبْنَ بِخُمُرِهِنَّ عَلَىٰ جُيُوبِهِنَّ ۖ

and to wrap [a portion of] their head covers over their chests

It is the responsibility of Muslim women to heed this command at all times. As for the imposition of dress currently happening in Iran, where women and girls rebelling against the headscarf or hijab are being punished for it, I believe this is more the result of the Iranian government seeking power and control than safeguarding the faith. After all, trying to control a population by enforcing religious mores through fear almost always leads to a rebellion against the faith by the masses. Islam, if practiced in its rightful manner, should instill more love for the faith as it improves the lives of its adherents; it does not take away basic freedoms. I will add, however, that Islam does not support encouraging young women to bare their bodies in the name of freedom. These permissive and potentially exploitative practices are also dangerous. One side imposes hijab; the other normalizes bikinis and sexual exploitation.

I can recall a time when I was visiting Saudi Arabia, back in the days when all women were covered from head to toe. My friend and I, on the way to a restaurant in Madinah for lunch, passed by a row of stores that were displaying beautiful dresses for women on mannequins. I was puzzled since I never saw anyone wearing dresses like these in public, so I asked my friend: "Who are these meant for?" He told me that the dresses were famous and purchased by local women all the time to be worn at home and at women-only exclusive parties in function halls. I learned that women love to dress up and look nice at home and among other women.

However you feel about what you have learned in this chapter, my purpose has been to provide an honest explanation of how Islam deals with these issues under Shariah law.

Muslims and non-Muslims can only coexist when we cast a light on our respective differences and practices without demonizing them, which brings to mind the first time I spoke by invitation at a church in Florida. It was early on in my tenure as imam of Fort Myers, and I was extremely nervous about how I would be received and whether I would be able to convey my message adequately. At the time, the American response to 9/11 was going full throttle, with the recent invasion of Iraq in addition to the war in Afghanistan. As I entered the church, a Muslim man dressed in a white traditional Pakistani garment, sticking out amidst a congregation of Christians dressed like, well, Floridians, my nervousness only increased. When congregants and audience members came to greet me, I shook the hands of men and placed my hand on my heart when greeting women, responding according to my instincts and my teaching. In Islam, we are taught that respecting the opposite gender means not touching any woman who isn't a relative or spouse, because she is honorable to herself, family, and Allah. Then one woman stepped up to greet me, opening her arms and embracing me—and I let her. I didn't feel that it was right to abruptly and publicly tell her that I couldn't touch or hug her. After the program, which, in my nervousness, went by in a blur, I made a general comment to the audience that I was glad to meet with them, but that if any woman approached, she should know that I wouldn't be shaking her hand or touching her because of the aforementioned reasons. As I mingled after the talk, a woman from the congregation came up to me and said, "That is such an amazing thing. I wish my religion had it."

CHAPTER 8

Is Shariah a Threat to the West?

By Imam Azhar Subedar

Ask the average Westerner how Islam proliferated throughout the Arab world, parts of Africa, Asia, and Europe during the Caliphate period, and most would assume that the religion was spread by the sword—in the past and now. There is an almost universal perception by non-Muslims that our ultimate goal is domination. Given the images of Bin Laden wielding a gun in a cave and threatening the non-Muslim world on video, livestreams of beheadings by members of ISIS in Syria, calls for jihad on Twitter (now X), and chants of "death to America" from crowds in Iran, and that point of view is understandable.

Yet despite these open signs of animosity toward the West by some Muslims, there has been a noticeable reduction in mass killings and murders by lone wolves done in the name of Islam. And war and destruction waged by Muslim countries against *all* non-Muslims (or "infidels") is virtually nonexistent.

In this chapter, I'll examine the fear of Muslim domination from the West and also from the perspective of Muslims themselves. I'll examine the question of what happens to Muslims who leave the faith, and if they are then considered enemies of Islam. I'll talk about how Muslims reconcile a situation in which the civil laws of their country conflict with those of Shariah.

I'll also illuminate the concept of jihad, a term many people first hear about on the news or through social media. When news breaks about Muslims involved in suicide or car bombings and killings, often at the behest of the Taliban, Al Qaeda, ISIS, and the like, these incidents only reaffirm the belief that Islam is a religion founded on violence and spread by the sword. In these pages, I've done my best not to duck these difficult topics, nor succumb to political correctness or obfuscation to make my answers more acceptable.

Let's start with the word *jihad* itself, which means "struggle." Struggle has many modes and shapes, including but not limited to war. Yet jihad is often considered to be one and the same as "holy war." Interestingly, the phrase "holy war" is nowhere to be found in either the Quran or the Hadith, nor is it rooted in Islamic teachings. Jihad, when used in the context of war, is described through divine instructions and reasons why one would engage in war in the first place. Jihad is not allowed unless certain conditions are met. Everlasting virtue and rewards are promised to anyone who engages in war under these circumstances, and a person who dies during war is deemed a *shaheed* (martyr). This is separate from a situation in which a person or people who, for whatever selfish reasons, rally their people to engage in war without the Divine's permission or command. It is important to separate human justification for war from Allah's command or permission to engage in the same.

Let's now consider jihad within the context of the foundational teaching of Islam. (First impressions tend to stick, right?) The first revelation of the Quran (96:1-5) is *"Read in the name of thy Lord who created . . ."* meaning that reading—or learning—Allah's words is the path to productive and long-lasting personal change. Change begins with the individual, not others. The first revelation was not "Go kill the infidels," which many mistake as the goal of Muslims and the purpose of following Islam.

During the first 13 years of Islam's founding in Makkah, a period during which many of those who declared their devotion to Islam were persecuted, there was never a command in the Quran for the faithful to kill others or retaliate in any way, even to defend themselves. This, despite the fact that those who declared their devotion to Islam were threatened with murder (and often murdered), boycotted, and otherwise persecuted.

(Quran 2:109)

وَدَّ كَثِيرٌ مِّنْ أَهْلِ ٱلْكِتَـٰبِ لَوْ يَرُدُّونَكُم مِّنْ بَعْدِ إِيمَـٰنِكُمْ كُفَّارًا حَسَدًا مِّنْ عِندِ أَنفُسِهِم مِّنْ بَعْدِ مَا تَبَيَّنَ لَهُمُ ٱلْحَقُّ ۖ فَٱعْفُوا۟ وَٱصْفَحُوا۟ حَتَّىٰ يَأْتِىَ ٱللَّهُ بِأَمْرِهِ ۗ إِنَّ ٱللَّهَ عَلَىٰ كُلِّ شَىْءٍ قَدِيرٌ

Many of the People of the Scripture wish they could turn you back to disbelief after you have believed, out of envy from themselves [even] after the truth has become clear to them. So pardon and overlook until Allah delivers His command. Indeed, Allah is above all things, competent.

Instead, after 13 years of continued persecution in Makkah, Muslims had no choice but to leave their hometown. They had no other option since they couldn't retaliate or defend themselves in any way, given that there were no verses revealed by Allah permitting them to do so.

In utter desperation, the Prophet Muhammad sought a safe haven, which ended up being Madinah, north of Makkah, where he had been promised safety by the inhabitants. But once all the Muslims had safely migrated in small groups in the darkness of night, the remaining nonbelievers of Makkah doubled down on their resolve to kill Muhammad and his followers, despite their peaceful departure. It was only then, more than 14 years after the beginning of Islam, when Muslims were establishing their community in Madinah and living in harmony with their neighbors (including Jews and nonbelievers), that the first command for (defensive) war was revealed:

(Quran 22:39,40)

أُذِنَ لِلَّذِينَ يُقَـٰتَلُونَ بِأَنَّهُمْ ظُلِمُوا ۚ وَإِنَّ ٱللَّهَ عَلَىٰ نَصْرِهِمْ لَقَدِيرٌ ٱلَّذِينَ أُخْرِجُوا مِن دِيَـٰرِهِم بِغَيْرِ حَقٍّ إِلَّا أَن يَقُولُوا رَبُّنَا ٱللَّهُ ۗ وَلَوْلَا دَفْعُ ٱللَّهِ ٱلنَّاسَ بَعْضَهُم بِبَعْضٍ لَّهُدِّمَتْ صَوَٰمِعُ وَبِيَعٌ وَصَلَوَٰتٌ وَمَسَـٰجِدُ يُذْكَرُ فِيهَا ٱسْمُ ٱللَّهِ كَثِيرًا ۗ وَلَيَنصُرَنَّ ٱللَّهُ مَن يَنصُرُهُ ۚ إِنَّ ٱللَّهَ لَقَوِىٌّ عَزِيزٌ

Permission [to fight] has been given to those who are being fought because they were wronged. And indeed, Allah is competent to grant them victory. [They are] those who have been evicted from their homes without right—only because they say, "Our Lord is Allah." And were it not that Allah checks the people, some through others, there would have been demolished monasteries, churches, synagogues, and mosques in which the name of Allah is much mentioned. And Allah will surely support those who support Him. Indeed, Allah is Powerful and Exalted in Might.

To reiterate, Muslims were invited to Madinah; they did not take it by force. In contrast, the nonbelievers of Makkah were determined to storm Madinah. Hence, the revelation of the verses of war.

Many of the verses throughout the Quran promoting jihad, deployment, or military activity—which are few and far between (only 1.09% of the entire Quran), yet portrayed as the bulk of the message—are tied to specific events during the Prophet's life. For example:

In Chapter 8, al-Anfal (The Spoils of War):

(Quran 8:39)

وَقَٰتِلُوهُمْ حَتَّىٰ لَا تَكُونَ فِتْنَةٌ وَيَكُونَ ٱلدِّينُ كُلُّهُ لِلَّهِ ۚ فَإِنِ ٱنتَهَوْا۟ فَإِنَّ ٱللَّهَ بِمَا يَعْمَلُونَ بَصِيرٌ

And fight with them until there is no more persecution and religion should be only for Allah; but if they desist, then indeed Allah sees what they do.

(Quran 8:65)

يَٰٓأَيُّهَا ٱلنَّبِىُّ حَرِّضِ ٱلْمُؤْمِنِينَ عَلَى ٱلْقِتَالِ ۚ إِن يَكُن مِّنكُمْ عِشْرُونَ صَٰبِرُونَ يَغْلِبُوا۟ مِا۟ئَتَيْنِ ۚ وَإِن يَكُن مِّنكُم مِّا۟ئَةٌ يَغْلِبُوٓا۟ أَلْفًا مِّنَ ٱلَّذِينَ كَفَرُوا۟ بِأَنَّهُمْ قَوْمٌ لَّا يَفْقَهُونَ

O Prophet, urge the believers to battle. If there are among you twenty [who are] steadfast, they will overcome two hundred. And if there are among you one hundred [who are] steadfast, they will overcome a thousand of those who have disbelieved because they are a people who do not understand.

These verses (and others in this chapter) pertain to the events surrounding the Battle of Badr, the first military expedition in Islam, which occurred in the land of Badr, more than 100 kilometers outside of Madinah, in the 15th year of Islam, 624 CE, the 2nd year of the migration.

In Chapter 3, Aal-Imran (The Family of Imran):

(Quran 3:121)

وَإِذْ غَدَوْتَ مِنْ أَهْلِكَ تُبَوِّئُ ٱلْمُؤْمِنِينَ مَقَـٰعِدَ لِلْقِتَالِ ۗ وَٱللَّهُ سَمِيعٌ عَلِيمٌ

*And [remember] when you, [O Muhammad], left your family
in the morning to post the believers at their stations for the
battle—and Allah is Hearing and Knowing.*

The verses that follow this serve as a reminder for what transpired during the Battle of Uhud, right outside of Madinah, in the 16th year of Islam, 625 CE, the 3rd year after migration.

In Chapter 33, al-Ahzab (The Clans):

(Quran 33:16)

قُل لَّن يَنفَعَكُمُ ٱلْفِرَارُ إِن فَرَرْتُم مِّنَ ٱلْمَوْتِ أَوِ ٱلْقَتْلِ وَإِذًا لَّا تُمَتَّعُونَ إِلَّا قَلِيلًا

*Say, [O Muhammad], "Never will fleeing benefit you if you
should flee from death or killing; and then [if you did], you
would not be given enjoyment [of life] except for a little."*

(Quran 33:26)

وَأَنزَلَ ٱلَّذِينَ ظَـٰهَرُوهُم مِّنْ أَهْلِ ٱلْكِتَـٰبِ مِن صَيَاصِيهِمْ وَقَذَفَ فِى قُلُوبِهِمُ
ٱلرُّعْبَ فَرِيقًا تَقْتُلُونَ وَتَأْسِرُونَ فَرِيقًا

*And He brought down those who supported them among the
People of the Scripture from their fortresses and cast terror into
their hearts [so that] a party you killed, and you took
captive a party.*

These verses are tied to the siege and subjugation of the Banu Qurayzah. This Jewish tribe had a covenant with the Prophet Muhammad, which they broke when they sided with the enemy during the Battle of the Coalition Forces (also known as the Battle of the Trench), which occurred in the 18th year of Islam, 627 CE, the 5th year of migration.

In Chapter 9, at-Tawbah (The Repentance):

(Quran 9:14)

قَـٰتِلُوهُمْ يُعَذِّبْهُمُ ٱللَّهُ بِأَيْدِيكُمْ وَيُخْزِهِمْ وَيَنصُرْكُمْ عَلَيْهِمْ وَيَشْفِ صُدُورَ قَوْمٍ مُّؤْمِنِينَ

Fight them; Allah will punish them by your hands and will disgrace them and give you victory over them and satisfy the breasts of a believing people.

(Quran 9:38)

يَا أَيُّهَا الَّذِينَ آمَنُوا مَا لَكُمْ إِذَا قِيلَ لَكُمُ انفِرُوا فِي سَبِيلِ اللَّهِ اثَّاقَلْتُمْ إِلَى الْأَرْضِ ۚ أَرَضِيتُم بِالْحَيَاةِ الدُّنْيَا مِنَ الْآخِرَةِ ۚ فَمَا مَتَاعُ الْحَيَاةِ الدُّنْيَا فِي الْآخِرَةِ إِلَّا قَلِيلٌ

O you who have believed, what is [the matter] with you that, when you are told to go forth in the cause of Allah, you adhere heavily to the earth? Are you satisfied with the life of this world rather than the Hereafter? But what is the enjoyment of worldly life compared to the Hereafter except a [very] little.

(Quran 9:73)

يَـٰٓأَيُّهَا ٱلنَّبِىُّ جَـٰهِدِ ٱلْكُفَّارَ وَٱلْمُنَـٰفِقِينَ وَٱغْلُظْ عَلَيْهِمْ ۚ وَمَأْوَىٰهُمْ جَهَنَّمُ ۖ وَبِئْسَ ٱلْمَصِيرُ

O Prophet, fight against the disbelievers and the hypocrites and
be harsh upon them. And their refuge is Hell, and wretched is
the destination.

These verses and others in this chapter describe the commands issued after the Conquest of Makkah, which includes the announcement to terminate all indefinite pacts and treaties with all the tribes of Arabia, while those treaties that had a stipulated period would be honored but not renewed. This announcement had been made to this effect, in addition to the nonbelievers not being allowed to perform the annual pilgrimage after that year, by Abu Bakr when on pilgrimage at the end of the 9th year after migration. This chapter also discusses the battle of Hunain in the 8th year after migration and also provides the instructions for the battle of Tabuk, a military demonstration against the Byzantine Empire in 630 CE, the 9th year after migration.

Understanding the timeline of these various events described in the Quran can make it easier to put them into context. Even when the Quran goes as far as to say *"fight against the disbelievers and the hypocrites and be harsh upon them,"* it isn't issuing a green light for jihad on the world. It is about saying "enough is enough" and taking action against those who have chosen to tyrannize and oppress others as their way of life.

At one point Allah commands the killing of the nonbelievers after the passing of the sacred month without restrictions, as is set down in (9:5):

(Quran 9:5)

فَإِذَا ٱنسَلَخَ ٱلْأَشْهُرُ ٱلْحُرُمُ فَٱقْتُلُواْ ٱلْمُشْرِكِينَ حَيْثُ وَجَدتُّمُوهُمْ وَخُذُوهُمْ

وَٱحْصُرُوهُمْ وَٱقْعُدُواْ لَهُمْ كُلَّ مَرْصَدٍ ۚ فَإِن تَابُواْ وَأَقَامُواْ ٱلصَّلَوٰةَ وَءَاتَوُاْ

ٱلزَّكَوٰةَ فَخَلُّواْ سَبِيلَهُمْ ۚ إِنَّ ٱللَّهَ غَفُورٌ رَّحِيمٌ

And when the sacred months have passed, then kill the polytheists
wherever you find them and capture them and besiege them
and sit in wait for them at every place of ambush. But if they
should repent, establish prayer, and give charity, let them [go]
on their way. Indeed, Allah is Forgiving and Merciful.

The goal is not to annihilate an entire people's existence but to end an entire *way* of existence—specifically, the history of tyranny, oppression, and injustice in the holy land of monotheism, in addition to the practices and the ways of nonbelievers. Those who wished to align their ways with the path of monotheism were welcomed to stay, while those who didn't were allowed to leave. The inhabitants of Makkah who had an indefinite treaty or no treaty at all were given four months to decide, while those who had a treaty were given the period of time specified by the treaty. Each of them, however, got respite until the "sacred months" were over, during which, in Islam, war is forbidden. In other words, time was given, and no one was pressured one way or another.

How did Muslims go from having no permission to defend themselves in Makkah to being able to engage in defensive warfare in Madinah? Why, finally, could they engage in offensive warfare? The answer can only be understood through the timeline of what happened in the first 23 years of Islam, when there was a shift from seeking refuge from governing powers to actually becoming the governing power.

Migration to Madinah was a major turning point. Before Muhammad and his companions landed there, the two major Arab tribes of Madinah, the Aws and the Khazraj, had been engaged in a bloody feud. When representatives of these tribes visited Makkah, they asked Muhammad and his followers to come to their land. The tribes then asked Muhammad to begin arbitrating their affairs and eventually called on him to govern their society.

Muhammad introduced a new, more just form of government, one that aimed to uphold the rights of every citizen. That included the right to defend themselves against anyone actively threatening the stability, values, and health of society and its governing body. This new right to defensive warfare influenced how the Quran's war-related commands evolved over time.

To be clear, it was only after Muhammad came to power at the request of the citizens of Madinah that a treaty was signed between the Muslims of Madinah and the nonbelievers of his hometown, Makkah, which was later violated by the Makkans themselves. As a result, Allah granted Muslims permission to conquer Makkah by force if they faced any resistance. Upon entering the city of Makkah with an army of 10,000 troops, the Muslims *didn't* use force. Rather, the tribes of Quraish in Makkah surrendered to Muhammad and his compatriots.

Once the Muslims were in power in both Madinah and Makkah, they had a stake in defending the society and system they'd created. To that end, in the 22nd year of Islam, the only choices the Quran presented to its enemies were to become Muslim or be killed. Incidentally, this was a clear ultimatum given only to the tyrannical rulers and oppressors of their people. This wasn't a choice forced on every person in the society—and certainly not on people who were non-Muslims.

As for offensive war—i.e., a war fought for the protection of people and societies outside of the Shariah governing body (the Caliphate)—the Quran mandates that the existing Caliphate must fight for those who are unable to create a just system of government due to oppression by tyrannical leaders. The Quran clearly states this:

(Quran 4:75)

وَمَا لَكُمْ لَا تُقَاتِلُونَ فِي سَبِيلِ اللَّهِ وَالْمُسْتَضْعَفِينَ مِنَ الرِّجَالِ وَالنِّسَاءِ وَالْوِلْدَانِ الَّذِينَ يَقُولُونَ رَبَّنَا أَخْرِجْنَا مِنْ هَذِهِ الْقَرْيَةِ الظَّالِمِ أَهْلُهَا وَاجْعَل لَّنَا مِن لَّدُنكَ وَلِيًّا وَاجْعَل لَّنَا مِن لَّدُنكَ نَصِيرًا

And what is [the matter] with you that you fight not in the cause of Allah [for] the oppressed among men, women, and children, who say, "Our Lord, take us out of this city of oppressive people and appoint for us from Yourself a protector and appoint for us from Yourself a helper?"

This of course gives rise to the question of whether Muslims retain the authority to use force to uphold the command of jihad in today's world. I believe Allah's authorization to use force remains valid, but—and this is a big exception—only if the circumstances that initially gave rise to the command for defensive war reoccur. If there *were* to be a time and place where these circumstances arose, and if Shariah law were to return, the Muslims enforcing that law could indeed use force to protect its people and land, just as other nations of the world today protect their land, values, and government, if threatened. Unlike the laws of other nations, however, Shariah arises from Allah's command rather than from the interests of a particular people. That's why waging a war of aggression for the purpose of transforming non-Muslim lands to Muslim, simply to serve the interests of those in power, is not permitted.

Again, there are harsh verses in the Quran that *seem* to instruct Muslims to do barbaric things, and these verses are often used as propaganda to foster hate or to recruit and indoctrinate extremists. But context is everything, and not enough people read the words before and after these oft-quoted verses to better understand the history and situations that led up to them. These commands are specific to a certain time, place, and circumstances, circumstances that warranted revelations from Allah. These revelations are, in turn, now part of the Quran (but again, they are specific to those circumstances). They are also meant to be a framework for action if similar circumstances arise in the future. What they don't do is give license to practice harsh measures at any time or place.

In every instance where war is sanctioned in the Quran, it is to confront and eliminate injustice, oppression, and inequality. When these verses were revealed to the Prophet Muhammad, the Muslims were in a position of power and had a responsibility to ensure that justice and peace were established and upheld. Incidentally, Muslims are still under this obligation, as every person under Islam is responsible for *themselves* and accountable for what they do.

(Quran 2:217)

وَالْفِتْنَةُ أَكْبَرُ مِنَ الْقَتْلِ

And fitnah is greater than killing.

To put this verse into context, *fitnah* is understood here as civil strife that can cause disorder, resulting in disharmony and conflict within the community, which most certainly can lead to mass bloodshed. A disagreement as to who would be successor to the Prophet Muhammad, peace be upon him, caused the schism resulting in the two major sects of Islam, the Sunni and the Shia. It is the continuation of this fitnah that is the basis for the thousand-year-plus disharmony between the Sunnis and Shia, perpetuating Muslims' killing of Muslims. It is apparent that those of us of the Muslim faith need to mend these disputes as we move toward global reconciliation of Muslims and all other faiths.

Sadly, that has proven to be difficult, given the tribal divides that exist not only in the Muslim world but also in the United States. I'm talking about T-shirts, bumper stickers, and other swag labeled with the word *infidel*. Like a schoolyard taunt, this basically says to Muslims, "Yes, I'm an infidel. What are you going to do about it?" The assumption is that Muslims consider everyone who doesn't share their faith to be an infidel.

To go deeper, the term *infidel* (literally, "one who is unfaithful") was an ecclesiastical term in Christianity around which the Church developed a body of theology dealing with the concept of infidelity—not sexual, but in reference to the divide between people who were baptized and followed the teachings of the Church versus those who were outside the faith—i.e., enemies of Christianity.

Today, however, the term is widely believed to be the translation of the Arabic word *kafir,* a term that was actually used in the Quran to refer to farmers who concealed seeds or covered them with dirt when they tilled the earth, leading to the definition "conceal" or "cover."

(Quran 57:20)

ٱعْلَمُوٓاْ أَنَّمَا ٱلْحَيَوٰةُ ٱلدُّنْيَا لَعِبٌ وَلَهْوٌ وَزِينَةٌ وَتَفَاخُرٌ بَيْنَكُمْ وَتَكَاثُرٌ فِى ٱلْأَمْوَٰلِ
وَٱلْأَوْلَٰدِ ۖ كَمَثَلِ غَيْثٍ أَعْجَبَ ٱلْكُفَّارَ نَبَاتُهُۥ ثُمَّ يَهِيجُ فَتَرَىٰهُ مُصْفَرًّا ثُمَّ يَكُونُ
حُطَٰمًا ۖ وَفِى ٱلْءَاخِرَةِ عَذَابٌ شَدِيدٌ وَمَغْفِرَةٌ مِّنَ ٱللَّهِ وَرِضْوَٰنٌ ۚ وَمَا ٱلْحَيَوٰةُ
ٱلدُّنْيَآ إِلَّا مَتَٰعُ ٱلْغُرُورِ

*Know that the life of this world is but amusement and
diversion and adornment and boasting to one another and
competition in increase of wealth and children—like the
example of a rain whose [resulting] plant growth pleases
the <u>tillers;</u> then it dries, and you see it turned yellow;
then it becomes [scattered] debris. And in the Hereafter is
severe punishment and forgiveness from Allah and approval.
And what is the worldly life except for the enjoyment
of delusion.*

Other applications of the term *kafir* include one who conceals or
covers the truth of Allah by openly rejecting it.

(Quran 3:72)

وَقَالَت طَّآئِفَةٌ مِّنْ أَهْلِ الْكِتَابِ آمِنُوا بِالَّذِي أُنزِلَ عَلَى الَّذِينَ آمَنُوا وَجْهَ النَّهَارِ
وَاكْفُرُوا آخِرَهُ لَعَلَّهُمْ يَرْجِعُونَ

*And a faction of the People of the Scripture said [to each
other], "Believe in that which was revealed to the believers
[Muslims] at the beginning of the day and reject it at its end
that perhaps they will abandon their religion."*

This verse refers to the practice of some followers of divine
scriptures, whether the Torah or Christian Bible, who decided to

use Islam against the Muslims by embracing the faith to boost the morale of the Muslims, only to abandon Islam at the end of the day. The goal was to break the Muslims morale and push them to also abandon their faith.

Kafir, then, was never meant to be the slur people have made it out to be today. Neither is everyone who is outside the Muslim faith a kafir, or "infidel."

Additionally, there is a difference between a disbeliever and a nonbeliever.

In English, *disbelief* means to actively reject the truth, while *unbelief* refers to the "absence of belief." To put it another way, the word *kafir* has to do with knowledge: Anyone who knows the good in something and then goes on to reject it, concealing the reality of it to themselves and others, is a kafir.

That's precisely why it's incorrect to categorize all non-Muslims as *kuffar* (the plural of kafir). It's impossible to reject something if you aren't intimately familiar with it. That's the difference between unbelief and disbelief. Hence the lifelong mission of Prophet Muhammad, which was to spread the word of Allah by giving *Da'wah* (inviting others to Allah), so they may be made aware of what Islam is.

(Quran 16:125)

ادْعُ إِلَىٰ سَبِيلِ رَبِّكَ بِالْحِكْمَةِ وَالْمَوْعِظَةِ الْحَسَنَةِ ۖ وَجَادِلْهُم بِالَّتِي هِيَ أَحْسَنُ ۚ إِنَّ رَبَّكَ هُوَ أَعْلَمُ بِمَن ضَلَّ عَن سَبِيلِهِ ۖ وَهُوَ أَعْلَمُ بِالْمُهْتَدِينَ

Invite [everyone] to the Way of your Lord with wisdom and kind advice, and only debate with them in the best manner. Surely your Lord knows best who has strayed from His Way and who is guided.

So the question then becomes: How should Muslims see and deal with a kafir?

According to the Quran, believers must let disbelievers know that they are on a separate path—nothing more.

(Quran 109)

قُلْ يَـٰٓأَيُّهَا ٱلْكَـٰفِرُونَ لَآ أَعْبُدُ مَا تَعْبُدُونَ وَلَآ أَنتُمْ عَـٰبِدُونَ مَآ أَعْبُدُ وَلَآ أَنَا۠ عَابِدٌ
مَّا عَبَدتُّمْ وَلَآ أَنتُمْ عَـٰبِدُونَ مَآ أَعْبُدُ لَكُمْ دِينُكُمْ وَلِىَ دِينِ

1. Say, "O Kafirs, 2. I do not worship what you worship.
3. Nor are you worshippers of what I worship. 4. Nor will
I be a worshipper of what you worship. 5. Nor will you be
worshippers of what I worship. 6. For you is your religion, and
for me is my religion."

Although the two paths are different, that isn't a reason for a Muslim to treat a disbeliever differently, much less with violence.

(Quran 60:8)

لَّا يَنْهَىٰكُمُ ٱللَّهُ عَنِ ٱلَّذِينَ لَمْ يُقَـٰتِلُوكُمْ فِى ٱلدِّينِ وَلَمْ يُخْرِجُوكُم مِّن دِيَـٰرِكُمْ أَن
تَبَرُّوهُمْ وَتُقْسِطُوٓا۟ إِلَيْهِمْ ۚ إِنَّ ٱللَّهَ يُحِبُّ ٱلْمُقْسِطِينَ

Allah does not forbid that you be kind and just to those who
did not fight against you on account of religion, nor drove you
out of your homes. Surely Allah loves those who are equitable.

This verse takes the relationship between a believer and a disbeliever a step further, from "we are on different paths" to "equitable."

Why, then, does the Quran call for death to a kafir, if equitable treatment is what the Quran says? Why the contradiction?

When the Quran speaks of "killing the kafir," we should remember the following points:

1. This was commanded 14 years after the birth of Islam.

2. It was due to a particular group of pagans from the Makkan tribe of Quraish who were considered a threat to the system and the citizens' safety at large. In other words, they not only rejected Islam after knowing it for what it was, but threatened violence against Islam and Muslims when they knew neither was a threat, then went on to perpetrate violence.

(Quran 2:191)

وَٱقْتُلُوهُمْ حَيْثُ ثَقِفْتُمُوهُمْ وَأَخْرِجُوهُم مِّنْ حَيْثُ أَخْرَجُوكُمْ ۚ وَٱلْفِتْنَةُ أَشَدُّ مِنَ
ٱلْقَتْلِ ۚ وَلَا تُقَٰتِلُوهُمْ عِندَ ٱلْمَسْجِدِ ٱلْحَرَامِ حَتَّىٰ يُقَٰتِلُوكُمْ فِيهِ ۖ فَإِن قَٰتَلُوكُمْ
فَٱقْتُلُوهُمْ ۗ كَذَٰلِكَ جَزَآءُ ٱلْكَٰفِرِينَ

And kill them wherever you find them, and drive them out from whence they drove you out, and disorder is greater than killing. And do not fight with them at the Sacred Mosque until they fight with you in it, but if they do fight you, then slay them; such is the recompense of the Kafirs.

We also learn from this verse that preemptive strikes against anyone who is merely "perceived [as] a threat" are not permissible, and that though everyone has the right to defend themselves in an attack, any response can only match the attack and not exceed it.

Disbelievers who go beyond rejection to openly mock or criticize Islam can be put in prison. If they surpass that and instigate harm by actively threatening the governing body of Islam and its citizens, and then carry those threats out, they may be sentenced to death, so long as this judgment is passed by a judge in a society governed by Shariah law and enforced by the respective authorities and not by laypeople in the streets. In America, we would call this treason, an offense that exists at both federal and state levels and also carries a sentence of death.

What are the consequences if someone consciously decides to leave the Islamic faith?

That person is known as an *apostate,* or, in Arabic, a *murtad.* In contrast to a kafir, who is someone familiar with Islam and then goes on to reject it, a murtad is someone who was once a part of the faith and has left—think of it as akin to renouncing one's citizenship.

Under Shariah law, anyone who commits apostasy in an Islamic society will be given time and space to understand their decision and what it means. They will have access to Islamic scholars so they can open up about their concerns and seek clarity. Shariah does not position its followers to be judges nor enforcers of law as they deem fit. No one can kill someone merely because they have left the faith, since leaving does not hurt the faith. Why, then, should the people of the faith feel hurt? Muslims need to understand and act within these limits.

(Quran 5:54)

يَـٰٓأَيُّهَا ٱلَّذِينَ ءَامَنُوا۟ مَن يَرْتَدَّ مِنكُمْ عَن دِينِهِ فَسَوْفَ يَأْتِى ٱللَّهُ بِقَوْمٍ يُحِبُّهُمْ وَيُحِبُّونَهُ

O you who believe! Whoever from among you turns back from his religion, then Allah will bring a people, He shall love them, and they shall love Him.

In the absence of the Caliphate and the absence of Shariah law being practiced anywhere in a society today, it should be impossible for anyone to be killed for denouncing the faith. But that is not the case in too many Muslim countries today.

In countries like America, Muslims who decide to leave the fold should also have access to an Islamic scholar to discuss their motivations. I still remember one former student who left Islam due to the difficult circumstances he faced while growing up—circumstances that ultimately pushed him away from his belief in Allah. I also remember this student's parents, who would periodically break down and insist that I must persuade their son to take their faith back. My advice was to practice patience and allow their child to heal. And over the years, I continued to have sporadic discussions with this student, who eventually asked me to officiate his wedding in a Muslim ceremony. He had found his faith again.

Under Shariah law, an apostate will not face death for their decision unless they become a threat to the state or its people. They can face punishment in a Muslim country, however, if they publicly deny Islam, since that potentially undermines the system and religion of the land. If they choose to keep their decision private, they are entitled to be left in peace. And of course, none of the above applies in non-Muslim countries, which are governed by the rules of their respective governments.

(Quran 2:217)

وَمَن يَرْتَدِدْ مِنكُمْ عَن دِينِهِ فَيَمُتْ وَهُوَ كَافِرٌ فَأُوْلَٰٓئِكَ حَبِطَتْ أَعْمَٰلُهُمْ فِى ٱلدُّنْيَا وَٱلْءَاخِرَةِ ۖ وَأُوْلَٰٓئِكَ أَصْحَٰبُ ٱلنَّارِ ۖ هُمْ فِيهَا خَٰلِدُونَ

And whoever of you reverts from his religion [to disbelief] and dies while he is a disbeliever—(not killed)—for those, their

deeds have become worthless in this world and the Hereafter,
and those are the companions of the Fire, they will abide
therein eternally.

An apostate, in other words, should not face death as punishment. The punishment lies tomorrow with Allah and is for Allah to decide.

Despite this, in Muslim countries around the world, people *have* been killed for apostasy at the hands of the public and sometimes by those representing the government, without due process. But this is contrary to Shariah, and I resent such people and their actions.

I am a believer and follower of Islam, but the Shariah of Islam is not something that can be imposed on people outside the faith, whether they reside under the Caliphate or in countries such as America. Allah makes that clear in the Quran.

(Quran 2:256)

لَآ إِكْرَاهَ فِى ٱلدِّينِ ۚ

There shall be no compulsion in the religion.

In other words, no one can be compelled to accept Islam; it cannot be forced on those outside the religion.

To go further, some aspects of Shariah law, mainly the penal code, are not applicable in countries where another governing body with a code and system exists, including the United States. Civil Shariah can only be applied under Islamic governance; it cannot be upheld otherwise. Muslims still have the option to follow their religious law if it's not in conflict with civil law; they can also obtain guidance when it comes to personal or family matters, such as with wills and inheritance, trusts, arbitration, dissolving a marriage, and child custody. Along with spiritual growth, religious devotion, improvement of character and more, this aspect of Shariah has and can continue to be peacefully incorporated into Western culture.

The First Amendment of the Constitution allows freedom of belief and freedom of religious practice. As a Muslim, I believe this right exists so long as the adherents of a particular faith respect other people's rights. The Establishment Clause of the United States sets a limit, however: No religious tradition can be established as the basis of the country's laws. This includes Islam's Shariah, and Jewish Halakhah laws.

Several states have attempted to go further, however, either passing (or attempting to pass) laws designed to prevent courts from applying Islamic or "Shariah" law, as well as any "foreign" or "international" law. One amendment to the state constitution passed in Oklahoma mentions Shariah specifically, in addition to international law. Moreover, since 2010, more than 200 anti-Shariah law bills have been introduced in 43 states. These laws are less about preventing religious overreach—the U.S. Constitution already denies authority to any foreign law—than about fomenting suspicion and hatred of Shariah.

Shariah law, however, is not the problem. The problem is the Muslims and non-Muslims whose heinous actions, divisive chants, and threats fill the airwaves. Equally, government officials who stir the pot of Islamophobia and fear, particularly after an attack by Islamic terrorists, or who turn a blind eye to violence committed by white supremacists, are adding fuel to the fire rather than finding solutions to maintain a civil society.

Another thing to keep in mind: The so-called Islamic terrorist organizations of today and their ideologies are only a few decades old; Islam, as a religion, dates back millennia. Far from being about war and vengeance, the Quran presents a lifestyle for its adherents, including a system for governing their actions based on how things were done in the past. It is meant to provide a framework for living a life of virtue and good deeds; that is Shariah, and it has been in practice among Muslims, in the U.S. and abroad, for centuries. To be clear, I'm not referring to the penal law, but to the personal law; the one that holds me, a Muslim, to the highest standards before Allah, society, and myself.

Interpretations of Shariah as a threat to civilized Western society (or anywhere else, for that matter) only empower Islamophobes, which, in turn, emboldens Islamic extremists. No one wins. Everyone loses.

CHAPTER 9

Fears About Islam and Sharia

By Robert Gary

In the preceding four chapters, Imam Subedar has provided his honest insights into Islam, with a candor I have rarely seen when these topics are addressed. As his coauthor, I appreciate that candor, but I must still ask the question: Are his explanations reassuring, or do they confirm non-Muslims' worst fears? For 2 billion Muslims, the Quran is regarded as the direct word of Allah. As a nonscholar and a lay student of Islam, I can only say that the evidence as to whether Islam is a violent religion is found within the Quran itself. There are a number of verses, for example, that encourage fighting. Imam Subedar has explained that these verses must be read in the proper context. However, how can any Muslim do this if they are not getting the proper instruction from their imam? Just as it's tough to find devout Catholics or Evangelicals who deny that Jesus is the Son of God, faithful Muslims would never deny that the words in the Quran come directly from Allah—that these words are the *heart* of Islam.

If you want to understand Islam and Muslims, the text of the

Quran is where you begin and where you end. As I said earlier, simply begin reading the Quran and you have begun the journey to understanding what Allah communicated to the faithful. And the words that guide 2 billion of our fellow travelers on this planet cannot be ignored. Verse 6:115 states, *"The Word of your Lord is perfected in truth and justice. None can change His words."*

I find it notable that Imam Subedar never suggests ignoring or disobeying a command from the Quran. What he does do (sometimes successfully and sometimes not, in my opinion) is offer a different interpretation, or suggest that a particular passage must be read in context with other passages, or assert that the historical events that prompted a revelation are no longer applicable to the present (but could be in the future).

I have noticed, though, that Muslims who are strict in their adherence to the faith claim to follow the Quran more closely than other Muslims. From my own reading of the Quran (in translation), I've found many verses to be harsh and demeaning to women and seem, in my view, to incite Muslims to violence. As a Jew, I am also concerned about verses that are clearly anti-Semitic. Here is a limited sampling of translated verses from the Quran illustrating my concerns:

- Verse 4:34 states men are in charge of women and that a man is allowed to strike his wife.

- Verse 24:31 seems to say that (women) should not reveal their charms in public.

- Verse 24:2 states that an adulteress should be struck 100 times with a lash and is only fit to marry an adulterer (24:3).

- Verse 9:123 instructs believers to fight the disbelievers "near you."

- In verse 8:16, the Quran warns that believers who fail to fight disbelievers in battle will incur the wrath of God.

- In verse 8:12, there are these terrifying words: "When your Lord revealed to the angels: I am with you, therefore make firm those who believe. I will cast terror into the hearts of those who disbelieve. Therefore strike off their heads and strike off every fingertip of them."

- Verse 5:62,63 accuses the Jews of committing vile deeds and the rabbis of turning a blind eye.

I remain unapologetic about focusing on the fears and concerns that many non-Muslims (including myself) harbor regarding certain passages in the Quran—passages that seem to promote actions that are harmful to society or to certain groups. You may argue that the Hebrew Bible commands many things that faithful Jews ignore, such as animal sacrifice. In the same way, there's an argument to be made that certain passages in the Quran are too extreme to be taken seriously, or that Muslims may feel they are free to discard and ignore portions of the Quran that are inconsistent with their values.

The thing is, it's impossible to equate the Quran to the Hebrew Bible or the New Testament. Unlike those other sacred books, the Quran isn't a book at all. It's more of a bridge or even a direct conduit to Allah, almost akin to a religious teleporter. If that's tough to absorb, think of it this way: Ignoring the Quran's precepts is like your boss walking into your office and telling you to start work on a project. In contrast, the Christian and Hebrew Bibles would be more like reading a memo from your boss about starting the project. Compared with a word-of-mouth directive, a memo doesn't have quite the power and urgency, so it may be easier to put aside and ignore. Similarly, Muslims cannot look the other way or choose to ignore a directive from the Quran, since those directives are of divine (i.e., not human) origin. The rules cannot be filtered through a person's personal preferences; they *are* the voice of Allah, and they're meant to direct Muslims how to live.

America's Muslims and Muslims Abroad

It needs to be said that acts of violence committed by Muslims against non-Muslims are relatively rare, at least in the West (though the same can't be said for countries such as Iran or Afghanistan). The truth is, Muslims in the U.S., like the Jewish population in the U.S., are not monolithic. Numbering roughly 3.5 million people, they constitute about 1% of America's population. Of that, a majority are Sunnis, and most of the rest are Shiites. (Imam Subedar belongs to the former group.) The difference between those two groups can be difficult for Westerners to discern, so here's a bit more background: The split in Islam between the Sunnis and the Shiites occurred following the death of Muhammed in 632 CE, and the political ramifications of that split continue to this day. The Sunnis believed that Muhammed had not picked a successor and that the leader of the Muslims should be selected from within the group of his closer followers. They selected Abu Bakr, who was close to Muhammed and an early convert to Islam. In contrast, those who are now Shiites believed that Ali Ibn Abi Talib, a blood relative of Muhammed—his cousin and son-in-law—was designated by God to be his successor.

While both the Sunnis and Shiites (also known as Shia) believe the Quran is the word of God, the Shiite spiritual leaders are called clerics and are led by a Grand Ayatollah who, theoretically, holds the final word on religious issues. The Sunnis have no such hierarchy; their spiritual leaders are called imams and each imam, speaking from their respective pulpit, is considered the final authority on any given topic. This means that where an imam receives training is critically important. In the U.S. (where Shiites and Sunnis tend to coexist peacefully), many imams have been trained through the fundamentalist Wahhabi of Saudi Arabia, a less tolerant sect of Islam that teaches its students and future imams ideas that are often incompatible with Western values and even antithetical to the beliefs of more moderate Muslims. As the final authority for the congregation, the imam's views become essential in how their congregation sees the world.

Incidentally, the rise of Shiite Iran as a power in the Islamic world posed a threat to Saudi Arabia and other Sunni nations dominant in the Gulf, leading to some degree of clandestine cooperation between these countries and Israel. (Israel, like America, views a nuclear Iran as a threat to the world.) Often, it seems there is little agreement in the Arab world over who is even a true Muslim. Many extremist groups, like ISIS and Al Qaeda, claim they are carrying out the will of Allah, while moderates accuse the extremists of being little more than criminals. The Sunni and Shia barely consider one another to be legitimate Muslims.

Yet despite this division, Saudi Arabia is important to *all* Muslims, even those residing in the United States. The heart of Islam is in Sunni-dominated Saudi Arabia, and the influence of Saudi Arabia looms large over the American Muslim community. The deserts of Saudi Arabia are where Muhammed lived and where Muslims believe he received the revelations from the angel Gabriel, revelations that comprise the Quran. For Muslims, Mecca remains the holiest city, where, once a year, millions of Muslims converge at the Ka'bah located at the Great Mosque of Mecca. The Ka'bah contains a black stone believed to have been placed there by Muhammed. The Ka'bah and the black stone are not worshipped but are a physical symbol of the unity of Islam.

As indispensable as Saudi Arabia is to the origins and traditions of Islam, it is only recently that the monarchy there has signaled some readiness to potentially break from the grip of the Wahhabis. Through its young de facto leader, Muhammed bin Salman, the country seems to be distancing the kingdom from the Wahhabis and even attempting to rein in their influence. This could weaken the Saudi monopoly on determining the ideology of Islam. It could also push Muslim nations toward embracing a more moderate form of Islam.

And Saudi Arabia *is* changing. There are efforts to liberalize laws that restrict the rights of women and loosen the strict hold that the fundamentalists have had on so many facets of citizens' lives. It also appears that Saudi Arabia is not only reaching out to other Muslim nations but is quietly forging ties with Israel against Iran (or at least they were, before the October 7, 2023, attacks by Hamas). The war in Gaza and perhaps other factors have brought Iran and Saudi Arabia closer together and further isolated Israel. Nevertheless, it's worth taking a closer look at how the origins of Islamic extremism took hold within Saudi Arabia, amidst its historic tolerance of the Wahhabis and the sect's fundamentalist version of Islam.

The roots of Wahhabism go back to the very beginning of the Kingdom of Saudi Arabia, when the Saudi government—essentially, the royal family—agreed to provide protection and support to the Wahhabi radical clerics in exchange for the Wahhabis' not challenging the Saudi royal family—essentially a "you leave us alone and we'll support you" policy. I believe the Saudis' desire to hold primary influence in the Muslim world is part of what motivated them to encourage the export of Wahhabism to America and beyond.

America would no doubt welcome religious reforms within the Saudi kingdom as well as the weakening of the Wahhabi message from the pulpits of American mosques. By speaking out and encouraging moderation, in these pages and elsewhere, Imam Subedar, for one, has shown the courage necessary to challenge the teaching of this extreme form of Islam that is entrenched in so many mosques in this country. But he cannot fully succeed until Muslims take on sweeping reform from within.

The big question is, who will be able to provide a unified, more moderate message to the world's imams? There are certainly organizations (and even countries) that would seek to fill the vacuum created in Saudi Arabia by the recent hostility between the Saudi government and its home-grown brand of Wahhabi fundamentalism. The megaphone must fall into the hands of those who will deliver a message of tolerance and acceptance of all religions, and reject violence and armed jihad.

I worry that, instead, more extremist splinter groups will rise to the fore. Take the Taliban: My understanding is that the Taliban's particular take on Sharia came from India, where some Muslim scholars built a seminary in a town called Deoband. More seminaries started spreading near the border between India and Pakistan. Some of the graduates of these seminaries ultimately became what we now know of as the Taliban, including the Taliban's founder, Mullah Muhammad Omar. The Taliban was also influenced by the Wahhabis of Saudi Arabia, which remain an influential group across the world, including in the U.S.

If one Islamic splinter sect or even governing body can practice and interpret the Quran in a violent way, so can another—just look at Hamas, the Muslim Brotherhood, Al Qaeda, and ISIS. I'm not saying that Islam has a monopoly on extremism. In the U.S., there is a growing threat from violent white Christian nationalists and malevolent authoritarian government. That's why moderates of all stripes—Muslim, Jewish, Christian and others—need to come together to fight extremism, including terrorism committed in the name of religion, racism, or political beliefs.

Muslims Must Obey U.S. Laws

Under our criminal and civil system of governing, Muslims and non-Muslims alike must obey all laws, not just the ones they are comfortable with. Imam Subedar assures us that Muslims must obey the civil laws of the nation in which they reside; they cannot toss them aside for Sharia. But for devout Muslims, the Quran's rules may hold a much more compelling moral authority than legislation passed by any secular government. So, I ask, would it be possible to incorporate Sharia law into Judeo-Christian culture, given the role the Quran and Sharia play for Muslims, even those living in non-Muslim-majority countries? I'm skeptical about that.

Imam Subedar tells us that the violent verses have to be read in the context of the times. These verses still are to be obeyed, but only if circumstances arise that are similar to those that occurred in the past, during Muhammed's time. But who decides? The imams? Imam Subedar tells us that Sunni Islam is not hierarchical—that each individual mosque is its own self-contained entity with its own imam. Does that mean it's up to each individual imam to decide that jihad might be called for? Where are the guardrails to help Muslims decide whether a particular imam's call for jihad or violence is appropriate? The transparency just isn't there.

Sharia remains the law of choice for Muslims, even if it cannot be openly followed. As I read the English translations of the Quran, it seems to me that much of what is commanded is not only against what most in the U.S. would consider civilized conduct between men and women, but would also constitute a crime of domestic violence under the laws of the United States. Can verse 4:34, which permits a man to strike his wife under certain conditions, be expunged from the Quran? It cannot. If it is in the Quran, it cannot be altered. Moreover, many of these concepts require a scholar to be interpreted correctly (especially if they are being read in translation). Which begs the question: What are Muslims and readers of the Quran who are not scholars and do not read the Quran in Arabic supposed to make of these verses?

And so, a conflict exists between the laws of the U.S. and the Quran, which is the sacred word of Allah. While Imam Subedar makes it plain that he is not suggesting that Sharia law supplant the laws of the United States (or any country under a non-Muslim government), the Quran explicitly states that it is the "guide" for mankind, the basis for deciding between right and wrong—meaning there is no need for a separate system of civil law independent of Sharia. Quran 4:59 says, *"O you who believe! Obey Allah, and obey the Messenger [Muhammed] and those charged with authority among you. If you differ about anything within yourselves, refer it to Allah and His Prophet [Muhammed], if you believe in All and the Last day."*

Under Sharia, it is up to Allah to resolve all differences, meaning there is no need to bother with man-made laws to resolve conflicts. But the Quran takes the obligation to observe Sharia law a step further in Quran 9:112, saying *"...the happiest people reinforce good and prevent evil."*

The question is, what is evil? Is every individual who doesn't believe in the Quran (i.e., infidels) considered evil? How far does the obligation to prevent evil go?

Imam Subedar contends that Sharia, as he defines it, is already present in America. Its objectives, as he puts it, are reforming society; establishing justice for all humans; promoting the well-being of all communities; and creating an environment that fosters self-development, where "everyone can thrive and reach their full potential." Given that the Sharia is very specific and is the governing principle for many of the world's Muslims today, does that mean Muslims in America feel they must reform the entire society?

Imam Subedar said no to that question. He has told me, "No, Muslims should not enforce their values to reform any society or to prevent what they deem as evil. The administration of civil law is the responsibility of the governing body. As for their values, Muslims must hold themselves to the standards of what is good and evil in Shariah, irrespective of where they live."

What about when there is a conflict between civil law and what Muslims perceive as evil?

The Problem Areas

Imam Subedar has addressed three aspects of Sharia law that Western non-Muslims would see as antithetical to a civilized society, including the Islamic penal code and criminal justice issues, as well as harsh penalties such as amputation for theft or beheading for disobeying Islamic law. He also addresses women's issues, including the fear that Islam and Sharia law support misogyny, as well as the subject of spousal abuse and violence against women. Then there is the language concerning jihad, Islamic extremism, and who, exactly, is considered an infidel. I would add another item to this list, which is Islam's apparent intolerance of other religions as well as the numerous seemingly anti-Semitic verses in the Quran.

Criminal Justice and the Penal Code

Though Imam Subedar rejects the Taliban's extreme version of Islam, he does support the imposition of whatever penalties are found in the Quran. He acknowledges that there are penalties in practice in Muslim communities—but not in the Quran—that Westerners and/or non-Muslims would likely see as brutal or barbaric, namely the penalties for violating Islamic law and culture, including public stoning, floggings, beheadings, and amputations.

Even if we confine ourselves to punishments referenced in the Quran, Imam Subedar views these as more effective deterrents to crime than those found within Western criminal laws.

To my mind, the question is not whether these measures are effective deterrents of crime, adultery, and other socially undesirable behaviors. I will also set aside the argument as to whether these penalties constitute crimes against humanity, because that standard is determined by a particular culture. However, I can state with absolute confidence that these practices would never gain acceptance in the West. The very idea of government-sanctioned amputations or beheadings is shocking to the sensibilities of the average non-Muslim as well as to most who live in the U.S. or other Western countries, where gratuitous violence and maiming are considered off-limits as forms of punishment. In contrast, the Taliban, even today, allows a member of a victim's family to execute a convicted murderer with a single bullet to the head. We also know the Taliban has displayed the dead bodies of some accused kidnappers post-execution. The Taliban claims these punishments are authorized by Islamic law. Most non-Muslims have no way of disputing that claim. And to my knowledge, Islamic nations have not openly and loudly criticized the Taliban for its brutal punishments.

There is, of course, substantial support for the death penalty in some Western countries—as long as the human body is left intact. Beheadings, in other words, are not an option, whereas many consider lethal injection or gas to be a more "acceptable" method of administering capital punishment. That may be because we have grown accustomed to the idea of putting someone to death this way, while Islamic-sanctioned punishments are unfamiliar and therefore more disturbing. The issue is not as clearly defined as barbarism versus civilized behavior, much less good versus evil. I also have to point out that it is primarily America's poor and people of color who inhabit our prisons' death rows—another circumstance that should give us pause in carrying out brutal penalties.

My coauthor confirms that Islam allows "a life for a life" in the case of murder. Perhaps more surprisingly for some readers, he also explains that the Quran allows for forgiveness, even in the case of murder (Quran 2:178). To be clear, in Afghanistan, it is possible under Sharia law for the family of a murder victim to accept compensation from the perpetrator in lieu of punishment. If that money is not accepted, the punishment is execution (Quran 5:33).

Jewish readers may recognize that the Torah in Leviticus 24:19–21 also commands an eye for an eye, though this philosophy is certainly no longer enforced or practiced by any governments or Jewish groups. Yet as I write this, the Taliban is imposing Sharia law in Afghanistan, where the Quran (in 5:38) mandates that thieves have their hands amputated. Imam Subedar explains that according to Sharia, anything valued at $10 or more technically warrants this punishment. In today's world, there are very few things worth less than $10.

So how can Muslims and non-Muslims coexist given these different ways of looking at crime and punishment? Once we move beyond the judgmental position that one side is right and the other is wrong and recognize that we are simply different, we create a safe space for coexistence. While I argue that Sharia is not now and never could be compatible with Western culture, I'm not prepared to describe an entire religion of 2 billion people as any less well intentioned or honorable than those who believe and act the same way I do.

Sharia and Women

Would applying Sharia law in Western countries significantly impact women's rights? I ask this question not because my coauthor suggests that Sharia replace the domestic laws of the United States or any other non-Muslim country. My concern is what laws might be imposed should a Muslim majority eventually come to power. Our book champions the principle that understanding can only be enhanced once the unvarnished truth is revealed.

Here are some difficult truths regarding women and Islam.

Spousal Abuse

Violence against women, both inside and outside the home, is a major problem in both Western and Islamic cultures. But to my eyes, the Quran, in some cases, appears to condone striking one's wife when she is disobedient or threatens desertion (4:34): "*admonish them and leave them alone in the sleeping places and beat them . . .*" Imam Subedar delves into the multiple meanings of the Arabic word *darb* for "beat" or "strike." However, when I searched different translations, I found uniformity regarding the right of a man to strike his wife:

> "*As for women of whom you fear rebellion, convince them, and leave them apart in beds, and beat them. Then, if they obey you, do not seek a way against them. Surely, Allah is the Highest, the Greatest.*" (Mufti Taqi Usmani)

> "*As to those women on whose part ye fear disloyalty and ill-conduct, admonish them (first), (Next), refuse to share their beds, [And last] beat them (lightly); but if they return to obedience, seek not against them Means [of annoyance]: For Allah is Most High, great [above you all].*" (Yusuf Ali)

> "*As for women of whom you fear rebellion, admonish them, and remain apart from them in beds, and beat them. Then if they obey you, do not seek ways to harm them. Allah is Exalted, Great.*" (Tafheem-ul-Quran – Abul Ala Maududi)

You will note that each of these translations calls for the "beating" of disloyal and rebellious women. Of course, this begs the questions: How do you define "disloyal and rebellious," and who makes that determination—the irritated husband? Putting aside that problematic issue, many Muslims, particularly non-Arabic-speaking Muslims who may not have access to Imam Subedar's multiple translations of *darb*, are left believing that this verse directs a husband to "beat" a disobedient wife. (I will not go into the additional admonition to avoid them in bed.) I would ask Imam Subedar if he agrees that many translations of 4:34 do indeed direct a husband to beat his wife, and if there is a statement in the Quran that directly forbids striking a "disobedient" wife. In Western society, even the concept of a "disobedient wife" is jarring and discordant. And what rights does a woman possess against a husband she perceives as disloyal, rebellious, and disobedient?

Women and the Hijab

Women in Saudi Arabia, Iran, and Afghanistan do not have the right to decide what they will wear in public places. Despite assurances to the contrary, at press time, the Taliban in Afghanistan is requiring all Muslim women to be completely covered, as well as banning them from universities and working for NGOs. We have all been witness to the brave struggle of Iranian women seeking the right to dress as they choose. After a brief pause, prompted by nationwide protests in Iran, the government there is once again deploying the morality police to enforce its version of proper modest Islamic dress for women and girls. The justification for these measures is that they are required by the Quran. No room for nuance there.

Sharia and Marriage

Sharia law also seems to dictate who a woman can and cannot marry (e.g., by declaring outsiders off-limits). Quran 2:221 says, "*Do not marry idolatrous women unless they join the faith. A maidservant who is a believer is better than an idolater even though you may like her. And do not marry your daughters to idolaters until they accept the faith. A servant who is a believer is better than an idolater even though you may like him. They invite you to Hell, but God calls*

*you to Paradise and pardon by His grace. And He makes His signs
manifest that men may happily take heed."*

I take this to mean that according to Sharia law, the only men
a Muslim woman can marry are Muslim men. Quran 2:221 goes
on to say the daughters of Muslims are forbidden to marry non-
Muslims. This is true even though apparently a Muslim man can
marry a Jew or a Christian, as stated in 5:5. *"The chaste believing
women and the chaste women of the people who were given the Book
before you, are lawful to you . . ."* Does this mean that a Muslim
man can marry a Christian or a Jew, or does it mean they can do so
only if their future spouse converts, as required in 2:221?

Under the mandates of this surah, if Sharia law were to suddenly
be installed in the U.S., most American men would be barred from
marrying any Muslim, a stricture that hearkens back to a time when
interracial marriage was illegal in America. I ask Imam Subedar,
does this passage not seek to tell a tale that goes back to a dark time in
America where men and women were not free to marry whomever
they choose?

Of course, in the U.S., Sharia does not formally control who
Muslim women can marry, as my coauthor has pointed out
numerous times. But given the prohibitions of the Quran against
marrying outside the faith, are Muslim women and men expected
by their families and by Muslim culture at large to marry only
Muslims?

And what does Islam say about the right of gay people to marry in
America? Is that also forbidden? And for those who see themselves
as transgender, would they have the right to alter their body to
express the gender they feel themselves to be? My understanding is
that Islam forbids anyone from altering the body they were given
by Allah, making transgender rights particularly problematic in

an Islamic society. These issues are hot topics fueling the raging culture wars in America. I suspect our far-right brethren would be surprised to find they are aligned with Muslim voters on many of these issues, seeking to limit individual freedoms of LGBTQ+ people.

Women, Sharia, and Equality

As a former trial attorney, I have concerns about the Quran's command that requires two women to be a witness but only one man. There is certainly no comparable rule in the laws of United States civil procedure, which governs the rules of evidence and trials. Imam Subedar explains that this dilution of a woman's testimony is not because women are less valued than men, referring to the Quran to back up his explanation that the intelligence of women isn't being called into question. Rather, he argues, the verse is meant to protect women—if one woman errs, the other can remind her. Since giving false testimony is punished so harshly in Islamic society, potentially stripping a person of their place and credibility in the community (not to mention condemning them in the afterlife), Imam Subedar contends that Allah declined to place that burden or those consequences on women, who may not be well versed in financial and contractual matters (or, at least, weren't at the time of this particular revelation). One woman can therefore back up the testimony of the other, making it difficult for what they say to be deemed false in the eyes of a judge.

The explanation that women should not have this extra burden and responsibility is one that is familiar to me as a Jewish man. Orthodox Judaism traditionally requires 10 people for a minyan—the minimum number required for a service in a synagogue. Women, however, are not counted as part of that 10. The usual explanation is that women should not be burdened with this responsibility. In reality, whether women are members of the Orthodox Jewish community or the Muslim community, when they are bound by different rules than men, they often end up with the short end of the stick.

Child Marriage and Polygamy

Imam Subedar also takes issue with the widespread perception that Islam condones child marriage, pointing to the fact that the Quran commands that to be married, females must be of reproductive age. But the solution to the sexual abuse, marriage, and rape of children is not to equate the age of consent to a child's first menstruation, which can happen as young as 8 years old.

As for polygamy, Imam Subedar points out that under Sharia law, a man can marry up to four women, justifying this as a limitation on sexual partners that will help restrict the spread of STDs.

But given that, in the West, the divorce rate and widespread adultery are as much the rule as the exception, the proposed solution cannot be worse than the problem. Imagine the outcry from women's rights organizations if men were allowed four wives while women all had to share the same man.

I still vividly remember one experience in March of 2016, when my wife, Karen, and I were at the Taj Palace Hotel in Mumbai, India, at the very moment Prince William and Kate Middleton were commemorating the rebuilding of the hotel. (In 2008, a Muslim terrorist group had carried out a series of 12 coordinated attacks, including the bombing of the hotel, in which 39 people died.) From a balcony, we watched the royal couple welcome the elite of Indian society. Watching with us were two women from Saudi Arabia who, despite being totally covered with only their eyes showing, were obviously as excited about watching the reception as Karen and I were.

Karen learned from the women that they were sister wives staying at the Taj with their husband (singular). It struck me then as it does now the disparity between what men and women are allowed. Why are Muslim men permitted to have four wives and women only one husband? Imam Subedar's argument about how having multiple wives cuts down on cheating apparently doesn't apply to women and their sexual needs. The Institute for Family Studies reports that 13% of all married women have committed adultery. Would that number drop if women could have four husbands? We will never know.

Granted, Western nations are also grappling with difficult issues, including child marriages, not to mention rampant sexually transmitted diseases and unwanted pregnancies. It is beyond debate that society would be better off without these problems. The question is whether practices such as polygamy and the marriage of children (even if they are postpubescent), which are condoned by Islam, institutionalizes practices that have no place in modern society. Living with societal problems is very different from a religion (or government) endorsing or approving problematic practices. Western culture looks to religion to provide a high moral standard, though we need look no further than the Catholic Church's scandals to see that this ideal doesn't always prevail. Yet if Islam's values were to be adopted by the West, the subsequent treatment of women, including the acceptance of polygamy, would upend the moral structure that is the foundation of the family in the West.

Rather than condemning the 100 lashes, Imam Subedar instead suggests that the harsh penalty for adultery is justified, because under Sharia, false accusations, lies, and slander are themselves punished by 80 lashes, and so these punishments would occur only rarely. I would suggest that marriage counseling might be a better approach to deterring potential adulterers.

The Islamic world sees the open acceptance of pornography and the commercialization of sex in movies in the West as immoral and degrading to women and corrosive to society. Premarital sex, as well as sexual freedom and experimentation, have become normalized in Western culture, though not everyone in the West approves of them. Many in the West accept these things not because they are beneficial to society but because they have become the norm.

Yet Americans would never accept the Quran's solutions for these societal problems. America is not Iran or Saudi Arabia or Afghanistan. Imagine if a Western government began meting out public floggings and stoning or decided to implement "minor" amputations of the toes and fingers as a deterrent for theft.

The Meaning of the Terms *Jihad* and *Infidel*

There are verses in the Quran that seem to describe suicide bombers receiving rewards for their sacrifice. Quran 3:145 in particular troubles me: *"No soul can die except by Allah's permission, the term (of life) being fixed as in writing. If any do desire a reward in this life, We shall give it to him: and if any do desire a reward in the Hereafter, We shall give it to him. And swiftly shall We reward those (who serve us) with gratitude."*

It appears that the Quran promises that Muslims will be rewarded for killing non-Muslims. And since these words presumably come directly from Allah, I wonder who the "We" is in the passage above? If no soul can die except by Allah's permission, wouldn't this include someone who is the victim of a suicide bombing—an acknowledgment that claiming a life in this way is permitted? And what about the promise that anyone who dies advancing the cause of Islam will be rewarded? To me, it looks as if the answers to these troubling questions can be found in Quran 3:157: *"If you are killed or die, in the cause of Allah, forgiveness from Allah is far better than all (the wealth) they can accumulate."*

What message is a faithful Muslim getting from this passage, other than if they die for the cause of Islam, they will be rewarded?

Even more stark in its brutality, Quran 8:12 unequivocally states that Allah *"shall cast terror into the hearts of infidels. Strike off their heads, strike off the very tips of their fingers!"*

Passages like the one above could be and have been used by terrorist groups and extremists to justify barbaric acts and spread terror. Certainly the widely publicized videotaped beheadings by ISIS achieved exactly that.

There is no shortage of examples of the Quran calling for violence. Quran 5:33 says, *"Those that make war against God and his apostle and spread disorder in the land shall be slain or crucified or have their hands cut off on alternate sides or be banished from the land."*

These passages are known to every radicalized Muslim. As a non-Muslim, it is hard not to be concerned about the power of these passages and their powerful impact on a young person seeking to carry out what they perceive as a commandment from Allah. The power of the Quran on a radicalized Muslim was grimly illustrated by the 2025 New Year's Day massacre on Bourbon Street in New Orleans, in which a man claiming allegiance to ISIS plowed into a crowd of revelers, killing 14. In its January 3 edition, the *New York*

Post, a widely read conservative tabloid, ran a picture of the terrorist's residence in which his Quran is open to verse 9:111. According to the *Post,* the passage "expounds on Muslims' responsibility to kill Allah's enemies, and to be willing to die for that mission in return for eternity in paradise."

Thus, one man acting alone is able to discredit and bring condemnation down upon an entire religion and its followers. But it also illustrates how the violent passages of the Quran can be interpreted by someone who has been radicalized and seeks to become a martyr. To reach that single man, ISIS has in place a sophisticated online presence that includes a weekly newsletter, *al-Naba.* Therein lies the conflict for those of us who are outside the Islamic faith and are witnessing the devastating acts of a radicalized Islamic terrorist. Does the fault lie with Islam and the violent verses of the Quran? With the radicalization of the mentally vulnerable by a rogue terrorist organization? Or with the failure of mainstream Islam to rout out a deadly and destructive force co-opting its identity for its own murderous goals? Before 9/11, none of this was part of the American psyche.

Given Americans' experience of 9/11, the question of whether Islam is violent under certain circumstances becomes unavoidable. Imam Subedar does not dispute that the Quran contains violent verses that, in one form or another, order the killing of infidels, albeit under certain conditions. I cite the following:

(Quran 2:190) *"Fight in the way of God those who fight you, but do not transgress. Indeed. God does not like transgressors."*

(Quran 2:191) *"And kill them wherever you find them and expel them from wherever they have expelled you, and fitnah [persecution] is worse than killing. And do not fight them at al-Masjid al-Haram until they fight you there. But if they fight you, then kill them. Such is the recompense of the disbelievers."*

(Quran 2:193) *"Fight them until there is no [more] fitnah [persecution] and [until] worship is for God. But if they cease, then there is to be no aggression except against the oppressors."*

The phrase in 2:91, *"kill them wherever you find them,"* is not only unnerving but raises the question of who, exactly, "them" is. Is it anyone who rejects Islam? Is it, as some Hadiths indicate, any Muslim who leaves Islam? If so, how does this square with the Quranic verse 2:256, which says, *"there is to be no compulsion in religion?"* Are there different standards for how to treat nonbelievers—Christians, Jews, and those who leave Islam? Imam Subedar has provided insight into the definition of an infidel, but I still wonder how a Muslim might view me, a non-Muslim. Am I an "infidel"? If not, am I somehow less worthy than a fellow Muslim? This is a dilemma faced by all religions that imbue their followers with special qualities denied to those of other faiths.

But when I look at what the Quran says regarding how Muslims should treat nonbelievers, I can only conclude that Muslims who aspire to be both good neighbors and citizens of the West do so not because of the Quran but in spite of it.

Take this example, from 9:5: *"But when the forbidden months are over then fight and kill the pagans wherever you find them, attack them, and stay waiting for them in every stage: But if they repent, and establish regular prayers, and practice charity, then make it easy for them: Verily, Allah is oft forgiving. Most Merciful."*

Or this less-than-comforting passage, which distinguishes between the standard for killing a Muslim or a non-Muslim. In Quran 4:92: *"a believer should never kill a believer."*

But that rule is somewhat modified in 17:33, which says: *"And do not take life—Which Allah has made holy—Except for just (and true) cause."*

One way that Imam Subedar seeks to explain passages is by talking about the Doctrine of Abrogation, in which earlier passages are struck and replaced by newer passages or completely removed altogether, as was the case for Quran 2:106, a verse on stoning an old man and an old woman: *"Whatever verse we abrogate or cause to be forgotten, we bring a better verse than it or like it."* If this refers to the verses revealed later in the Quran, which tend to be more violent and less tolerant than earlier ones, that gives me little comfort, since unlike the earlier, more peaceful, verses, these later verses can't be cast aside.

Imam Subedar states: *"Again, there are harsh verses in the Quran that seem to instruct Muslims to do barbaric things, and these verses are often used as propaganda to foster hate or to recruit and indoctrinate extremists. But context is all, and not enough people read the words before and after these oft-quoted verses to better understand the history and situations that led up to them. These commands are specific to a certain time, place, and circumstances, circumstances that warranted revelations from Allah. These revelations are, in turn, now part of the Quran (but again, they are specific to those circumstances). They are also meant to be a framework for action if similar circumstances arise in the future. What they don't do is give license to practice harsh measures at any time or place."*

Imam Subedar also explains that verses authorizing violence against non-Muslims should be considered inactive until a situation arises that is similar to the original incident that provoked the revelation, hundreds of years earlier. But in my years of reading translations of the Quran, I've never been able to find a hint that any command should be limited by time or circumstances. Without such explicit limitations, how is a Muslim to know which orders to obey and which are no longer applicable? I ask again: Who has the authority to determine when contemporary conditions justify the violence authorized by the Quran? In this vacuum, ISIS, Al Qaeda, and other extremist organizations have felt free to take the words of the Quran literally. How could they read the mandates of the Quran any other way unless they'd had the benefit of Imam Subedar's years of advanced Islamic education? How can a young Muslim in Pakistan, Jordan, or the United States put these words into context without a knowledgeable guide? For me, my coauthor's "time, place, and circumstances" response raises many more complex and troubling questions than it answers.

Rather than parsing the Quran, wouldn't it be better to root out extremism where we find it, starting with (but not limited to) every mosque that condones violence in Islam's name? It is the responsibility of Islam to police its own community, isolating and eradicating extremists and their ideas and warding off recruitment of young people to an extreme ideology. To the extent that there has been a condemnation of violence within the Muslim community, it appears to have been weak and ineffective.

But let's assume that Imam Subedar's explanations are correct (and I do), and that the peaceful Islam he describes is, in fact, the dominant message disseminated from the mosques of America. All I know is what I have read, and what I have read cannot be interpreted as peaceful. That's not to say that Muslims who are our neighbors, local business people, and friends are not peaceful. It would seem that America's Muslims are more focused on their quality of life than executing the letter of the law set forth in the

Quran. But to the uninitiated, the language in the Quran remains disturbing.

My point is that vigilance (but not overreacting) may be warranted. And when I point out that the language of the Quran sets Muslims and non-Muslims against each other, as I do throughout this book, that doesn't mean we can't coexist. On the contrary, I believe we must coexist, even if certain aspects of Islamic ideology seem problematic to those in the West.

Anti-Semitism and Islam's Intolerance of Other Religions

I am a nonreligious Jew. However, I attend Friday night services, observe all the holidays, and strongly identify with the culture. For me, the essence of my Judaism is being part of that unbroken chain of fellow Jews that stretches back in time and forward, guaranteeing the preservation of the Jewish people. I am also interested in what the Quran says about Islam's relationship to Judaism, as well as to Christianity.

First, Islam sees both Jews and Christians as "people of the book." Like Islam, they are Abrahamic religions. The Quran 3:67 says that Abraham was neither a Jew nor a Christian but "surrendered his will to Allah," meaning that, according to the Quran, Abraham was a Muslim and that Jews, Christians, and Muslims all share a common sacred book. Muslims believe the final and correct version of that book is the Quran. Quran 5:48 says, *"We sent to you [Muhammed] the Scripture with the truth, confirming the Scriptures that came before it, and with final authority over them."*

Indeed, many verses of the Quran contain passages similar to those found in the TaNaKh (Hebrew Bible) and New Testament and refer to stories from both. In fact, as the Quran points out, Muhammed was accused by nonbelievers of having copied the Quran from the Bible. Quran 8:31 says, *"Whenever our revelations are recited to them, they say, 'We have heard them. If we wished we could produce the like. They are nothing but the fables of the ancients.'"*

The Quran explicitly states (in 10:37) that it is a more complete explanation of the Bible. That doesn't account for the fact that while some stories are similar on the surface, their conclusions tend to be very different. For instance, Quran 4:157 (as I read it) says Jesus was not crucified: *"And [for] their saying 'Indeed, we have killed the Messiah, Jesus, the son of Mary, the messenger of Allah.' And they did not kill him, nor did they crucify him; but [another] was made to resemble him to them. And indeed, those who differ over it are in doubt about it. They have no knowledge of it except the following assumption. And they did not kill him for certain."*

And Quran 23:91 states that Allah never fathered a son: *"Allah has not taken any son, nor has there ever been with Him any deity. [If there had been], then each deity would have taken what it created, and some of them would have sought to overcome others. Exalted is Allah above what they describe [concerning Him]."*

Then there is Quran 61:6, which says: *"And of Jesus son of Mary, who said to the Israelites: I am set forth to you from God to confirm the Torah already revealed and to give news of an apostle that will come after me whose name is Ahmad [Muhammed]."*

In other words, the upshot is that Jesus predicted that Muhammed would follow after him.

The common roots of Judaism, Christianity, and Islam are often cited as a basis for why these religions should be tolerant of one another. In fact, their common origins can also become a source of conflict.

The Quran states that the words in the current-day Hebrew Bible are incorrect because they were changed by those who were supposed to preserve the word of God—specifically, that the Jews adulterated and changed the language of the Torah. For example, in Quran 62:5, the verse seems to say (in my English translation) that the Torah was entrusted to the Jews, but they refused to bear it and were "like a donkey laden with books." Quran 5:13 states that the Jews "changed the words from their places" and forgot a "good part of the message." The Quran also indicates that the Jews believe Ezra is the son of God. Verse 9:30 states: *"The Jews say Uzair (Ezra) is the son of God and the Christians say Messiah (Christ) is the son of God."* Do Muslims believe that the Jews view Ezra as the son of God? If not, how can this passage be explained? I have never met a Jew who believes that Ezra is the son of God.

I wonder if Imam Subedar considers the Quran a correction of both bibles?

Clearly, the Quran takes positions that run counter to Judaism and Christianity, though there is some overlap among the three. And while every religion claims to have the only correct interpretation of its texts, only the Quran contains verses that explicitly state that the other guy's (namely Christians' and Jews') texts were compromised.

Imam Subedar explains that the point of the Quran's criticism of Jews is to make an example of them—i.e., to demonstrate how bad behavior will be punished to prevent someone else from doing the same. But this presumes that the Jews' (and in some cases the Christians') behavior is wrong, a presumption that has contributed to hostility between Muslims and Jews, as well as Muslims and

Christians. I fear it also contributes to the possibility of terrorism against non-Muslims, as well as to the spread of Islamophobia.

Here, I'll point out that there are also problematic verses in the Hebrew Bible. Exodus 21:28, for example, calls for stoning as punishment (among other examples). No modern Jewish person, or rabbi, for that matter, believes that God would approve stoning someone to death, despite what the Bible says. And in most modern versions, the wording has been changed to mesh with modern values.

In contrast, all Muslims are exposed to verses in the Quran that attack Jews.

- Quran 5:60 declares that Jews are "cursed."

- Quran 5:62 says Jews "compete with each other in sin and hate," eat "forbidden things," and "Evil is the things they do."

- Quran 5:66 accuses the Jews of not following the Torah truthfully and says that for many of them, "evil is that which they do."

Of course, the rancor that now exists in the Middle East between Muslims and Jews may not be related to the Quran at all, but rather to the State of Israel. The Iranian cleric I met with in Shiraz ushered me out of his mosque only when our conflicting attitudes toward the State of Israel became clear.

Recently, I asked Imam Subedar if there was a verse in the Quran that supported Jews and Muslims working together. He answered by citing Quran 3:64: *"Say, 'O People of the Scripture, come to a word that is equitable between us and you—that we will not worship except*

Allah and not associate anything with Him and not take one another as lords instead of Allah.' But if they turn away, then say, 'Bear witness that we are Muslims [submitting to Him].'"

Parsing this verse, I agree that when the Quran says "People of scripture," it is referring to the Jews, and that there is a suggestion that Jews and Muslims work together—but isn't that only if Jews convert to Islam?

There are a number of troubling verses in the Quran that go further, seeming to actively promote intolerance:

- Quran 53:29, for instance, encourages Muslims to shun those "who turn away from Our Message and desire nothing but the life of this world."

- Quran 3:28 says believers should "not take for friends or helpers unbelievers rather than believers."

- Quran 5:57 cautions believers to not take for friends or protectors those who mock Islam whether or not they have received the scriptures or are unbelievers.

If Islam seeks to discourage interactions with other faiths, how are we to unite?

In either case, if the harsh verses about Jews are to be moderated, the call for tolerance must come from the imams and clerics as they lead their respective mosques. I say this because of the unique influence a Sunni imam has on his congregation. As noted, since there is no hierarchy in the Sunni Islamic power structure, the final authority of Islam rests in the voice of the imam. And an imam in America who is able to speak to his flock in English has the additional weight that comes from being understood. Arabic may be the language of the Quran, but very few American Muslims speak or understand it. The congregation is dependent on the imam to convey the meaning of the Arabic words in the Quran. If the imam teaches tolerance, that is the message the congregation hears. But if the message is one of intolerance, there is little in Sunni Islam to counter it.

I am not naive. Religious leaders of *all* faiths are guilty of not practicing what they preach. That's different, however, from incorporating an objectionable or discriminatory practice into the dogma of a religion, such as Mormon (or Muslim) polygamy. The consequences of a religion adopting and allowing activities that are contrary to the values of their resident nation can be dire. If, for instance, the ritual of animal sacrifice by Jews or Christians were still practiced on a daily basis, you wouldn't expect Jewish or Christian animal lovers to accept those who practiced it. In our volatile society, a rash of protests would likely result, along with a societal rejection of that faith that could lead to alienation, hate, and "othering."

Why hasn't the Islamic world rejected these practices? I suspect the answer is that Muslims cannot reject any commands set forth in the Quran because they come directly from Allah. The challenge is, can people in the West reject those practices without rejecting those who, in good faith, support them? In today's fractured world, that's a tall order, given that, as a nation, we can't seem to come to an agreement regarding restricting gun registrations and limiting the sale of assault weapons, despite an epidemic of mass shootings. We are also fiercely divided on racial issues and LGBTQ+ rights. The far right is determined to condemn liberals as a threat to Christian traditional values, while liberals see the far right as a threat to democracy. What sort of response will my coauthor's revelation—that Islam endorses some of these brutal practices—have on a country that is already primed to hate the other?

The bond between Imam Subedar and myself suggests that it is possible for otherwise decent people with fundamentally different beliefs to accept one another. But accepting and promoting values that run contrary to the fabric of Western society becomes troublesome if those values are rooted in a religion's tenets.

CHAPTER 10

The Imam Cuts Through Misperceptions of Shariah

By Imam Azhar Subedar

(((Deep Breath)))

As I read through Bob's fears of Islam (i.e., his rebuttal of my explanation of Islam), I frequently found myself nodding. This isn't necessarily because I agreed with him but, rather, because of how often I have heard similar sentiments over the years.

My coauthor's concerns are a testament to how a handful of verses, no more than a couple of dozen out of more than 6,000 in the Quran, can, when misinterpreted, poison the minds and hearts of people across the globe against Islam. What I've hoped to do from the very beginning was not to sugarcoat any verse, even those often seen as problematic, but to give readers the knowledge and tools to stop the fear-mongering in the name of Islam.

Let me say this first: Every soul has the right to live peacefully and never feel threatened by another's way or ideology. But there is no denying that there is a problem with Islam—not the faith itself, but the rampant ignorance about it and, even more, the "propaganda" perpetuated in its name. That propaganda is akin to showing an apple to the masses and claiming, "This is a watermelon." Over time, you'll have people who will confidently claim that an apple is a watermelon, and believe it, buying into an alternative reality.

That is where Islam is today.

For now, I will say that my coauthor has made a compelling case, and one that is likely to resonate with those who already fear Islam. His arguments reflect longstanding concerns that have become embedded in the psyches of so many people who, perhaps understandably, don't know how to see Shariah and Islam in any other way.

Bob and I took up this task not to prove each other wrong or even to engage in a spirited debate, but to create a dialogue that fosters broader understanding. What I want from you, the reader, is for you to open your mind and consider how it is that a single topic can provoke such deeply opposing beliefs, fueling the fire of fear and mistrust.

How do we reconcile our differences? Our radical solution is: Don't even try. Instead, we provide disparate perspectives on the same subject. One is based on knowledge, the other, on information gleaned from reading the Quran—and also, perhaps, preconceived notions. Each results in a completely different understanding of the same subject. At the same time, open discussion, even when it's contentious, or raises more questions than it answers, will never be harmful to this nation or our world.

Do Muslims' practices have their challenges here in the West? Yes, they do. Will Muslims be able to fix them overnight? No, we won't. However, it is possible to begin a shift away from where we are to where we might possibly go, ideally toward greater global harmony.

As coauthors, we've tried to present the information in this book following a three-step process: First, I discuss the foundational knowledge of the matter of Shariah; second, Bob addresses the fears and misconceptions that surround it; and, finally, third, I will focus below on the facts that will dispel those fears that feel very real not just for my coauthor but for millions of Americans.

My goal in these pages is to round out the foundational knowledge of Shariah I've already provided. My hope is that you keep an open mind, even if what I say feels outside of your comfort zone. The bottom line: I don't believe that Islam needs to be reformed to remain relevant; what it needs is to be restored to its original roots and purpose through explanation by credible people so that it can be properly understood.

And so I begin.

(Mis)Understanding the Quran: The Chasm Between Us

After the terrorist attacks of 9/11, my coauthor asked himself, as many did, "What is Islam?" To answer, he did what many continue to do: He turned to the Quran. The problem, for the uninitiated, is that the Quran can leave people more confused than when they began. Other sources may also be inadequate or confusing, such as Islamic literature found in brochures or online, often because it is provided by experts but not well explained or because the "experts" themselves are not scholars of the faith. Instead of clarifying, they end up muddying the waters.

One factor that can make the Quran confusing at times is that most readers turn to translation rather than reading the original text. This may seem like quibbling, but there is a difference between the Quran in its original form and the various translations of it—the meaning can often get lost in the translation. The purpose of the Quran was never to be translated into every language but to propagate a lifestyle. For Muslims, the focus must be on the actions and lifestyle that Allah commands; it is not enough to merely comprehend words on a page. To put that into perspective, consider that Islam spread to parts of the world long before a physical copy of the Quran reached those areas, including not only Arab but non-Arab lands such as Indonesia. But Arabic and non-Arabic speakers alike understood that what was of primary importance in the Quran was not the language itself, but what it was asking: adherence to a particular lifestyle.

Who taught them that lifestyle? Those who brought Islam from Arabia, the followers of Islam. In the absence of those who learned directly from Muhammad or his companions, or a chain of teachers linking back to the earliest Muslims, who is left to teach that lifestyle today? Who can one *trust* to teach it? This question worries my coauthor. But the (reassuring) truth is that the Quran provides a system.

(Quran 9:122)

وَمَا كَانَ الْمُؤْمِنُونَ لِيَنفِرُوا كَافَّةً ۚ فَلَوْلَا نَفَرَ مِن كُلِّ فِرْقَةٍ مِّنْهُمْ طَائِفَةٌ لِّيَتَفَقَّهُوا فِي الدِّينِ وَلِيُنذِرُوا قَوْمَهُمْ إِذَا رَجَعُوا إِلَيْهِمْ لَعَلَّهُمْ يَحْذَرُونَ

And it does not beseem the believers that they should go forth all together; why should not then a company from every party from among them go forth that they may apply themselves

to obtain understanding in religion, and that they may warn
their people when they come back to them that they
may be cautious.

This verse instructs Muslims that a *select group* from within the community and the faith should go and learn the religion from teachers who themselves have learned it through a chain going back to the Prophet Muhammad. They are then obliged to come back to their people and impart that knowledge through their teachings and the way they live. But the truth is, not everyone is cut out for this task. Today, nearly every second Muslim feels the need to learn the jurisprudence (i.e., the legal philosophy) of Islam, along with the Arabic language, and other sciences. Learning and education certainly is a good thing, but the purpose of the learning matters, too. The goal of pursuing knowledge of Islam must be to become a better Muslim and nothing more. Too often, I see people delving into the Arabic language or the intricacies of Islamic jurisprudence and sowing differences of opinion and division. They may understand the words, but the right actions don't follow.

Knowing the Arabic language can be a plus, but it is not essential to living as a Muslim. Indeed, 82% of the Muslim world is non-Arab, which means most Muslims don't speak Arabic and therefore read the Quran in translation. That contributes to a muddying of the Quran's purpose or, more accurately, shifting its focus to words rather than actions or lifestyle.

You might ask, given what I've just said, how anyone can learn the lifestyle if they don't know Arabic. The answer: through the actions of their teachers and imams, who will teach through example and not merely words. Clearly, the responsibility of an imam or an Islamic leader can't be underestimated. (More on that shortly.)

But the upshot is that Islam is a religion of action, fueled by good character at the center.

According to the research of Professor Reima Al-Jarf of King Saud University, in Riyadh, Saudi Arabia, the earliest Persian translation of the Quran appeared in the 7th century; the earliest Latin translation is from 1143; and the English translation was done in 1649. In other words, the Quran was translated various times over centuries, by both non-Arab and Arab Muslims, but not in the early days of the spread of Islam. In addition, many English translations of the Quran differ: Some translators used "older," more archaic English words and constructions; others used simple modern English; others added commentary to the mix. To make things even more complicated, still others translated the meaning of the verses by paraphrasing, while others gave a word-for-word translation.

Before these translations were available, Muslims learned Islam through the lifestyle taught by those who lived it, and who themselves had learned from those who lived it before them. This lifestyle went back to the companions of Muhammad, who learned it from the Prophet Muhammad himself. That is the description of "the chain" I alluded to above. That consistency and consensus protected it from becoming a hostage of nepotism and favoritism, as did the sheer numbers of people demonstrating and teaching the Shariah lifestyle.

Which brings me back to my argument that only the most qualified, trustworthy people must be recruited to become scholars. These students of the faith are then tasked with steeping themselves not just in the words of the Quran but also in its guidelines for how to live, so they can become exemplary members of their communities once they return from their studies. Relatedly, it is worth noting that Allah sent prophets to the prophets' own people.

(Quran 2:67)

وَإِذْ قَالَ مُوسَىٰ لِقَوْمِهِ

And when Musa (Moses) said to his people

(Quran 6:83)

وَتِلْكَ حُجَّتُنَا آتَيْنَاهَا إِبْرَاهِيمَ عَلَىٰ قَوْمِهِ

And this was Our argument which we gave to Ibrahim
(Abraham) against his people

(Quran 7:59)

لَقَدْ أَرْسَلْنَا نُوحًا إِلَىٰ قَوْمِهِ فَقَالَ يَا قَوْمِ

Certainly We sent Nuh (Noah) to his people, so he said:
O my people!

(Quran 35:24)

وَإِن مِّنْ أُمَّةٍ إِلَّا خَلَا فِيهَا نَذِيرٌ

And there was no nation but that there had passed
within it a warner.

The definition of the word *understand* in the following quoted
verse is "the way one should live."

(Quran 12:2)

إِنَّا أَنزَلْنَاهُ قُرْءَٰنًا عَرَبِيًّا لَّعَلَّكُمْ تَعْقِلُونَ

Indeed, We have sent it down as an Arabic Qur'an that you
might understand.

Islam consists of actions and values that, as they became more
widespread, were formally collected into a code of behavior. Arabic

grammar classes or intense religious debates were not required to understand them.

Who Is Responsible for Teaching Islam Today?

As with all religions, the practices of individual Muslims in America vary widely. It all comes down to how each person views the role of faith in their life. Some Muslims attend the mosque and pray daily; others do so weekly or seasonally. From my perspective as an imam, typically, a family's connection to the mosque is what most influences the way they practice Islam at home and in society at large. The more a family attends the mosque, the more likely they are to observe traditional Islamic practices in dress; in their interactions with others in general society (and their treatment of loved ones); and, of course, in their manner of prayer, whether before meals or before sleeping. That doesn't mean that people who don't attend the mosque on a regular basis are not religious. But in my observation, those who do attend regularly seem to more easily integrate their faith into their everyday life than those who do not. In short, a mosque is a hub where a positive Islamic environment is both established and nurtured by the congregation's shepherds—i.e., their imams.

Scholars and imams, as I have said, are responsible for educating their community about the Islamic lifestyle that is the foundation of Islamic teachings. They are responsible for teaching their community about their religious needs and duties and enlightening them through faith on matters of the moment, hour, or season. These teachings will and must evolve over time and according to location.

It's fair to ask how much progress these scholars and imams have made—both in America and around the world, and among Arabs and non-Arabs—in educating their communities and helping congregants *understand and live out* their faith. I am sorry to say, not much at all.

To be clear, many, if not all, of these leaders are teaching basic Islamic knowledge to their congregants, including seasonal celebrations (Ramadan, or the Islamic New Year) as well as general topics on an array of contemporary issues. This knowledge is disseminated through nightly sessions after prayer or during the weekly (Friday) sermon, or, sometimes, through courses created to teach certain subjects, such as Islamic core beliefs, history, or jurisprudence. However, transmitting knowledge to the Islamic community goes beyond the mere teaching of books or subjects. It also requires leaders to have an intimate knowledge of the virtues and vices that exist within their congregants so they can work to root out those vices (individually and collectively) while encouraging the virtues. Of course, that's only possible if the imam invests his time and energy toward getting to know the people in his congregation, learning about their day-to-day lives and problems as if he were an intimate family member. In other words, human failings such as prejudice, intolerance, lying, backbiting, racism, etc., must be addressed individually to allow each person to become a better version of themselves. Thus an effective imam must be not only a spiritual leader but a personal pastoral counselor.

What I propose is to develop our communities more strategically, so that instead of constantly teaching religious subjects (such as the method of fasting taught on the first night of Ramadan), we proactively address contemporary issues and events in the world around us, whether addressing suicide prevention or what to do when a mosque is attacked or an atrocity is committed in the name of Islam. Instead of merely reacting to such events and playing catch-up, every imam has a moral responsibility to correctly guide their congregation on how to act on a regular basis. Only by taking on that moral obligation can Muslim leaders in the West shift the narrative. And they must. Any person invested in their community will absorb the ups and downs and important issues happening within a community, including issues that are likely to create conflict or difficulty. Being plugged in in that way allows leaders to be proactive, heading off dangers before they strike. Just as it only helps to learn CPR in advance rather than waiting until someone starts choking, a good leader knows his congregants' vulnerabilities—whose lives need saving, so to speak.

There are a couple of factors preventing this from happening. The first is a shortage of Islamic scholars serving the critical needs of the growing Muslim communities across America.

Even before 9/11, mosques across America were suffering from a lack of formally educated scholars and leaders. After the attacks, it became exponentially more difficult to attract qualified scholars and leaders. So mosques have been forced to improvise, taking on half-baked pseudo scholars who have learned the religion haphazardly, maybe with a few sporadic in-person classes (or maybe even on YouTube). That presents a danger for all communities and all faiths. I call this the phenomenon of blind men leading blind people into a dark forest. How can we expect mosques to serve and educate their congregants, much less thrive, under these conditions? All communities lose if they can't depend on their religious leaders to guide them in the right direction.

And even when America produces true Islamic scholars on its shores, along with many who graduate abroad and return to this country, the vast majority end up leaving the mosque within their first five years of service or go into other areas such as business, pursuing a different career path altogether.

Why are those trained and educated to lead communities abandoning those very communities and opting to enter other careers? I believe that's due to the current way that mosques are structured and function—the second factor preventing real community growth. Unlike the majority of churches, nearly every mosque in America is a creation of its own community and runs independently of other mosques in the country and the dictates of religious bodies in other countries. I see this as a bittersweet arrangement. The sweet part is that this community-based structure enables each mosque to (theoretically) focus on the needs and priorities of its community without pressure from outside structures. The bitter part has to do with who holds the power to make decisions within that community. You may be surprised to know that it's not the scholars or the most religious folks; it's apt to be the most affluent members of the community, or the founders, who feel the need to hold on to control no matter how out of touch they are from the community's current needs. Their primary concern is to ensure that money continues to flow into the mosque's account, which necessitates catering to the largest financial donors as opposed to what the imam sees as the community's greatest needs. This hampers a mosque's independence and effectiveness, since you can be sure that the biggest donors to the mosque are the ones getting their way, not the imams. Both of these factors—the shortage of Islamic scholars and the structure of mosques today—make it all too easy for ignorance to prevail.

The muck on this heap of issues is the growing culture of "celebrity imams"—people who have perhaps been educated but are more known for their large social media followings. (This is particularly true in American Muslim communities, but it also occurs in other parts of the world.) Often these Hollywood-style imams have *Shaykh* or *doctor* or *PhD* as their titles, which sounds more appealing to many than the traditional *imam*. And there's no denying that many are compelling, articulate speakers who command a global audience. But despite their good work and service, it's tough for these people to impact any community on a foundational level because they cater to crowds rather than to individuals—they have a top-down effect rather than a bottom-up impact. You could even say that these celebrity imams are perceived more as entertainers than true imams. A community member may walk away from a celebrity lecture feeling they have learned something but still end up ill equipped to make the inner changes that the faith and the heart require.

Can American Muslims restructure their mosques by importing models of systems from abroad? Sadly, no. Outside the West, Islamic leaders are typically appointed (and monitored) by the governments of their respective countries. Not surprisingly, they tend to say and do and teach what the government-appointed religious bodies tell them to—delivering sermons that have been preapproved by the government, for example. There is no freethinking; if an imam goes off script, he can lose his title and possibly be punished.

It is primarily due to this model that extremism emerged: Some of these government-run mosques failed to attend to the needs of the community, and extremists rushed in to fill that void. Mosques did not foster their community's growth and education, at least beyond what higher-ups instructed. As a result, every desperate faith-loving person ended up being vulnerable to the words of extremists outside the mosque, where care and services were held out as enticements.

Even when an imam is running and controlling their community-built mosque (as opposed to the one built and run by the government body), too often, that imam develops a cult-like following, splintering off from other Muslims who don't see eye to eye with them. Just as troubling, these imams often find that discrediting others is the shortest path to enhancing themselves and gaining followers, and so they allow hatred to take precedence over the needs of the community.

As with other religions, Muslim communities are not immune to corruption. The sad fact is, the great majority of Muslim congregants are unaccustomed to an imam who considers their welfare their top priority, so it's no wonder that when one does come along, it's tough for that person to prove they are the real deal. Here in America, where elected boards can hire and fire imams at will, mosques can seem more like corporations, at least in terms of their structure. They are run by (volunteer) board members who, while elected, may not be qualified, or, if they're not getting paid, basically phone it in because "Hey—I'm just a volunteer!" Over the years, it has sometimes seemed to me that too many board members are more interested in the title than the work.

If you run a business and you have "volunteers" at the helm, you and I know where it will end up: in an abyss. Speaking more tangibly, these mosques tend to change course whenever new members are elected, which is every two or four years, with the imam riding the waves of their ever-changing wishes. No wonder it is difficult to find an imam willing to devote himself to a community for five years or more. The younger, non-immigrant generation of imams in particular aren't willing to be bullied and pushed around. Instead, they opt to stand down, resign, and move on to other centers. If they get burned again, they walk away from established mosques and set up their own places of education and worship which, if those expand, inevitably run into the same problems. And so the cycle continues, and it will go on until someone can put a stop to it and start anew.

I believe we need real solutions to these long-standing problems, including hiring executive directors to run the main operations of the mosque. This will free up the (volunteer) board's time and reduce the risk of conflict.

What I'm saying is that many of the problems of Islam today arise because of how our mosques are run, both here and abroad. I am sure this problem is not unique to Islam. But as a community servant who has spent most of my time in the trenches with individuals who live in that community, I am intimately familiar with the needs of my congregants. For any imam, knowledge of the faith and experience of direct service is what provides the insight necessary to understand the spiritual life and demands of their particular congregation. The sad part is that in my experience (and that of other imams), the resentment from the board and their unprofessionalism often impedes progress instead of allowing mosques to flourish. This hurts both the imam and the community, though the imam is almost always the target of the congregation's blame.

For example, during my second post as an imam in Port Charlotte, Florida, one of my goals was to build a broader understanding of Islam in the wider community. To that end, I served in many volunteer posts, including as a spiritual director at the University of

Tampa and as the only Muslim advisor to the Florida Department of Education on behalf of the Muslim community. I also took on countless interfaith speaking engagements. All of these commitments meant I had to spend some time outside the mosque, which, ultimately, was seen by the board as conflicting with my contract. My contract stated that I had to lead all five prayers, every day, six days a week. Compromise for the greater good was not an option. Ultimately, I was told to either do what was stated in the contract or go elsewhere and follow my "dreams." So that is what I did.

I ended up in Texas with the same dream and aspiration: to empower the next generation of Muslims to be confident in their faith and the best leaders they are capable of being. Whether leading their families, their business, or simply themselves, it should always be through the lifestyle of the faith. Yet after five and a half years, that relationship also ended. I am someone who makes my thoughts on community matters clear. Truth be told, I often hold opinions that go against the norm, refusing to stay silent or nod in approval. I don't express views that serve the special interests of the few over the many. In other words, like all religious leaders, I face many challenges at the grassroots level, and I'm not always able to overcome them.

I have the utmost respect for Islamic scholars who do take on the post of imam and who endure in spite of the difficulties. Certainly, they are not doing it for the love of power nor for the money. (Surveys show that compared with clergy in other religions, imams are the lowest-paid and the most overworked.) The few who choose to do it despite the realities on the ground do it only for the love of the community and a selfless resolve to serve their Lord.

All of this makes it difficult for imams to honestly address crucial and controversial issues, however, including the ones my coauthor mentions. Unfortunately, the wrong people often end up filling the void—either that, or no one addresses difficult issues at all, and silence prevails.

As is the case with any religion, if a religious text (in this case the Quran) is interpreted by the wrong people, it can become a tool for harm and manipulation. Verse 3:7 makes it clear that though the Quran contains sections that are self-explanatory, there are also sections that require interpretation, and not just by anyone.

(Quran 3:7)

هُوَ ٱلَّذِىٓ أَنزَلَ عَلَيْكَ ٱلْكِتَـٰبَ مِنْهُ ءَايَـٰتٌ مُّحْكَمَـٰتٌ هُنَّ أُمُّ ٱلْكِتَـٰبِ وَأُخَرُ مُتَشَـٰبِهَـٰتٌ ۖ فَأَمَّا ٱلَّذِينَ فِى قُلُوبِهِمْ زَيْغٌ فَيَتَّبِعُونَ مَا تَشَـٰبَهَ مِنْهُ ٱبْتِغَآءَ ٱلْفِتْنَةِ وَٱبْتِغَآءَ تَأْوِيلِهِۦ ۖ وَمَا يَعْلَمُ تَأْوِيلَهُۥٓ إِلَّا ٱللَّهُ ۗ وَٱلرَّٰسِخُونَ فِى ٱلْعِلْمِ يَقُولُونَ ءَامَنَّا بِهِۦ كُلٌّ مِّنْ عِندِ رَبِّنَا ۗ وَمَا يَذَّكَّرُ إِلَّآ أُوْلُوا۟ ٱلْأَلْبَـٰبِ

It is He who has revealed the Book to you [O Muhammad];
some of its verses are decisive, they are the basis of the Book,
and others are allegorical. As for those in whose hearts is
deviation, they will follow that of it which is allegorical, seeking
discord and seeking to give it [their own] interpretation. And
no one knows its interpretation except Allah. And those firm in
knowledge say, "We believe in it. It is all from our Lord." And
no one will be reminded except those of understanding.

This verse alludes to the fact that not all parts of the Quran are self-explanatory. Many portions benefit from an expert explanation, someone who also understands the limits of their individual interpretation. When qualified and well-educated experts and explanations are lacking, misinterpretation abounds. Finally, there are parts of the Quran that can only be interpreted by Allah, such as the words *Alif-Laam-Meem* that appear in the beginning of Quran 2.

Of course, while a qualified scholar should always be the starting point of any interpretation of the Quran, anyone is welcome to try to interpret the Quran themselves, as my coauthor is doing and has done. No one has the power to stop nonscholars from interpreting away, as the denizens of ISIS and the Bin Ladens have also been doing for quite some time now.

I compare it to an ordinary person who Googles the answer to a medical question. That person isn't necessarily a threat to medicine or to the safety of every human being, just as ordinary people (nonscholars) interpreting the Quran aren't a threat to the world order or to Islam. The threat emerges when Googlers decide they themselves are as knowledgeable as doctors, or when interpreters of the Quran are granted legitimacy as "experts" and given an open forum and access to a global crowd of listeners. That's part of the reason why everyone should have enough understanding of the Quran so that they can separate true authorities from pretenders. That's one of my goals in this book: providing that basic understanding.

As for my coauthor, he is correct in his conclusion that Muslims are not allowed to reject any command of the Quran because it would mean rejecting the word of Allah. At the same time, it must be understood that Muslims are also not allowed to twist or misrepresent those exact words for their own purposes, because that would change the words of Allah and the reason these words were revealed.

At the end of the day, Muslims want to not only practice their religion but to live it, in their lives and within their hearts. In fact, they feel that Allah speaks to them through their heart. Who will help them live those words correctly, particularly when it's not always possible to interpret the meaning of certain verses in the Quran for the here and now? As I've said, that task must fall to those who have studied the Quran in depth and are qualified to judge which parts are self-explanatory and which require context from other verses and/or incidents surrounding their revelation. Some verses may not make sense immediately but will become clear at a later time. The validity of the word of Allah (the Quran) is universal and eternal. To contextualize it, we need learned people to assist us in understanding it at all times throughout the ages.

The terrorists who belong to Al Qaeda and ISIS are *not* those people—they are *not* Islamic scholars. Many cannot read or understand Arabic. They do not know what Allah is saying to them in the Quran, and they certainly do not understand what Allah is asking of them as Muslims; they are merely using the Quran to further their evil agendas, manipulating the word of Allah to justify their violent tendencies. Any sane, educated scholar of the faith will tell you that.

Women and the Islamic View on Marriage in the West: Shariah-Based Marriages vs. Current Trends and Culture

In modern-day America and in many Western nations, being able to marry someone you love, irrespective of gender, is lawful and indeed even becoming the norm. In Islam, however, the purpose of marriage is to find peace with someone with whom you can potentially procreate. Therefore, marriage is only acknowledged to be valid between a cisgender woman and a cisgender man, who, infertility issues notwithstanding, should be able to reproduce under typical circumstances.

(Quran 4:1)

يَـٰٓأَيُّهَا ٱلنَّاسُ ٱتَّقُواْ رَبَّكُمُ ٱلَّذِى خَلَقَكُم مِّن نَّفۡسٍ وَٰحِدَةٍ وَخَلَقَ مِنۡهَا زَوۡجَهَا وَبَثَّ

مِنۡهُمَا رِجَالًا كَثِيرًا وَنِسَآءً ۚ وَٱتَّقُواْ ٱللَّهَ ٱلَّذِى تَسَآءَلُونَ بِهِۦ وَٱلۡأَرۡحَامَ ۚ إِنَّ ٱللَّهَ

كَانَ عَلَيۡكُمۡ رَقِيبًا

O humankind, fear your Lord, who created you from one soul
and created from it its mate and dispersed from both of them
many men and women. And fear Allah, through whom you
ask one another, and the wombs. Indeed Allah is ever, over
you, an Observer.

What, then, of gay marriage? Some readers may be surprised
to hear that two men or two women legally becoming a couple in
America does not violate Shariah law. That's because while gay
marriage is allowed in America, it is not *imposed* on all Americans.
Under my faith, I would not be allowed to marry a man, but it
isn't a problem if those outside of Islam choose to do this. I have
my way, you have yours; regardless of what others want to do or
are permitted to do, my faith provides me with a framework for
deciding what is right, and same-sex marriage does not fall under
that framework. Another example: Under Shariah, demonstrations
of love and sexuality are supposed to remain behind closed doors,
within a private sphere. That doesn't mean people of other faiths/
walks of life can't engage in public displays of affection, as they do
in the West.

Unless individuals are living in and governed by an Islamic
country ruled by Shariah, the laws of Islam cannot prevent anyone
from living their life in a way that feels true to them, as long as they
are respectful of others. On the other hand, when it comes to sex,
marriage, and gender, the will of Allah *can* be acknowledged and

adhered to by Muslims, even if they live outside of a country where Shariah is officially practiced or a Caliphate exists.

And while I'm discussing marriage and sensitivities surrounding love and sex in modern America, I'll pause to make a comparison: In 2015, same-sex marriage was legalized in the U.S., taking its place beside heterosexual marriage. That doesn't mean, however, that Americans can do whatever they want when it comes to marriage. America does not allow polygamy, an accepted practice in Islam. That's a clear indication that secular law in the U.S. also has its boundaries, regardless of the First Amendment guarantee of freedom of expression. So here's a provocative question: Since most Americans feel that people should be able to love who they want, why can't polygamy be one of those expressions of love? I don't know the answer to that. What I do know is that some people believe it has to do with finances—that financially, polygamy keeps women in a less-than-optimal position. To my mind, that reasoning only strengthens the case for following Shariah, which commands that a man is never absolved from his financial responsibility toward his wife/wives, regardless of the woman's financial standing.

(Quran 4:34)

ٱلرِّجَالُ قَوَّٰمُونَ عَلَى ٱلنِّسَآءِ بِمَا فَضَّلَ ٱللَّهُ بَعْضَهُمْ عَلَىٰ بَعْضٍ وَبِمَآ أَنفَقُواْ مِنْ أَمْوَٰلِهِمْ

Men are in charge of women by [right of] what Allah has given one over the other and what they spend [for maintenance] from their wealth.

Shariah guards against the possibility that women will be taken advantage of in a polygamous marriage. That makes me wonder if the general Western bias against polygamy stems from an outdated notion that women can't take care of themselves. Think about it: In the case of polyandry (women having multiple husbands), would people worry that the male partners would be taken advantage of financially? I don't think so. The point of my short rant is to expose the double standard in so many of our assumptions.

Let me acknowledge here that some readers might be wondering, as my coauthor does, why Islam doesn't permit a woman to have multiple husbands if one man can have multiple wives.

The answer, to my mind, is simple. Allah did not grant that permission in Islam. And when the creator of humans tells us what we need as humans, it isn't for us to question His wisdom or decisions. There's also the practical issue that it would be difficult for a woman with multiple husbands to determine the father of her child unless those husbands agreed to DNA testing, which could also deprive her of financial support.

Surprisingly, in the U.S., one in five adults believes that polygamy is morally acceptable, according to a 2020 Gallup poll. This number has almost tripled since the question was first asked in 2003. Yet the United Nations Human Rights Committee calls for polygamy to be "abolished wherever it continues to exist." If a person can have multiple sex partners and still be married to one person (as in an open marriage), shouldn't it be okay to have multiple marriage partners for men, or, as some believe, for women?

The point of marriage under Shariah is to promote healthy companionship over sexual needs alone. That's an important thing to note, especially when it comes to temporary liaisons. In Islam, the marriage ceremony makes a couple's personal commitment to another person public before the community and before God. Indeed, tying the knot is valued so highly that a newly married person is considered to have completed half their faith on their journey toward meeting Allah.

That is also why, in Islamic culture, pornography and open sexual exploitation are not welcome in society. Also not condoned by Shariah: the practice of having multiple partners (boyfriends, girlfriends, casual dates, significant others, open relationships, baby mamas/daddies), which is often how potential partners in the West meet each other, and how many families begin— or end up. To my knowledge, the sanctity of marriage and the legal protection it provides is the preferred arrangement for all religions.

Divorce and Marriage in Islam

Islam teaches us everything from how to conduct ourselves as individuals, and our role in the family, to the right way to govern society. If specific opportunities to apply the teachings arise in one's personal life or within the community (as they did during the Caliphate), followers can use these commands as a framework for action. That doesn't mean, however, that faithful Muslims must implement the Quran to the letter at all times no matter what. Take divorce for example. Quran 2:229 to 2:242 describes the process of divorce as follows:

(Quran 2:229)

ٱلطَّلَٰقُ مَرَّتَانِ ۖ فَإِمْسَاكٌ بِمَعْرُوفٍ أَوْ تَسْرِيحٌ بِإِحْسَٰنٍ ۗ وَلَا يَحِلُّ لَكُمْ أَن تَأْخُذُوا۟ مِمَّآ ءَاتَيْتُمُوهُنَّ شَيْئًا إِلَّآ أَن يَخَافَآ أَلَّا يُقِيمَا حُدُودَ ٱللَّهِ ۖ فَإِنْ خِفْتُمْ أَلَّا يُقِيمَا حُدُودَ ٱللَّهِ فَلَا جُنَاحَ عَلَيْهِمَا فِيمَا ٱفْتَدَتْ بِهِۦ ۗ تِلْكَ حُدُودُ ٱللَّهِ فَلَا تَعْتَدُوهَا ۚ وَمَن يَتَعَدَّ حُدُودَ ٱللَّهِ فَأُو۟لَٰٓئِكَ هُمُ ٱلظَّٰلِمُونَ

Divorce is twice. Then, either keep [her] in an acceptable manner or release [her] with good treatment. And it is not lawful for you to take anything of what you have given them unless both fear that they will not be able to keep [within] the limits of Allah. But if you fear that they will not keep [within] the limits of Allah, then there is no blame upon either of them concerning that by which she ransoms herself. These are the limits of Allah, so do not transgress them. And whoever transgresses the limits of Allah—it is those who are the wrongdoers.

The goal of Shariah is to teach its followers to absorb core values first—revering God, following His commands, and holding oneself accountable at all times. Ideally, these values serve as a moral compass in times of confusion; they are not meant to be weapons against peace, or a means of taking over the world, and they don't have to be adopted completely at every instant, much less enforced.

That makes sense, especially because certain Muslim values do seem to conflict with American values. But this doesn't have to be a problem if each person's beliefs are respected and each of us is free to practice our own culture and faith. Quran 2:221, for instance, forbids all Muslims from marrying idolators or polytheists since they don't fit the Quran's monotheistic core value system. It may surprise readers to learn that this command does not prohibit Muslim men from marrying devout Christians or Jews (people of the book) who uphold the values taught by their faith; if they live by what I have defined as their Shariah, they are suitable partners for Muslim men.

Devout Jews and Christians can marry Muslims, and vice versa, as implied in the following passage.

(Quran 5:5)

ٱلْيَوْمَ أُحِلَّ لَكُمُ ٱلطَّيِّبَـٰتُ ۖ وَطَعَامُ ٱلَّذِينَ أُوتُوا ٱلْكِتَـٰبَ حِلٌّ لَّكُمْ وَطَعَامُكُمْ حِلٌّ
لَّهُمْ ۖ وَٱلْمُحْصَنَـٰتُ مِنَ ٱلْمُؤْمِنَـٰتِ وَٱلْمُحْصَنَـٰتُ مِنَ ٱلَّذِينَ أُوتُوا ٱلْكِتَـٰبَ مِن
قَبْلِكُمْ إِذَآ ءَاتَيْتُمُوهُنَّ أُجُورَهُنَّ مُحْصِنِينَ غَيْرَ مُسَـٰفِحِينَ وَلَا مُتَّخِذِىٓ أَخْدَانٍ ۚ
وَمَن يَكْفُرْ بِٱلْإِيمَـٰنِ فَقَدْ حَبِطَ عَمَلُهُۥ وَهُوَ فِى ٱلْءَاخِرَةِ مِنَ ٱلْخَـٰسِرِينَ

This day [all] good foods have been made lawful, and the food
of those who were given the Scripture is lawful for you and
your food is lawful for them. And [lawful in marriage are]
chaste women from among the believers and chaste women
from among those who were given the Scripture before you,
when you have given them their due compensation, desiring
chastity, not unlawful sexual intercourse or taking [secret]
lovers. And whoever denies the faith—his work has become
worthless, and he, in the Hereafter, will be among the losers.

In America, there are no barriers to marrying into different religions. At the same time, my Shariah has identified who I can marry: a woman who shares my religion or who is a devout Christian or Jew. And for women, a Muslim man. For me, these are Allah's boundaries, which, as a Muslim, I respect and accept.

At the same time, as a Muslim American, I don't have a right to object to other people's marriage choices. All individuals have the right to do as they please (as long as they're not hurting anyone or breaking the law). No one should impose their values on another or be made to feel uncomfortable at the hands of another.

I also want to consider the fairy-tale depiction of marriage that most Americans grow up absorbing, and how that influences the way many Westerners think about marriage. We are not only taught that it's necessary to throw an elaborate wedding, but that the goal should be ending up with a spouse who has perfect looks, a prestigious job, and money, and who will make us happy for the rest of our years. Truth be told, these criteria are unreachable for the majority of people. They shouldn't be required.

To go further, I see these fairy-tale perceptions of marriage and its legal complexity as obstacles to organic, fulfilling relationships. Too often, the mere cost associated with fulfilling societal expectations for a wedding, and then a marriage, results in the crumbling of the one thing marriage is all about: the relationship. And then the laws and the courts, not to mention the divorce attorneys who suck couples' hard-earned money out of their pockets, leave married people with two bleak options: to accept the reality and fight out the divorce, or to be quiet and live in misery. A prison sentence in either case, really.

Contrary to what most Westerners believe, in Islam, marriage is always the decision of the couple involved; if two people like each other and want to explore a relationship, all they need to do is to inform their families, then go to the courts to register their decision before two witnesses. They may also decide to hold a small and simple ceremony, but in general, there is no complex process or undue wedding expense involved. The marriage may last a long time or it may not, but regardless, marrying someone openly is a sign of valuing and respecting that person, rather than allowing them to feel used for sex alone.

The same can be said for divorce: It's simple. In Islam, it doesn't take years to end a marriage nor cost an arm and a leg to separate. While some couples in the West may choose the less expensive and contentious path of mediation, for the most part, too many tend to go down the road of vengeance, suing one another and racking up expenses and resentment.

Under Shariah law, a woman must present her reasons for seeking a divorce before a judge, and the judge may grant her the right to divorce. In contrast, a man can simply declare that he wishes to divorce and the matter is finished. What must be recognized, however, is that his financial responsibility toward his wife and children does not end with the divorce. Under Shariah, men have a duty toward their ex-wife and children based on their needs and the former husband's means.

(Quran 2:233)

. . . وَعَلَى ٱلْمَوْلُودِ لَهُ رِزْقُهُنَّ وَكِسْوَتُهُنَّ بِٱلْمَعْرُوفِ ۚ لَا تُكَلَّفُ نَفْسٌ
إِلَّا وُسْعَهَا ۚ

. . . and upon the father is the mothers' provision and their clothing according to what is acceptable. No person is charged with more than his capacity.

Whatever belonged to the woman before marriage remains hers after divorce, along with anything she earned during the marriage. The man is also entitled to whatever was his before marriage. But even if the former husband moves on and marries someone else, he will continue to be financially responsible for his former wife for a period of time defined by a judge. A woman, on the other hand, has no financial responsibility toward the man, which is why she must explain her reasons for calling it quits.

Other than finances, the involvement of the court is limited and, as I've said, based on the circumstances of the couple (including the number of children and other factors). As is true in the West, it is not a one-size-fits-all process. The job of any judge is to help divorcing Muslim couples iron out any sticky issues rather than prolonging the process. Lastly, after a divorce, under Shariah, the man is responsible for physically raising the boys after the age of 7 and the girls postpuberty (a framework provided in Shariah but not necessarily the final decision. That decision is based on the father's mental and physical ability and stability, which is determined by a judge). Ultimately, under Shariah, divorce doesn't grant men the right to say "I divorce you" and then walk away.

All that said, divorce is considered something couples should turn to only as a last resort. Instead, the Quran mandates mediation—that is, that couples make the effort to resolve their marital issues before jumping to divorce. A couple contemplating separation must present their case to family members for mediation or, if necessary, go to a third party for arbitration.

(Quran 4:35)

وَإِنْ خِفْتُمْ شِقَاقَ بَيْنِهِمَا فَابْعَثُوا حَكَمًا مِّنْ أَهْلِهِ وَحَكَمًا مِّنْ أَهْلِهَا إِن يُرِيدَا

إِصْلَاحًا يُوَفِّقِ اللَّهُ بَيْنَهُمَا ۗ إِنَّ اللَّهَ كَانَ عَلِيمًا خَبِيرًا

And if you fear dissension between the two, send an arbitrator from his people and an arbitrator from her people. If they both desire reconciliation, Allah will cause it between them. Indeed, Allah is ever Knowing and Acquainted [with all things].

If all efforts to resolve their differences fail, the couple is then able to dissolve the relationship. As referenced earlier, in Quran 2:229-242, a framework is given for everything from one's demeanor toward the other (before and after a divorce) to what one can take from the marriage, as well as for contingencies such as parental duties and financial support of children and the death of one of the divorced parties.

I feel it is sufficient to say that in Islam, it is possible to make marriage (and divorce) work without any threats or preconditions attached, based on a few simple conditions: A man keeps his assets; a woman keeps hers. The man will be financially responsible for his former wife and for the children for a period of time, and, physically, for raising his children until they become adults. These responsibilities are understood and accepted. There is generally no need to enforce these rules or hand out penalties; it's just what people do. The Islamic system of divorce allows the former couple the time, space, and financial flexibility to pursue new paths while continuing to fulfill their financial obligations, or having those obligations met (i.e., through child support and alimony). No one is imprisoned after a marriage has been terminated, either literally or figuratively.

In contrast, in the U.S., suing for divorce can create stress far beyond the emotional strain of two people splitting up. For that, I blame the government's overinvolvement in the process. The state should not have a hand in determining the details of a couple's divorce agreement—say, that each member of a couple is legally entitled to 50% of their combined assets, regardless of the earning situation in that particular marriage.

Of course, it makes sense to have some legal framework in place to manage difficult circumstances and complicated finances—for example, if one partner suddenly dies with no will. The purpose of any governing system should be to ensure safety and stability for its citizens, not the opposite. To my mind, government overreach begins when citizens doubt the system and fear getting caught up in it, as many do when it comes to contested divorces that end up in court.

People, especially people who are divorcing, will inevitably have disagreements and thus need to defer to the courts to resolve those disagreements. But I suggest that the current framework of marriage and divorce in America is too narrow. We need a broader way of thinking about it, one that perhaps allows and legitimizes anyone who wishes to exit a relationship and enter into another (legal) relationship, or, for that matter, who wishes to maintain multiple relationships without breaking a law or doing something unlawful.

I also wonder why getting into (and out of) a relationship in the U.S. requires a legal license and a legal dissolution (filing divorce papers) when, as of June 2021, Governor Abbott of Texas signed a bill that made it legal for anyone to carry a weapon (including a gun) regardless of whether they have a license. I find it ironic that it's considered perfectly fine to carry something that can cause another person's death—no license required—while one can't marry without a license.

At the end of the day, divorce is a personal matter. In a nation where discussions of how much control the government should have in one's personal life are at a fever pitch, why isn't the requirement that marriages be dissolved legally considered to be a similar intrusion?

The Question of the Right Age for Marriage

Another tricky issue raised by my coauthor is that Islam grants any female of reproductive age the right to marry. But if our current dating culture is okay with a middle schooler being in a dating relationship, and if more than half of U.S. teenagers have sex by age 18, then why prohibit marriage at a young age? The truth is, Islam and the West see the purpose of marriage differently. In Islam, sex is a part of the bigger picture of a marital relationship—just one element of a life of commitment and trust. That's precisely why a commitment through marriage is required before couples can have sex. In the West, sex education (including how to have safe sex) is taught in many elementary schools, presumably because it is considered okay for kids to explore their sexuality.

To go further, why not trust someone under 18 to marry when, in some states, we allow underage individuals to change their gender, so long as their parents approve it? To be clear, under Shariah, Muslims are taught that our body is a trust from Allah, our creator. We don't have the right to alter our bodies; there are limits to what we can do in everyday life.

I believe that when it comes to the sex or gender of an individual, Allah doesn't make mistakes. The current trend of transitioning to another gender brings to mind a promise the devil himself made before Allah when he was thrown out of heaven: that he would destroy the human race. Allah recaps the devil's promise in the Quran.

(Quran 4:119)

وَلَأُضِلَّنَّهُمْ وَلَأُمَنِّيَنَّهُمْ وَلَآمُرَنَّهُمْ فَلَيُبَتِّكُنَّ آذَانَ الْأَنْعَامِ وَلَآمُرَنَّهُمْ فَلَيُغَيِّرُنَّ خَلْقَ اللَّهِ ۚ وَمَن يَتَّخِذِ الشَّيْطَانَ وَلِيًّا مِّن دُونِ اللَّهِ فَقَدْ خَسِرَ خُسْرَانًا مُّبِينًا

*And I will mislead them, and I will arouse in them [sinful] desires, and I will command them so they will slit the ears of cattle, and I will command them **so they will change the creation of Allah.** And whoever takes Satan as an ally instead of Allah has certainly sustained a clear loss.*

I'm not saying here that it is ideal or advisable for adolescents to marry. What I wonder is why society considers it acceptable for an adolescent to, say, have sex, explore their sexuality, change their gender, but not freely decide to marry? These two standards *are in conflict*; that is my objection. Another example of conflicting standards: In the U.S., young adolescents are allowed to make decisions about their body as if they were adults when, in many states today, adult women are not able to freely decide to keep their baby or have an abortion.

From what I've seen, people who oppose minors being able to transition come from all different religions and cultures. To my mind, this broad-based opposition has to do with this issue taking up what I consider to be an outsized political space in our society. I don't condemn those who choose to transition, but I don't have to validate that practice, say, by putting "he/his" in my email signature. Shouldn't the fact that gender surgery is legal be validation enough? Shouldn't everyone feel safe to stand by the decisions they make or the positions they take, politically correct or not?

Violence Against Women

Finally, I want to talk about the widespread perception that in Islam, women are ill-used second-class citizens. Certain translations of the Quran, when referring to women, even state, "Strike them," as my coauthor points out.

But if "striking" or "beating" a woman is indeed permitted in Islam because of a specific verse in the Quran, the Prophet Muhammad would have had no problem hitting his wives. But he didn't hit his wives. The fact that Muhammad's own wife, Aishah, states, "he never beat any of his wives" is evidence of that.

The confusion here stems from problematic translations of the Quran. Over time, those translations seep into and influence culture and may become difficult to confront or even change. Most people in non-Arabic-speaking Muslim countries today rely on translations, which vary widely, and consequently miss the Quran's broader message about daily actions and lifestyle, or even fall into a culture or lifestyle that contradicts the essence of Islam and its teachings. As I stated earlier, I believe the imams of today need to clarify and redefine seemingly troubling verses so that their congregations understand the point of commands and/or instructions from Allah, especially those pertaining to women. Simply put: Under Shariah, there is no justification for abuse.

Take, for instance, the words of Muhammad in his famous farewell sermon, when the Prophet addressed all believers in his first and final pilgrimage in Arafat, highlighting the most important aspects of his message, including:

> *"O people, it is true that you have certain rights with regard to your women, but they also have rights over you. Remember that you have taken them as your wives only under Allah's trust and with His permission. If they abide by your right then to them belongs the right to be fed and clothed in kindness. Do treat your women well and be kind to them for they are your partners and committed helpers."*
> (Hadith, Musnad Ahmad 19774)

The trouble/confusion comes with several Hadith, which do contain descriptions of beating women. Before I get to those, I would also ask Muslim readers, some of whom have absorbed the widespread belief in Islamic culture that it is okay to beat women, to be extra patient here as I go back in time.

Prior to the advent of Islam in Arabia, it was common practice in

Makkah to bury one's daughter alive, since having a daughter was considered to be a stain on one's honor and family name. It was Islam that stopped this practice.

(Quran 81:8,9)

وَ إِذَا الْمَوْ ءُودَةُ سُئِلَتْ بِأَيِّ ذَنبٍ قُتِلَتْ

And when the girl [who was] buried alive is asked,
For what sin she was killed?

More explicitly, on the Day of Judgment, when every soul is resurrected, Allah states that He will inquire what sin the (buried) little girl committed to be given such a punishment. This warning eventually created a culture in which girls were nurtured; that was part of what one did in order to be admitted into Paradise.

The Prophet Muhammad said:

"If anyone has a female child, and does not bury her alive,
or slight her, or prefer his children (i.e. the male ones) to her,
Allah will bring him into Paradise."
(Hadith, Abu Dawood 5146)

And, in another Hadith:

"Anyone who has three daughters and provides for them,
clothes them and shows mercy to them will definitely enter
Paradise." (Hadith, Adab Al-Mufrad 78)

After the advent of Islam in Makkah, those who embraced the Islamic faith realized that certain practices they were accustomed to were not in compliance with the values of their new religion (despite the absence at that time of an explicit command against them). Hence, they abandoned such actions—burying girls, beating wives—as best they could. But once they moved to Madinah, some fell back to beating their wives, even going so far as to seek permission from Muhammad to do so. One Hadith, below, describes what happened at that time:

> *"The Prophet Muhammad said, 'Do not beat the female slaves of Allah.' [A female slave simply means a woman. Men and women in Islam see themselves as slaves/servants of Allah. The context here is one's wife/wives.] When Umar, a companion, came to the Prophet and complained: 'The women have become very daring towards their husbands,' Muhammad gave permission to beat them. Then many women went to the family of Muhammad (his wives) complaining of their husbands, and the Prophet Muhammad said, 'Many women have gone round Muhammad's family complaining of their husbands. Those who take to beating their wives, are not the best among you.'"*
> (Hadith, Abu Dawood 2146)

My question here is that if it was permissible to beat women (one's wife), why did the people need to get approval from the Prophet to do so? Moreover, if the people who beat their wives were condemned by Muhammad after the first day (*"You are not the best of us"*), why, 1,400 years later, do so many Muslims continue to feel they can do it?

Imams have a responsibility before Allah to guide their congregations toward what is best and what is right, which means they need to take the lead in changing attitudes around beating women. That is sometimes easier said than done.

Recently, I was part of a panel discussion of scholars speaking before an audience of young Muslims. One of the female attendees asked why Islam permitted striking a woman; I responded by pointing out the flawed translation of the word *darb*. Some of the other scholars on that panel condemned me for my statements, cutting me off while I was in the middle of explaining, declaring that I was wrong and that Shariah supported the opposite of what I was saying (beating women). At the moment he interrupted me, there was a gasp in the audience; the young people seemed to be stunned by his disrespect. The two other scholars on the panel weren't bothered; they were in such strong agreement that Shariah supports beating one's wife that they had no compunction about cutting me off. I tell this story to give a sense of the passion that surrounds this topic in the Muslim world.

So you may be surprised to learn that despite the disagreements, we panelists went for dinner afterward, where I brought the topic up again. Once again, two of the learned scholars at the table stated their belief that striking one's wife was permissible under the faith. However, when I pushed for clarity and a definition of what type of beating, and with what instrument, and how many times, I suddenly sensed some hesitation in the air. One stated that the translation of the verse meant to nudge one's wife with his shoulder, expressing dissatisfaction and anger; another spoke about what is commonly found in the commentary of the verse, where using a wife's scarf for a "beating" is described—in other words, hitting is not involved; the purpose is to express disgust. To my mind, these vague descriptions are a testament that something isn't right in terms of the explanation of this verse. If the Prophet Muhammad instructed us to beat our spouse, wouldn't he have taught us exactly how it should be done? But that clarity is absent in the divine sources of Shariah.

Sadly, due to the widespread belief among many Muslims that

beating women is in fact legislated by Islam, physical abuse of women (a wife or daughter), often leading to murder, is a norm in certain countries, such as Pakistan. Often, bystanders will watch as the act is carried out, all while the woman screams for her life. There are too many cases to describe, as almost all of them are swept under the rug by the officials and the media. Why? I blame the bulk of it on the misinterpretation of what the religion permits through the translation of a verse that isn't in sync with the practice of the Prophet Muhammad. If Shariah were practiced in its true form, such inhumanity and heartlessness would never exist, much less prevail. Such heartless humans do not fit the description of animals; they are worse.

(Quran 7:179)

وَلَقَدْ ذَرَأْنَا لِجَهَنَّمَ كَثِيرًا مِّنَ الْجِنِّ وَالْإِنسِ ۖ لَهُمْ قُلُوبٌ لَّا يَفْقَهُونَ بِهَا وَلَهُمْ أَعْيُنٌ لَّا يُبْصِرُونَ بِهَا وَلَهُمْ آذَانٌ لَّا يَسْمَعُونَ بِهَا ۚ أُولَٰئِكَ كَالْأَنْعَامِ بَلْ هُمْ أَضَلُّ ۚ أُولَٰئِكَ هُمُ الْغَافِلُونَ

And We have certainly created for Hell many of the jinn and mankind. They have hearts with which they do not understand, they have eyes with which they do not see, and they have ears with which they do not hear. Those are like livestock; rather, they are more astray. It is they who are the heedless.

When it comes to reestablishing the true meaning of the "striking/beating" verse, which, unfortunately, carries centuries of incorrect beliefs and practices behind it, Muslims have a lot of work to do. It is going to take time and understanding for today's scholars in both the West and East to absorb and teach the correct meaning. Difficult as it is, I consider this work to be wholly worthwhile.

Allah assigned a role for husbands just as He did for wives. An imbalance in these positions or a violation of these decreed roles can lead to the kind of chaos we are seeing now. Men, in Islam, have been given a responsibility that has a level of respect attached to it. I applaud all men who, despite the push in today's world to lead an independent lifestyle, happily marry and work hard to raise and provide for their families. Society should never undermine this reality, nor should we shun it. Between the narrative of abusive men and rebellious women, we are losing the sanctity of marriage. Every person has a duty to fix themselves and do their part to uphold a relationship from their end. That's why it is up to people—or, rather, believers—to carry forth the shift in how to conduct themselves according to Islam and to teach this conduct to subsequent generations in order to abolish the ignorant ways of the past.

Jihad, Laws, and the Fear of Global Domination

America has a growing and vibrant Muslim population of 3.5 million people who are dedicated to Shariah law, meaning that Muslims here are already living what they believe and practicing it for themselves, allowing their actions of faith to serve as an example to those around them (rather than indoctrinating or compelling anyone to do as they do). There is no command compelling them to impose their religion on others; they are simply following the command in the Quran to practice their faith.

That *doesn't* mean they shouldn't follow the laws of the country in which they live. I'll repeat here what I've said before: All citizens should and must obey the laws of their respective countries, and Islam doesn't command Muslims otherwise. Every new American citizen must pledge to uphold the Constitution, including Muslim

Americans. The Quran commands us to fulfill our pledge and word, whatever that pledge may be.

(Quran 5:1)

يَـٰٓأَيُّهَا ٱلَّذِينَ ءَامَنُوٓاْ أَوْفُواْ بِٱلْعُقُودِ

O you who believe! fulfill all obligations (contracts).

Penal Law vs. American Law

This brings me to practices such as public stoning, floggings, or amputations. My coauthor is correct that there is no room in Western culture and civilization for these practices, despite their being sanctioned under Shariah law. Only in an Islamic country under an Islamic governing body (i.e., Caliphate) that follows the laws of Islam to the letter can Shariah be practiced in its entirety. The very definition of an "Islamic" governing body is one that follows Shariah law through and through, including civil law. Moreover, only that governing body, whether the Caliph or the courts, can decide when modern conditions demand Quranic mandates for enforcing the penal code or, for that matter, for waging war.

Any Muslim who believes Shariah should be implemented to a "T" in America is not in fact a follower of the Shariah of Islam because of the simple fact that the penal code is not applicable under the American law and judicial system.

Does that mean Muslims in America who follow the law of the land rather than Shariah civil law are discarding the Shariah or, worse, disobeying Allah by rejecting the Quran (as my coauthor assumes)? It does not. Moreover, any imam in America who stands before their congregation and calls for jihad, or the chopping off of a thief's hand, is overstepping their authority. Finally, if Muslims were to assume a leadership role in this country (beyond any Muslims already serving in Congress), they would not be able to substitute Shariah for the Constitution. Islamic civil law (i.e., the penal code) will never and should never replace America's governing laws, even if those leaders practice Shariah in their own lives.

I say this not because the current U.S. justice system is perfect. Indeed, it is flawed and dysfunctional in its own way, with formerly incarcerated individuals suffering the weight of punishment long after they are released, sometimes forbidden from voting in elections, to name just one common "legal" injustice.

If an individual has served their time, why can't they be accepted back into society, with all the attending rights and privileges? Instead, individuals are forced to disclose their history to potential employers, and employers are allowed to refuse to hire them because of that history, making it difficult for these individuals to build a life outside of prison. So while it's unlikely that a criminal in the U.S. will be punished by having a limb amputated, or by being lashed with a whip, or stoned (as they would under Shariah law), they are treated brutally in other ways, never able to move on, handicapped by their past and unable to get a second chance at life.

For these reasons and others, despite everything I've said, I do believe there is a place in Western society for Shariah law, troubling verses or no, just as there is a place for our current system of government, despite its many flaws. Fixating on the very few passages in the Quran that deal with meting out justice, as my coauthor sometimes does, misses the overall message. Moreover, whether or not Shariah is the law of the land, it can be used as a viable basis for finding solutions to some of the trying problems in our world, problems that affect all of us. I'm talking about creating a culture of respect for others, in part based on the teachings and beliefs of Islam and Shariah law and the way of life it promulgates.

Meanwhile, for those who adhere to, embrace, and practice the Islamic faith, Shariah continues to shape Muslims' values, including where they worship, how and what they eat, and the clothing they wear. You may also be surprised to learn that the Shariah of practicing Islam has been present in America from the 1800s and maybe even earlier. Many Muslims who came to this beautiful land for exploration, business, or trade, and even those who were forced to come through slavery, did not necessarily leave their religion or beliefs behind, even as they adopted a new nationality.

You've likely seen this where you live or when you travel: Muslims practicing their faith, say, by praying five times a day or, perhaps, Orthodox Jews walking to synagogue (instead of driving) during Sabbath. In America, religious laws continue to exist and exert influence, but they are not the same as civil laws, nor should they be, for Muslims or any other religious group.

Yet maybe all of us can benefit from what Shariah has to offer. Qays ibn Sa'd, a companion of Muhammad, reported:

> *"A funeral passed by Prophet Muhammad, and he stood up.*
> *It was said to him, 'It is a Jew.' The Prophet said,*
> *'Was he not a soul?'"* (Hadith, Bukhari 1250)

Going further, the Prophet strictly warned against mistreating people of other faiths.

> *"Beware! Whoever is cruel and hard on a non-Muslim*
> *minority, or curtails their rights, or burdens them with more*
> *than they can bear, or takes anything from them against*

their free will; I (Prophet Muhammad) will complain
against the person on the Day of Judgment."
(Hadith, Abu Dawood 3052)

Being a devout Muslim does not mean enforcing capital punishment. There is always a process involved. One thing to know is that circumstances at the time of revelation set a precedent for future decisions, serving as a framework for similar circumstances in the future (though *not* as a green light for continuing these practices). I'm talking about verses such as the one below.

(Quran 8:39)

وَقَٰتِلُوهُمْ حَتَّىٰ لَا تَكُونَ فِتْنَةٌ وَيَكُونَ ٱلدِّينُ كُلُّهُ لِلَّهِ ۚ فَإِنِ ٱنتَهَوْاْ فَإِنَّ ٱللَّهَ بِمَا يَعْمَلُونَ بَصِيرٌ

And fight with them until there is no more persecution and
religion should be only for Allah; but if they desist, then indeed
Allah sees what they do.

This was originally commanded during the Battle of Uhud, right outside of Madinah, in the 16th year of Islam/the 3rd year of migration, and it was meant to serve as a guide for the future if—and only if—similar circumstances arose. So what were the circumstances back then? Before the people of Makkah invaded Madinah, an agreement was made by all parties in Madinah, including the Muslims who had migrated there, the Jews, and the nonbelievers to collectively defend the city against invasion. The command in 8:39, above, reflects Allah's approval of defensive war back then, at that time, under those circumstances.

Taqiyya and the Myth of Holy War

At one point in time, I harbored the hope that if Osama Bin Laden were captured, our lives would eventually return to normal—or, at least, the normal that existed before 9/11. My hopes were put to test in real time on a flight to Florida from New York City one evening on May 1, 2011. I'd flown in from Saudi Arabia that morning and had a connecting flight to catch with JetBlue on my way home. I vividly remember sitting in front of the window by the gate as the sun set, slumped in my chair, exhaustion washing over me. After boarding, I was quite happy to realize that there were many empty seats, so I found a row close to the back and, after takeoff, stretched out for a nap. Thousands of feet above the ground, under the dark night sky, I was abruptly woken to the sound of cheers. When I sleepily sat up, unsure where I was, I saw passengers giving each other high-fives and whooping with joy. I clicked on the in-flight TV and started flipping through the channels, all featuring the same breaking news: President Obama's announcement that the U.S. military had located and killed Osama Bin Laden. As a Muslim with a beard dressed in Islamic garb, I suddenly felt self-conscious about my appearance. Slowly, I lay back down and stayed there, now wide awake and aware of a new reality: While Bin Laden might now be gone, the results of his actions would live on, and all Muslims, peaceful or not, would continue to pay the price for his hatred.

Yet it never occurred to me to conceal the truth of my faith from others, a process known as *taqiyya,* to which my coauthor alludes when describing our first encounter. Taqiyya is not a Sunni concept, so I can't address it from my (Sunni) perspective. But could it be possible that normal, working-class, family-loving Americans who also happen to be Muslims are hiding something from their fellow Americans? Are they on standby, merely waiting for a signal to expose who they truly are by bombing and killing "the infidel," as some believe? No, they are not.

What I can say is that Muslims are permitted to hide their faith only when their lives are threatened because of their religion. If someone puts a gun to a Muslim and says, "Renounce your faith or die!" they can and should renounce it, verbally at least, as long as they remain true to their beliefs in their heart.

(Quran 16:106)

مَن كَفَرَ بِٱللَّهِ مِنۢ بَعْدِ إِيمَٰنِهِۦٓ إِلَّا مَنْ أُكْرِهَ وَقَلْبُهُۥ مُطْمَئِنٌّۢ بِٱلْإِيمَٰنِ وَلَٰكِن مَّن شَرَحَ بِٱلْكُفْرِ صَدْرًا فَعَلَيْهِمْ غَضَبٌ مِّنَ ٱللَّهِ وَلَهُمْ عَذَابٌ عَظِيمٌ

Whoever disbelieves in Allah after his belief, except for one who is forced [to renounce his religion] while his heart is secure in faith. But those who [willingly] open their breasts to disbelief, upon them is wrath from Allah, and for them is a great punishment.

This verse explains how concealing one's belief is permissible when one's life is threatened.

But the fact remains that non-Muslims often distrust the motives of Muslims, as Bob brings up when he refers to this particular passage in the Quran:

(Quran 3:28)

لَّا يَتَّخِذِ ٱلْمُؤْمِنُونَ ٱلْكَٰفِرِينَ أَوْلِيَآءَ مِن دُونِ ٱلْمُؤْمِنِينَ ۖ وَمَن يَفْعَلْ ذَٰلِكَ فَلَيْسَ مِنَ ٱللَّهِ فِى شَىْءٍ إِلَّآ أَن تَتَّقُوا۟ مِنْهُمْ تُقَىٰةً ۗ وَيُحَذِّرُكُمُ ٱللَّهُ نَفْسَهُۥ ۗ وَإِلَى ٱللَّهِ ٱلْمَصِيرُ

Let not believers take disbelievers as allies rather than
believers. And whoever [of you] does that has nothing with
Allah, unless you guard yourselves against an apprehension
from them. And Allah warns you of Himself, and to Allah is
the [final] destination.

Frankly, before working on this book, I'd never looked at this and the previous verse from quite this angle, but I have to say, the anti-Muslim propaganda machine has done a good job of painting Islam according to their liking by twisting verses like the ones above in a way that leads to Bob's interpretation.

Let me provide an explanation of this verse. As I alluded to earlier, a *kafir* is someone who openly rejects Allah after understanding who Allah is. A kafir can also be someone, who, after their open rejection, vocalizes their hatred and possibly even instigates harm against the religion. My point is, it is a broad definition. And I have to ask, why would a believer in Allah take a kafir as a close confidant and ally? On the other hand, you might choose to be pleasant to someone, maintain a cordial relationship, or even forge a formal friendship, all of which are separate from making that person your ally and close confidant.

My coauthor appears to suggest that, according to the Quran, all Muslims must treat people outside the faith as kafir, and, to go further, that they must be hiding malicious motives toward them, as the Quran says, "guard yourselves against an apprehension from them."

Yet neither of these two verses contains the idea of lying to people to blend in and hide one's malicious intent, as Bob sees it. In fact, his interpretation misses some important context, which is why anyone would bond with an enemy, much less tell an open enemy who they truly are and what they believe when they know that person could pose a threat to them, Muslim or not. Soccer lover that I am, I'll use the analogy of a player telling the opposing goalkeeper which direction they intend to shoot the penalty in a sudden death situation. They just wouldn't do it. In the same way, it makes sense to keep "disbelievers who harbor hatred against your very essence" at arm's length, which is quite different from plotting against them while smiling to their face.

In Islam, we are taught that we have but one enemy. It isn't a people, a religion, or a culture. Our enemy is the devil, Iblis, and Muslims are supposed to keep their guard up against him at all times. Iblis was once a noble jinn who worshiped Allah throughout the universe. He rose in rank from teacher of the angels to gatekeeper of Paradise. Ultimately, he disobeyed Allah and was exiled from heaven. He had a final wish, which Allah granted: to live till the end of time in order to take each human and jinnkind down with him to the hellfire. Hence, the command to "call to good" or "forbid from evil" means calling to the good of which the devil disapproves and forbidding the evil that he condones.

The widespread fear of "Islam" that has been keeping my coauthor and many others awake at night for the past two decades comes courtesy of ISIS and its propaganda. ISIS claims that "their Islam" is the right way, so once again, let me provide clarity on the true faith of Islam. Take the claim of the recent pretender Abu Bakr al-Baghdadi, the late leader of ISIS, that it was possible to create a new Caliphate. In truth, that's like believing that any Tom, Dick, or Harry who claims they are Jesus is in fact Jesus. No one from the Muslim-majority countries, neither the governments nor their faith leaders, gave al-Baghdadi or ISIS legitimacy; that is proof enough that ISIS and Baghdadi don't speak for or represent Islam. Their actions aren't Shariah; they are criminal. The world needs to trace the proof back to those who backed them and who didn't.

In addition, Muslims across the globe have loudly and clearly condemned and continue to condemn terrorism, even though it makes no sense for us to feel that each one of us is responsible for what a few do in our name. And yet we are still called to answer to unfair accusations. Islam is not a religion of violence. My coauthor has his own concerns, based on certain verses in the Quran that concern killing, warfare, and attitudes toward those who are not Muslim. That's understandable. And the best way for people who fear our 1,400-year-old religion, to counter that fear, is to learn more about it. Only then will people be able to see how the name of Islam has been hijacked and used for the advancement of terror and fear.

As I pointed out in my description of jihad, the term *holy war* does not exist in the Quran, Hadith, or Islam.

The concept of holy war—defined by the *Encyclopedia Britannica* as *"any war fought by divine command or for a religious purpose"*— has of course played a role in many religions and is also found in the Bible, in the Book of Joshua.

The first holy war likely began in October 312 CE, when the Roman emperor Constantine saw a vision of the cross in the sky with the inscription *in hoc signo vinces* (in this sign you will win). Constantine, trusting the vision, had the cross inscribed on the armor of his soldiers, who won the battle against a pagan army despite being greatly outnumbered. Historians regard this as a turning point in the fortunes of Christianity.

Then, of course, there were the Crusades, which lasted from 1095 until 1291 CE, a series of Western holy wars fought to capture the sacred places in the Holy Land from the Muslims who lived there— battles intended to right past wrongs done against Christianity.

The first Crusade was initiated by Pope Urban II in 1095. He raged at the capture of the holy places and the treatment given to Christians and ordered war to restore Christianity. He also absolved of their sins those who took part in the Crusades.

While there were no Crusades in Islamic history, the Quran certainly contains verses that may seem related to such warlike events. One such verse, pointed out by my coauthor, says:

(Quran 2:194)

ٱلشَّهْرُ ٱلْحَرَامُ بِٱلشَّهْرِ ٱلْحَرَامِ وَٱلْحُرُمَٰتُ قِصَاصٌ ۚ فَمَنِ ٱعْتَدَىٰ عَلَيْكُمْ فَٱعْتَدُواْ عَلَيْهِ بِمِثْلِ مَا ٱعْتَدَىٰ عَلَيْكُمْ ۚ وَٱتَّقُواْ ٱللَّهَ وَٱعْلَمُوٓاْ أَنَّ ٱللَّهَ مَعَ ٱلْمُتَّقِينَ

The Sacred month for the sacred month and all sacred things are [under the law of] retaliation; whoever then acts aggressively against you, inflict injury on him according to the injury he has inflicted on you and be careful [of your duty] to Allah and know that Allah is with those who guard against evil.

This tells us that as humans, we Muslims will not shy away when violence is inflicted on us. It's akin to the Old Testament philosophy of an eye for an eye: If people are intent on hurting you, you will respond in kind, but only after exhausting every other possibility (ignoring your enemy, turning a blind eye, exercising patience). Standing up for yourself is always necessary. Using strength in response to harm inflicted should be a last resort.

Not unrelatedly, I happen to live in Texas, a state that permits open carry of firearms, as I mentioned already. I have often wondered who, exactly, has harmed those who choose to carry a gun. If the answer is, as I suspect, no one, I have to ask why they are carrying firearms. The carriers may very well answer that the mere possibility that someone could hurt them is reason enough for their bearing arms. In the Quranic verse I refer to above, Allah commands Muslims to be ready to defend themselves in cases where the laws of the land are not protecting them, but the main edict is to use violence for self-defense only, not to be an aggressor.

My coauthor also sees the following verse as disturbing:

(Quran 2:191)

وَٱقْتُلُوهُمْ حَيْثُ ثَقِفْتُمُوهُمْ وَأَخْرِجُوهُم مِّنْ حَيْثُ أَخْرَجُوكُمْ ۚ وَٱلْفِتْنَةُ أَشَدُّ مِنَ ٱلْقَتْلِ ۚ وَلَا تُقَٰتِلُوهُمْ عِندَ ٱلْمَسْجِدِ ٱلْحَرَامِ حَتَّىٰ يُقَٰتِلُوكُمْ فِيهِ ۖ فَإِن قَٰتَلُوكُمْ فَٱقْتُلُوهُمْ ۗ كَذَٰلِكَ جَزَآءُ ٱلْكَٰفِرِينَ

*And kill **them** wherever you overtake **them** and expel **them** from wherever **they** have expelled you, and fitnah [strife] is worse than killing. And do not fight **them** at al-Masjid al-Haram (the sacred sanctuary in Makkah) until **they** fight you there. But if **they** fight you, then kill **them**. Such is the recompense of the **disbelievers**.*

Bob wonders who the Quran is referring to when it refers to "**them**," and "**they**" above; he also takes issue with the command to "strike upon their necks," below:

(Quran 8:12)

إِذْ يُوحِى رَبُّكَ إِلَى ٱلْمَلَٰٓئِكَةِ أَنِّى مَعَكُمْ فَثَبِّتُوا۟ ٱلَّذِينَ ءَامَنُوا۟ ۚ سَأُلْقِى فِى قُلُوبِ ٱلَّذِينَ كَفَرُوا۟ ٱلرُّعْبَ فَٱضْرِبُوا۟ فَوْقَ ٱلْأَعْنَاقِ وَٱضْرِبُوا۟ مِنْهُمْ كُلَّ بَنَانٍ

*[Remember] when your Lord inspired the angels, "I am with you, so strengthen those who have believed. I will cast terror into the hearts of those who disbelieved, **so strike [them] upon the necks** and strike from them every fingertip."*

To address my coauthor's first question, "them" and "they" in Quran verse 2:191 refers to the Makkans—namely, Quraish tribespeople. Makkah was conquered by the Muslims after the resident tribes violated the truce they had written and cosigned along with Muhammad in Hudaibiyah a couple of years earlier. Specifically, as Muhammad and his believers were traveling to Makkah from Madinah to perform pilgrimage, in the 19th year of Islam (the 6th year of migration), they were intercepted by members of the Quraish tribe and barred from entering Makkah. That's when a treaty was written up, one that declared a ceasefire between the parties for a period of 10 years. Two years later, one of the clauses was violated. It so happened that Banu Khuza's tribe, an ally of the Muslims, and Banu Bakr, who were with the Meccan Quraish tribe, clashed in a fight. In this way, a vital clause of the treaty was breached, hence opening the doors for the conquest of Makkah (as described earlier) and the choice presented to the people therein to stay or leave, with ample time given to make that decision.

(Quran 9:28)

يَا أَيُّهَا الَّذِينَ آمَنُوا إِنَّمَا الْمُشْرِكُونَ نَجَسٌ فَلَا يَقْرَبُوا الْمَسْجِدَ الْحَرَامَ بَعْدَ عَامِهِمْ هَـذَا ۚ وَإِنْ خِفْتُمْ عَيْلَةً فَسَوْفَ يُغْنِيكُمُ اللَّهُ مِن فَضْلِهِ إِن شَاءَ ۚ إِنَّ اللَّهَ عَلِيمٌ حَكِيمٌ

O you who have believed, indeed the polytheists are unclean [in their belief], so let them not approach the sacred mosque after this, their [final] year. And if you fear privation, Allah will enrich you from His bounty if He wills. Indeed, Allah is Knowing and Wise.

Furthermore, to clarify, in verse 8:12, which refers to striking them upon their necks, it is evident in the beginning of the verse that Allah is commanding the angels, and not all Muslims, to strike the necks of their enemies. Specifically, when Muslims were under attack by the people of Makkah, Allah sent angels down to defend the believers. In both verses, in other words, it's necessary to understand the past circumstances and the details as to who is being commanded to do what to glean the true meaning of the verses—as is true of so much of the Quran.

Some of what's in the Quran is part of our history, including the commands to Muslims to take retaliatory measures after the conquest of Makkah. We need to understand history to understand the struggle that people endured in the past so we can live our faith without fear in the present.

More specifically, on the day of the conquest of Makkah, Muhammad said:

> *"Allah has made Makkah a sanctuary since the day He created the Heavens and the Earth, and it will remain a sanctuary by virtue of the sanctity Allah has bestowed on it till the Day of Resurrection. Fighting in it was not made lawful to anyone before me nor will it be made lawful to anyone after me, and it was not made lawful for me except for a short period of time."*
> (Hadith, Bukhari 603)

Every time we read this passage, Muslims are reminded of this incident and the struggles our forebears endured—much the same way that Americans celebrate July 4th—to commemorate the American fight for independence.

In life, context is everything, and the same holds true for the Quran. My goal, in this book, is to help provide the context and to show that, though the Quran's relevance continues, explanations of its contents can evolve, as interpretations of the Constitution shift for modern times. My only caveat is that correctly interpreting some of the verses requires a level of knowledge of the Quranic text that is only possible through extensive study.

My coauthor, of course, doesn't take issue with all of the Quran. In his view, the verses that were revealed to Muhammad in the earlier Meccan period—the first 13 years of Islam, when Muhammad was a new prophet, and he and the believers were persecuted mercilessly, suffered ridicule, were forced from their homes, and boycotted into starvation—tend to have a more peaceful tone. In contrast, the verses Muhammad received in the Madinah (post-migration) era, where Muhammad and his followers had found more stability in their new society and the message of Islam began to spread far and wide, seem, to Bob, to be less tolerant of non-Muslims and more apt to preach or condone violence. For example, the verses revealed in the first period instruct Muhammad to "only convey his message" to the people while the later revelations instruct him to take up arms against them. However, when these verses are understood in the context of the incidents behind their revelation, it's clear that Bob's beliefs are unfounded.

The Meaning of Abrogation

My coauthor wonders whether the more violent verses that were revealed later abrogate (or override) the more peaceful earlier-revealed verses. He worries that the more violent verses truly define Islam and the Quran as an extremist ideology suited only to zealots. To understand this concern, it is essential to know that the Quran had two periods of revelation: Makkan (revealed earlier) and Madinan (revealed later). In light of this, my answer to him is that the later verses do not override the earlier verses—and that the Quran is *not* focused on preaching violence. To go back in history again, the first 13-year period of revelation in Makkah was meant to introduce monotheism to a pagan people, with stories of previous prophets and nations and reflections on the creation of one God, in addition to Allah introducing Himself as the One true God. During the following 10 years—the Madinah period—the rules and laws of life for believers are laid out more explicitly, including instructions on how to defend oneself in war while adhering to the rules of engagement. To put this another way, the first 13 years were about communicating the true foundation, message, and heart of Islam. The laws and injunctions that came later were about giving Muslims detailed instructions on how to go about their daily lives in a complex, always evolving world, so Muslims would understand exactly how to live life and honor the rights of others so as to please God and enter Heaven in the afterlife.

Still, 99% of all the commands in the Quran came down in the final 10 years (post-migration). In my coauthor's view, the latter commands regarding war override the more peaceful premises of the earlier revelations, thereby abrogating them. The truth is that these two sections can and do coexist equally. To explain that, I want to delve deeper into what abrogation really means.

As for specific verses (as opposed to the two separate periods of revelation), it is important to understand that in the Quran, certain verses were revealed initially, then overwritten (removed and replaced, or removed altogether) by Allah during the course of the 23-year revelation. This is known in Arabic as *naskh*. Only Allah was able to abrogate or remove a verse, and then only during the course of revelation. Once Allah completed the Quran, abrogation was no longer possible. The Quran is now complete. No part of the existing Quran can abrogate or cancel out another part, nor can anyone abrogate any portion of it. In short, no human has the right to abrogate a verse, passage, or any part of the Quran.

(Quran 6:115)

وَتَمَّتْ كَلِمَتُ رَبِّكَ صِدْقًا وَعَدْلًا ۚ لَّا مُبَدِّلَ لِكَلِمَاتِهِ ۚ وَهُوَ السَّمِيعُ الْعَلِيمُ

And the word of your Lord has been fulfilled in truth and in justice. None can alter His words, and He is the Hearing, the Knowing.

This means that Makkan period verses cannot be overruled by the ones revealed later in Madinah; for one thing, their subject matter is different. The core values and tenets revealed in the first 13 years are the fundamentals of Islamic belief. Take those away and there is no meaning behind any command.

Interestingly, radical fundamentalists who cling to a few verses— e.g., "kill them wherever you overtake them"—are doing the same thing Islamophobes do: ignoring the message and overarching theme of Islam and the revelation of the Quran.

Suicide Bombers

Another concern expressed by my coauthor comes from verses similar to the following:

(Quran 43:32)

أَهُمْ يَقْسِمُونَ رَحْمَتَ رَبِّكَ ۚ نَحْنُ قَسَمْنَا بَيْنَهُم مَّعِيشَتَهُمْ فِى ٱلْحَيَوٰةِ ٱلدُّنْيَا ۚ وَرَفَعْنَا بَعْضَهُمْ فَوْقَ بَعْضٍ دَرَجَٰتٍ

Will they distribute the mercy of your Lord? **We** *distribute among them their livelihood in the life of this world, and* **We** *have exalted some of them above others in degrees.*

My coauthor wonders about the word *we*. To explain, when Allah is speaking in the Quran, He frequently uses the plural *We* rather than *I*.

(Quran 15:9)

إِنَّا نَحْنُ نَزَّلْنَا الذِّكْرَ وَإِنَّا لَهُ لَحَافِظُونَ

Indeed, it is We who sent down the Qur'an and indeed, We will be its guardian.

That *We* troubles my coauthor and others because, he believes, it suggests that Allah is including others alongside Himself, presumably even suicide bombers or other extremists. That is incorrect. First, when Allah uses the plural tense, He is referring only to Himself, His majesty, and His glory. Essentially, "We" is an honorific, referring to Allah's majesty alone and not to anyone else, especially suicide bombers.

Which brings me to Osama Bin Laden and the suicide bombers he commanded on 9/11. First, it is important to understand that before killing others, suicide bombers are already determined to kill themselves. But in Islam, suicide is prohibited.

(Quran 4:29)

وَلَا تَقْتُلُوٓاْ أَنفُسَكُمْ ۚ إِنَّ ٱللَّهَ كَانَ بِكُمْ رَحِيمًا

And do not kill yourselves. Indeed, Allah is to you ever Merciful.

According to the teachings of Islam, anyone who commits suicide is prevented from entering Paradise—and worse. The Prophet said, as stated in a Hadith:

> *"He who commits suicide by throttling shall keep on throttling himself in the Hell-Fire forever and he who commits suicide by stabbing himself shall keep on stabbing himself in the Hell-Fire."* (Hadith, Bukhari 1365)

In Islam, we believe that death is the continuation of our lifelong journey to meet our Creator, Allah. According to Islamic teachings, living a life that is pleasing to Allah will grant us admission to Paradise. For true believers, however, Paradise is not the aim; the goal is to see Allah with one's eyes in Paradise, as this is exclusive for the inhabitants of Paradise alone. Hence, good actions and deeds in this world will grant someone admission to Paradise, uniting them with Allah. Muslims who die in the course of teaching, or providing aid after a tragedy, or who are otherwise doing good for Allah, meet the definition of *shaheed,* or martyrs. Similarly, a person who dies on a battlefield during a war while fighting for a just cause is also considered a martyr. But killing an innocent person just because they are different from you is not a good deed. Suicide bombers and rogue militants need to be reminded of that, because their cause is selfish, unjustified, tyrannical, and, most of all, cowardly. People who kill others without justifiable cause, such as during an unjust war or in a terrorist attack on innocent civilians, are not martyrs; they are criminals.

Self-defense, on the other hand, is not violence. When others threaten the livelihood, safety, and rights of innocent people, it's imperative to stand up to those bullies and confront them by whatever means necessary, even if that means war.

Islam Is Not a Political Movement

There is a widespread perception among non-Muslims that the Quran is political—a book with an agenda that faithful Muslims will use as a guide when they take over existing governments in non-Muslim countries. My coauthor and others also worry that if Muslims become the dominant majority, those who don't comply with Allah's commandments will be punished. The confusion is understandable. The Quran *is* meant to be a message for all of humanity. But its tenets are applicable only to those who embrace Islam and the Quran as their way of life. When the Quran states that it is for all humankind, it is referring to the fact that there is no limit to who can benefit from its words; its gifts do not discriminate.

(Quran 81:27,28)

إِنْ هُوَ إِلَّا ذِكْرٌ لِّلْعَٰلَمِينَ لِمَن شَاءَ مِنكُمْ أَن يَسْتَقِيمَ

It is nothing but Good Counsel for everyone in the world, for everyone of you who wishes to follow the Straight Way;

That doesn't mean that everyone must adopt it, nor that the goal of Islam is world domination. Muslims must use their Islam to reform only themselves, not society as a whole. As I've said, the Quran is both a spiritual guidebook and, for those who adhere to it, a way of life.

I want to tell the story of a former student of mine, Ramzy Kilic, who, like my coauthor, took a trip to meet with Terry Jones after Jones announced his hate campaign and intention to burn thousands of Qurans, causing Muslims to riot here and abroad and a fatwa to be issued for Jones's death. (Incidentally, the violent response from

Muslims to Terry Jones's threat was also a consequence of emotions running wild—and of ignorance.)

My student's attempt to speak with Jones was an attempt to do the opposite: to create clarity. And after his visit, Ramzy told me that he had been the first Muslim that Terry Jones had ever met or spoken with. He recounted his conversation:

"I explained to him what Islam is and what we believe as Muslims. He was not aware of how we believed in Jesus (peace be upon him). Despite this, his view is that of many hard-core evangelists who believe that the Bible is the inerrant word of God and all else is of the devil. I asked him if the Jews were of the devil, and he said yes. I did not feel that he had anger towards Muslims, but that he just wanted to make the point that anything outside Christianity was of the devil. I never felt threatened or disrespected. I asked him to remove the yard signs he had placed (depicting propaganda against Islam) but told him that my request was not meant to take away his freedom of speech, but to realize that his message and signage could encourage extremists to harm Muslims. He obviously refused and then later decided to double down by having 'International burn the Quran day,' which backfired on him, especially after we brought together all the other faiths in town to counter his day with 'International read the Quran day,' along with a promise to provide a copy of the Quran to anyone who asked for it."

Hate is founded on ignorance—and hate goes in both directions. Rogue groups of any faith should be rejected, along with their propaganda.

Fatwa

That brings me to the subject of *fatwa*, defined as a ruling meant to provide clarity and direction for a particular question, concern, or problem. It is like a doctor's prescription for a patient in that it is specific rather than something meant for the masses. And in the West, it is pretty much impossible to utter the word without thinking of the author Salman Rushdie. I can vividly remember when *The Satanic Verses* was published, though I was only a child at the time. Muslims in Canada protested this book along with other Muslims across the globe, and I went with my father to attend one of the local demonstrations. But even as a boy, I knew that the anger I witnessed all around me wouldn't be resolved with a fatwa calling for Rushdie's death nor by people taking justice into their own hands at the request of one man, the supreme leader of Iran. As a scholar, I can also say today that a fatwa wasn't meant to be used in this way—despite the impression of most non-Muslims (and many Muslims as well).

For one thing, a fatwa is nonbinding. To be more precise, it is a legal ruling given by a qualified Muslim (known as a mufti), a ruling specifically focused on an individual. What it is not is a blanket command to kill. And while a mufti does have the power to make a ruling, he has no power to enforce it.

The notion today, both inside and outside the faith, that fatwa plays an important role in governing the actions and faith of Muslims in general (aside from the one who seeks a fatwa), is flawed. Many Muslims even believe that a fatwa takes precedence over the direction and opinions of scholars in their respective communities. Similarly, many non-Muslims believe that a fatwa can be issued by just about anyone who appears to resemble a Muslim, even if it's issued by someone living in a cave or a tent, like Osama Bin Laden (who was never qualified to issue a fatwa in the first place). Any qualified mufti knows the boundaries of using fatwas and issuing them. My coauthor is one of the many people who equate Shariah and fatwa, but they are not one and the same. Shariah is made up of the consensus of learned people and juristic analogy, in addition to the Quran and Hadith, the four branches of Shariah that I defined in the beginning. Nothing and no one supersedes the Quran and Shariah law, including fatwa.

Islam Is Not Wahhabism

My coauthor also repeatedly expresses concern about Wahhabism and its impact on Muslims in America. What I want him and everyone else to understand, first and foremost, is that the Wahhabis, who originated in the Kingdom of Saudi Arabia, are not the face of Islam nor the Muslim world.

That may surprise both Muslims and non-Muslims. After all, the Islamic faith was born in Makkah (now in Saudi Arabia), home to two of the three holiest sites in Islam: the Great Mosque in Makkah and the Prophet's Mosque in Madinah. Yet Islam is not confined to any one people or country, and neither are its teachings. Indeed, Islam is a global religion; there are 56 Muslim countries and approximately 50 nations with a Muslim majority.

So where does that leave Wahhabism? It is an Islamic reform movement followed by Muslims in Saudi Arabia and in many countries around the world. For historical context, it was launched by Sheikh Muhammed ibn Abdul Wahhab in Central Arabia in the 18th century and was adopted by the Saud (ruling) family in 1744; it has dominated that country ever since. Wahhabi theology and jurisprudence are based on the teachings of a 13th-century theologian, Ibn Taymiyyah, and the legal school of Ahmad ibn Hanbal, a renowned jurist from the 8th century. Essentially, both sources stress the literal interpretation of the Quran and Hadith and the establishment of an Islamic society based only on these two bodies of literature. Not surprisingly, then, Wahhabis believe that they alone practice the correct Islam. They condemn all other practices and sources of interpretation as "innovations," and they don't mean that in a complimentary way.

Why, then, has Wahhabism been so successful in terms of becoming the "name brand" of Islam? Blame the relationship the Wahhabis forged with the Saudi monarchy, evident through two branches of law enforcement in the kingdom: 1) the civil police that enforce the law, and 2) the religious police that enforce not only their own interpretation of the religion, but also strict codes of public behavior—for instance, the mandatory observance of Islamic rituals and gender segregation.

To give you a sense of just how much authority Wahhabis have in Saudi Arabia, preservationists estimate that, since 1985, up to 95% of the historic and sacred sites around Makkah and Madinah have been razed by the government. Why? Islam prohibits the worship of shrines, tombs, and sacred objects, and over the years, the Wahhabis have found the behavior of passionate visitors to these sites to be offensive. So they instructed the Saudi rulers to destroy many of these early sites and objects. Wouldn't it have been a better idea to educate people as to the correct way to visit these historical sights— i.e., showing respect, not reverence?

I have seen this kind of authoritarian thinking up close, while on the way to the holy mosque in Makkah to do the *tawaf,* which is circumambulating the *Ka'bah* (house of Allah). That's when

I noticed several Wahhabi police harassing a man who, to my eyes, appeared helpless and defenseless. It hurt me to my core that this man was being treated this way, so I interjected and asked, "What's going on?" One of them pulled me aside while another approached and asked if I spoke Urdu or English. I said I could speak either. Yet another person approached and started schooling me in a harsh way about how touching the columns of the mosque and revering them is *shirk* (meaning treating something as equal to Allah) and therefore not acceptable. As people looked on, these religious policemen shifted their focus from the man I'd tried to defend, ganging up on me and basically accusing me of committing a major sin.

Later, I learned that this older man had been touching a specific pillar that was believed to be where the *Buraq*, a heavenly animal, was secured with a rope on the night the Prophet Muhammad made the journey to Jerusalem and then ascended to heaven. Perhaps this man was touching the pillar incorrectly, but the response of the police was reprehensible, as was their attempt to intimidate me for trying to help.

And yet, despite this kind of behavior and repressiveness, there's no doubt that the Wahhabis have shown great skill in propagating the message of this ultraconservative form of Islam. I'd go so far as to call them a veritable public relations machine, spewing forth free literature and Quran translations and interpretation books, along with cassettes, CDs, and videos. Arab Muslims, non-Arab Muslims, converts, and anyone curious to know about the religion have access to these materials. The fact that this public education is taking place in the land of Islam's origin only strengthens and legitimizes their message. Beyond that, the Muslim world flocks to Saudi Arabia for pilgrimage throughout the year. Millions of people enter and exit their ports, where they come into contact with Wahhabis distributing these materials far beyond their mosques.

Their ideology has also been spread via human ambassadors, courtesy of the free Islamic education courses provided by Saudi Arabia, attended primarily by young Muslim men from across the globe, who are invited to study in the kingdom with all their expenses paid. By educating the future generation of imams and scholars of the faith from around the world, including in America, the Wahhabis helped spread their brand of Islam everywhere—an astonishingly effective campaign.

But, as my father liked to say, nothing is free in this life.

The hard-line approach to Islam that characterizes Wahhabism is not the Islam that Prophet Muhammad taught to the world. But as long as millions of Muslims and non-Muslims consider it to be a legitimate representation of Islam, the leadership and authority of an entire faith will be ceded to a twisted ideology, one that often doesn't correspond with the true tenets of Islam.

And that's not the only problem for Islam. Bob suggests that another problem is the influential Deoband school of Islam, which dates back to 1867, dominating the Indian subcontinent as well as South Asia. Deobandism has used its educational curriculum to train scholars and imams throughout the world. The current Taliban are believed to be a product of the Deoband school; it may surprise you to know that I am also a product of that ideology. My institute in the U.K. followed the Deobandi curriculum, which, in my opinion and experience, does not inspire extremism. My criticism is that its cookie-cutter method of teaching has produced too many closed-minded scholars who aren't interested in engaging in the real world. Not only has this resulted in Deobandi scholars passing absurd fatwas, but it has kept them apart from the modern world, since they have long prohibited listening to the radio, using a microphone for prayer, or watching TV. And they've taken that mindset further even in recent times. Today, too many contemporary Deobandi scholars have a habit of automatically prohibiting things they don't know anything about (cryptocurrency is one example), simply because they aren't mentioned in our sacred text or because they are disinclined to do the legwork needed to understand what is involved before making a ruling. This is also a sign of closed-mindedness.

A notable difference between the Wahhabis and the Deobandis, however, is that the former are backed by a government and all that comes with that: funding, public education, promotion, and the stamp of legitimacy from the rulers of a country seen as the leader of Islam. In contrast, the Deobandis have a different, more decentralized structure (as opposed to the top-down structure of Wahhabis), which is why you will find the label "Deoband" worn by a wide array of Islamic practitioners, from the Taliban to present-day local imams in the West.

In recent years, the Saudi Crown Prince, Mohammad Bin Salman, better known as MBS, has made it clear that he wants to reshape the conservative face of his country into a new, more modern and progressive image. In his Vision 2030 declaration, he has said that he wants women to hold prominent political posts as well as be granted more personal freedoms, like being able to drive and go out alone. Another goal is to open the country to the world and encourage tourism, as evidenced by the Saudi Arabian travel billboards that have appeared in Times Square in New York City in recent years.

To accomplish all this, MBS is going after Wahhabism, accusing his kingdom's Wahhabi establishment of being out of date and of propagating a faulty interpretation of Islamic scriptures. Speaking on national television in 2021 during Ramadan, he defended his promotion of secular Western entertainment in the kingdom, which had long been condemned as heretical by Wahhabi clerics. He has also set about sidelining the kingdom's Wahhabi scholars and preachers who, nevertheless, still command millions of followers in the country and beyond.

As part of his 2030 vision, MBS is also working to restore more than 100 historical sites in Makkah and Madinah that were destroyed because of the Wahhabi influence. In an interview with Fox News, MBS was asked if he was trying to change Saudi laws to make them more "realistic." His response: "More realistic for us as Saudi, not for foreign people," which made it seem as if he were backpedaling. But then he went on to say that he believed current laws were "far away from realistic for us as Saudi," asking, rhetorically, "Do we have bad laws? Yes. Are we changing that? Yes."

To me, these words make it clear that he is focusing on the root of the problem with the Saudi legal system—which is Wahhabi ideology.

Still, the question remains: Given its repressive nature, why did Wahhabism remain uncontested for so long, both within the kingdom and beyond it? In a 75-minute meeting with editors and reporters at *The Washington Post* during his visit to the U.S. in March of 2018, MBS laid the blame for the dominance of Wahhabism squarely on the U.S. and Saudi Arabia's other Western allies, who, during the height of the Cold War, urged the country to invest in mosques and madrassas (Islamic religious schools) to prevent the Soviet Union from making inroads into Muslim countries by firmly embedding Islam into the population.

While the future of Wahhabism currently lies with MBS, what's clear is that there is a huge shift occurring, one that suggests that this sect is not long for the Saudi kingdom. In part, that has to do with demographics. The current movement to push Saudi Arabia in a more liberal direction is most likely to be taken up by young people, who comprise 63% of the Saudi population and are more likely to have visited America or trained, studied, or even lived there. What's certain is that nearly all of these young people have watched American sitcoms and movies and are connected to the same social media outlets as others in their generation around the world. More than their elders, they have a sense of what an open culture looks like. And as once-forbidden activities become normalized in their homeland, including going to movies, concerts, and clubs, they are likely to embrace these changes.

I am pleased that the iron grip of the Wahhabis is now being challenged by MBS in Saudi Arabia, a challenge that could potentially weaken Wahhabism in the kingdom, which may potentially weaken Wahhabi influence globally. Which leaves us with a troubling conundrum: As tempting as it is to celebrate the seeming move away from Wahhabism, right now, there is nothing to replace it. That's why I hope that Muslims around the world, including those who follow the Wahhabi ideology, can eventually find their way to a less extreme, more moderate form of Islam, one that emphasizes individuals' connection to their Creator and the Islamic way of life rather than repressing large swaths of the population (i.e., women) by not allowing them to drive, for instance. But whatever direction the faith moves in Saudi Arabia or elsewhere, the crucial thing to remember about Islam is that the Quran is the word of Allah for all time.

(Quran 16:89)

وَنَزَّلْنَا عَلَيْكَ ٱلْكِتَـٰبَ تِبْيَـٰنًا لِّكُلِّ شَىْءٍ وَهُدًى وَرَحْمَةً وَبُشْرَىٰ لِلْمُسْلِمِينَ

*and We have revealed the Book to you explaining clearly
everything, and a guidance and mercy and good news for
those who submit.*

What the Quran continues to explain clearly is that living a life
of moderation, not of extremism, must always be the lens through
which we attempt to understand the context of any verse at any
time.

(Quran 2:143)

وَكَذَٰلِكَ جَعَلْنَاكُمْ أُمَّةً وَسَطًا لِّتَكُونُوا شُهَدَاءَ عَلَى النَّاسِ وَيَكُونَ الرَّسُولُ عَلَيْكُمْ
شَهِيدًا ۚ

*And it is thus that We appointed you to be the community of
the middle way so that you might be witnesses to all mankind
and the Messenger might be a witness to you.*

Islam, today, needs restoration to that middle way, not reformation.
Regardless of the rapid cultural changes we are all experiencing
in today's society, the values of the Quran (exemplifying Islam
through one's upright character) remain the same for all Muslims.
What Muslims need to do is reaffirm their faith values. It is not
Islam that needs to be changed, restored, or modernized. Rather,
more Muslims, including religious leaders, need to be better
educated as to what Islam truly is. The general public, both
Muslim and non-Muslim, should be educated enough to be able
to recognize when any political figure, media outlet, or religious
leader is misrepresenting or hijacking the name of the religion

to serve their personal agendas. If this were the case, the Muslim world would not be experiencing the problems it faces today, nor would we have ongoing conflicts about the acceptability of each new social trend that comes up, whether the question of current fashions fitting under Islam's dress code, or whether marrying anyone you love should be acceptable because love should reign supreme. These questions continue to divide us. As fellow Muslims, our faith should unite us, not divide us.

By making this call for change, I know I am inviting condemnation and even putting myself at risk at the hands of Islamic fundamentalists. But the time has come to create a movement that makes it clear to the world that Islam is not and never has been a religion of extremists and terrorists, much less one that is bent on upending the world order by any means possible. What I'm calling for isn't radical; it's necessary, and it involves taking steps to restore the true meaning of Islam, one that will align the public's perception of our beautiful faith with reality.

Muslims, Jews, Christians, and Tolerance

The mutual friendship that my coauthor and I have built over the years is no anomaly. Muslims are allowed to befriend anyone outside their faith—with some boundaries. However, my coauthor Bob is one of many who see the verse below as a command from Allah forbidding Muslims from befriending people outside of Islam.

(Quran 5:51)

يَـٰٓأَيُّهَا ٱلَّذِينَ ءَامَنُوا۟ لَا تَتَّخِذُوا۟ ٱلْيَهُودَ وَٱلنَّصَـٰرَىٰٓ أَوْلِيَآءَ ۘ بَعْضُهُمْ أَوْلِيَآءُ بَعْضٍ ۚ وَمَن يَتَوَلَّهُم مِّنكُمْ فَإِنَّهُۥ مِنْهُمْ ۗ إِنَّ ٱللَّهَ لَا يَهْدِى ٱلْقَوْمَ ٱلظَّـٰلِمِينَ

O you who have believed, do not take those Jews and those
Christians as allies who are allies of one another. And whoever
is an ally to them among you—then indeed, he is [one] of
them. Indeed, Allah guides not the wrongful people.

Let me clarify.

Islam does teach its followers that Jews and Christians who
are allied with one another should not be taken on as protectors,
meaning that any alliance that might have been forged for personal
or worldly gain or that might result in compromising one's values,
teachings, and identity is forbidden.

That doesn't mean Muslims cannot befriend those outside
the faith, nor that everyone outside the faith is evil. Rather, Islam
inspires Muslims to take each other (i.e., believers) as protectors and
guarantors, trusting them or confiding in them over non-Muslims.
This is due to the history of betrayal against the Muslims in early
Islam (after migration to Madinah) even after an interfaith treaty
was signed to prevent this from happening. (Again, context is all.)

The verse above also refers to the fact that Islam will only get
stronger when Muslims support, protect, and encourage one another
above others. But it has nothing to do with the permissibility of
friendship. To put it into perspective, just because you're a Lakers
fan and I'm a Mavs fan doesn't mean we are, by default, enemies.
We just support different teams. With regard to befriending and
dealing with others who are outside the faith, in Quran 60:8, Allah
clarifies:

(Quran 60:8)

لَّا يَنْهَىٰكُمُ ٱللَّهُ عَنِ ٱلَّذِينَ لَمْ يُقَٰتِلُوكُمْ فِى ٱلدِّينِ وَلَمْ يُخْرِجُوكُم مِّن دِيَٰرِكُمْ أَن

تَبَرُّوهُمْ وَتُقْسِطُوٓا۟ إِلَيْهِمْ ۚ إِنَّ ٱللَّهَ يُحِبُّ ٱلْمُقْسِطِينَ

Allah does not forbid you from those who do not fight you because of religion and do not expel you from your homes— from being righteous toward them and acting justly toward them. Indeed, Allah loves those who act justly.

And in Quran 60:9, He clarifies who we cannot befriend:

(Quran 60:9)

إِنَّمَا يَنْهَىٰكُمُ ٱللَّهُ عَنِ ٱلَّذِينَ قَٰتَلُوكُمْ فِى ٱلدِّينِ وَأَخْرَجُوكُم مِّن دِيَٰرِكُمْ وَظَٰهَرُوا۟ عَلَىٰٓ إِخْرَاجِكُمْ أَن تَوَلَّوْهُمْ ۚ وَمَن يَتَوَلَّهُمْ فَأُو۟لَٰٓئِكَ هُمُ ٱلظَّٰلِمُونَ

Allah only forbids you from those who fight you because of religion and expel you from your homes and aid in your expulsion—[forbids] that you make allies of them. And whoever makes allies of them, then it is those who are the wrongdoers.

The command provides a framework for making individual assessments; it is not an overarching condemnation of a certain people, faith, or culture. If you need proof of this, look no further than my friendship with Bob.

The Quran also does not encourage hatred of Jews, despite what Bob believes. My coauthor refers to an array of verses that he sees as anti-Semitic and espousing violence against the Jewish people. The problem here isn't translation or interpretation, but a lack of context.

Let me explain. In two verses that are similar, Allah speaks of the high regard and virtue he once gave to Bani Israel, or, as we know them through the Quran today, "the Children of Israel."

(Quran 2:47) and (Quran 2:122) are identical verses:

(Quran 2:47), (Quran 2:122)

يَٰبَنِىٓ إِسۡرَٰٓءِيلَ ٱذۡكُرُواْ نِعۡمَتِىَ ٱلَّتِىٓ أَنۡعَمۡتُ عَلَيۡكُمۡ وَأَنِّى فَضَّلۡتُكُمۡ عَلَى ٱلۡعَٰلَمِينَ

*O Children of Israel, remember My favor which I have
bestowed upon you and that I preferred you over
the worlds.*

Who are the Children of Israel? They are a people to whom
Allah sent almost all prophets, including Moses and Jesus (peace
be upon them both). Allah selected them to receive His messengers,
His word, and His favors. But then something happened. A notable
number of them rejected the word, hurt the messengers, and even
killed some of them. They disregarded the countless favors that
Allah had bestowed. In return, Allah punished those among them
who had done wrong, but not the entire community of the Children
of Israel.

Bob states, "By way of example, Quran 5:60 says the Jews are
'cursed' and some of them were turned into 'apes and swine.'" But
while the verse actually names Jews, the reference is to *those* Jews
who were entrusted with the faith but who failed to uphold that
trust. They believed in the message but then betrayed the messenger
and God.

(Quran 5:60)

قُلۡ هَلۡ أُنَبِّئُكُم بِشَرٍّ مِّن ذَٰلِكَ مَثُوبَةً عِندَ ٱللَّهِ ۚ مَن لَّعَنَهُ ٱللَّهُ وَغَضِبَ عَلَيۡهِ وَجَعَلَ
مِنۡهُمُ ٱلۡقِرَدَةَ وَٱلۡخَنَازِيرَ وَعَبَدَ ٱلطَّٰغُوتَ ۚ أُوْلَٰٓئِكَ شَرٌّ مَّكَانًا وَأَضَلُّ عَن سَوَآءِ
ٱلسَّبِيلِ

*Say, "Shall I inform you of [what is] worse than that as a
penalty from Allah? [It is that of] those whom Allah has cursed
and with whom He became angry and made some of them
apes and pigs and slaves of Taghut (idols). Those are worse in
position and further astray from the sound path."*

To provide context to the answer I gave my coauthor when we first
met, Allah did transform some Jews into monkeys as punishment
for their disobedience to Him on Shabbat. The Quran documents
this occurrence as factual.

(Quran 2:65)

وَلَقَدْ عَلِمْتُمُ ٱلَّذِينَ ٱعْتَدَوْا۟ مِنكُمْ فِى ٱلسَّبْتِ فَقُلْنَا لَهُمْ كُونُوا۟ قِرَدَةً خَـٰسِـِٔينَ

*And you had already known about those who transgressed
among you concerning the sabbath, and We said to them, "Be
monkeys, despised."*

To be clear, those punished didn't become the bloodline of the
Jewish people today. They were punished and then they perished. In
a Hadith, the following is recorded:

*"A man once said, 'O Messenger of Allah, are the monkeys
and pigs that exist today those who have been transformed?'
The Prophet said: 'Allah does not enable those who have been
transformed to have offspring or children. The monkeys and
pigs existed before that.'"* (Hadith, Muslim 2663)

Another point to consider: If turning disobedient Jews into pigs
and monkeys is described in the Quran, what is the purpose of this
passage? Is it to humiliate the Jewish people? I assume that is why

Bob brought it up at that lecture, but that's not the case, as becomes clear in the next verse:

(Quran 2:66)

فَجَعَلْنَـٰهَا نَكَـٰلًا لِّمَا بَيْنَ يَدَيْهَا وَمَا خَلْفَهَا وَمَوْعِظَةً لِّلْمُتَّقِينَ

So we made them an example to those who witnessed it and those who came after it, and a lesson for those who fear Allah.

In other words, Allah is warning the followers of Islam that the same punishment would befall them if they disobeyed His commandments. In a Hadith, the Prophet Muhammad said to his people:

"Among this nation, people will be transformed into monkeys and pigs, swallowed up in the earth, and pelted with stones."
(Hadith, Tirmidhi 1802)

Such verses make it easy to assume, as my coauthor does, that Allah is bashing all the Jews. But the purpose of Allah speaking ill of those Jews (or anyone) in the Quran is to warn the followers of the Quran what will happen if they do the same. Allah is disciplining the Muslims and previous followers of the faith by reminding them of certain wrongs committed by some of the faithful.

Similarly, all the vices committed by the Children of Israel, including arrogance, disobedience, mockery, and so on, are described in the Quran to warn followers to stay vigilant against those traits in themselves. In a Hadith, the Prophet Muhammad warned:

"You will follow the ways of those nations who were before you, span by span and cubit by cubit so much so that even if

they entered a hole of a mastigure [lizard], you would follow
them.' We said, 'O Allah's Messenger! Do you mean the Jews
and the Christians?' He said, 'Who else?'"
(Hadith, Bukhari 7320)

Allah's goal is not to criticize Bani Israel, but to teach the faithful
of today how seriously Allah takes a violation of a trust. It is a
warning to be cautious, not a command to perpetrate harm on non-
Muslims. If it were, then why, in the same Quran, would Allah tell
us that he once favored them?

(Quran 45:16)

وَلَقَدْ آتَيْنَا بَنِي إِسْرَائِيلَ الْكِتَابَ وَالْحُكْمَ وَالنُّبُوَّةَ وَرَزَقْنَاهُم مِّنَ الطَّيِّبَاتِ
وَفَضَّلْنَاهُمْ عَلَى الْعَالَمِينَ

And We certainly gave the Children of Israel the Scripture and
judgment and prophethood, and We provided them with good
things and preferred them over the worlds.

Just as the followers of Moses and Jesus submitted, Allah is
asking Muslims to submit to Him. By definition, a Muslim is
someone who, upon receiving a revelation, submits to it. Recipients
of the Torah (in Arabic, the holy Jewish scripture is referred
to as the Tawrat) and the Bible (the Gospel of Jesus, in Arabic,
referred to as the Injil) were Muslims. That may sound odd, but
the word *Muslim* is a generic term for a devotee. It is not a name
for someone who practices Islam alone, as the word is customarily
used today.

Abraham, the father of all three major faiths (Judaism, Christianity,
and Islam), was commanded to submit, and he did.

(Quran 2:131)

إِذْ قَالَ لَهُ رَبُّهُ أَسْلِمْ قَالَ أَسْلَمْتُ لِرَبِّ ٱلْعَٰلَمِينَ

When his Lord said to him, "Submit—Be a Muslim," he said:
"I submit myself to the Lord of the worlds—I am a Muslim."

And that is why Allah states Abraham was a Muslim.

(Quran 3:67)

مَا كَانَ إِبْرَٰهِيمُ يَهُودِيًّا وَلَا نَصْرَانِيًّا وَلَٰكِن كَانَ حَنِيفًا مُّسْلِمًا وَمَا كَانَ مِنَ ٱلْمُشْرِكِينَ

Abraham was neither a Jew nor a Christian, but he was one
inclining toward truth, a Muslim [submitting to Allah]. And
he was not of the polytheists.

In reality, anyone who submits to the will of God is a Muslim. Muslim is a state of a people, not a type of people. All followers of the one true God, all the way to Abraham and even before, submitted to His will. Submission is Islam, and one that submits is a Muslim. Think of it as referring to someone as "a person of faith."

(Quran 3:64)

قُلْ يَٰأَهْلَ ٱلْكِتَٰبِ تَعَالَوْاْ إِلَىٰ كَلِمَةٍ سَوَآءٍ بَيْنَنَا وَبَيْنَكُمْ أَلَّا نَعْبُدَ إِلَّا ٱللَّهَ وَلَا نُشْرِكَ بِهِۦ شَيْئًا وَلَا يَتَّخِذَ بَعْضُنَا بَعْضًا أَرْبَابًا مِّن دُونِ ٱللَّهِ ۚ فَإِن تَوَلَّوْاْ فَقُولُواْ ٱشْهَدُواْ بِأَنَّا مُسْلِمُونَ

Say, "O People of the Scripture, come to an equitable
proposition between us and you—that we will not worship
except Allah and not associate anything with Him and not

take one another as lords instead of Allah. But if they turn away, then say, 'Bear witness that we are Muslims [submitting to Him].'"

In other words, Allah commands Muslims and those who were recipients of the previous revelations, namely the Jews and the Christians, to come together and find common ground, without compromise or pandering. And I believe we can certainly work together for a common cause, without Jews (or Christians) adopting the Islamic faith first (as Bob assumed earlier).

In the same way, the Quran is not considered to be a "correction" of the Bible, as Bob postulates. Rather, it is a continuation of revelation just as the New Testament is a continuation of the Old Testament. Additionally, the Quran serves to clarify any misinterpretations or misrepresentations that occurred in previous revelations.

(Quran 5:46)

وَقَفَّيْنَا عَلَىٰٓ ءَاثَٰرِهِم بِعِيسَى ٱبْنِ مَرْيَمَ مُصَدِّقًا لِّمَا بَيْنَ يَدَيْهِ مِنَ ٱلتَّوْرَىٰةِ وَءَاتَيْنَٰهُ ٱلْإِنجِيلَ فِيهِ هُدًى وَنُورٌ وَمُصَدِّقًا لِّمَا بَيْنَ يَدَيْهِ مِنَ ٱلتَّوْرَىٰةِ وَهُدًى وَمَوْعِظَةً لِّلْمُتَّقِينَ

And We sent, following in their footsteps, Jesus, the son of Mary, confirming that which came before him in the Torah; and We gave him the Gospel, in which was guidance and light and confirming that which preceded it of the Torah as guidance and instruction for the righteous.

This affirms that Jesus came to continue the message of the Torah.

How does the Quran speak of the Torah? In the most positive way:

(Quran 5:44)

إِنَّا أَنزَلْنَا ٱلتَّوْرَىٰةَ فِيهَا هُدًى وَنُورٌ ۚ يَحْكُمُ بِهَا ٱلنَّبِيُّونَ ٱلَّذِينَ أَسْلَمُواْ لِلَّذِينَ هَادُواْ وَٱلرَّبَّـٰنِيُّونَ وَٱلْأَحْبَارُ بِمَا ٱسْتُحْفِظُواْ مِن كِتَـٰبِ ٱللَّهِ وَكَانُواْ عَلَيْهِ شُهَدَآءَ ۚ فَلَا تَخْشَوُاْ ٱلنَّاسَ وَٱخْشَوْنِ وَلَا تَشْتَرُواْ بِـَٔايَـٰتِى ثَمَنًا قَلِيلًا ۚ وَمَن لَّمْ يَحْكُم بِمَآ أَنزَلَ ٱللَّهُ فَأُوْلَـٰئِكَ هُمُ ٱلْكَـٰفِرُونَ

Indeed, We sent down the Torah, in which was guidance and light. The prophets who submitted [to Allah] judged by it for the Jews, as did the rabbis and scholars by that with which they were entrusted with the Scripture of Allah, and they were witnesses thereto. So do not fear the people but fear Me, and do not exchange My verses for a small price. And whoever does not judge by what Allah has revealed—then it is those who are the disbelievers.

Why does the Quran speak about the earlier revelations? Because the Quran was sent by the same Lord.

(Quran 3:3)

نَزَّلَ عَلَيْكَ ٱلْكِتَـٰبَ بِٱلْحَقِّ مُصَدِّقًا لِّمَا بَيْنَ يَدَيْهِ وَأَنزَلَ ٱلتَّوْرَىٰةَ وَٱلْإِنجِيلَ

He has sent down upon you, [O Muhammad], the Book in truth, confirming what was before it. And He revealed the Torah and the Gospel.

Every one of the preceding revelations was a follow-up to the former, the New Testament to the Torah, and the Quran to the New Testament. Think of the Quran as an update, rather than a correction. Indeed, the goal of referring to those Old and New Testament revelations in such a positive light is to highlight the legitimacy given to them by Allah, albeit for a specific period in time. Ultimately, Allah gives that legitimacy to the Quran, which is the final, boundless revelation. The instructions and commands from Allah in the Quran overwrite the commands and instructions in the previous revelations for those who are willing to submit to His will.

Bob referenced the following verse, claiming that the Quran explicitly states that it is a more complete explanation of the Bible:

(Quran 10:37)

وَمَا كَانَ هَـٰذَا ٱلْقُرْءَانُ أَن يُفْتَرَىٰ مِن دُونِ ٱللَّهِ وَلَـٰكِن تَصْدِيقَ ٱلَّذِى بَيْنَ يَدَيْهِ وَتَفْصِيلَ ٱلْكِتَـٰبِ لَا رَيْبَ فِيهِ مِن رَّبِّ ٱلْعَـٰلَمِينَ

And it was not [possible] for this Quran to be produced by someone other than Allah, but [it is] a confirmation of what was before it and a detailed explanation of the [former] Scripture, about which there is no doubt, from the Lord of the worlds.

To answer my coauthor, the Quran is indeed complete and comprehensive—it includes *all* previous revelations, namely the Torah, the Psalms, and the Bible. My coauthor implies that Islam believes these are in need of correction. That is not correct. What these pre-Islamic revelations require is clarification. All of these are in need of clarification, not correction, as he alluded.

My coauthor is also concerned with this statement:

(Quran 9:30)

وَقَالَتِ ٱلْيَهُودُ عُزَيْرٌ ٱبْنُ ٱللَّهِ وَقَالَتِ ٱلنَّصَـٰرَى ٱلْمَسِيحُ ٱبْنُ ٱللَّهِ ۖ ذَٰلِكَ قَوْلُهُم بِأَفْوَٰهِهِمْ ۖ يُضَـٰهِـُٔونَ قَوْلَ ٱلَّذِينَ كَفَرُواْ مِن قَبْلُ ۚ قَـٰتَلَهُمُ ٱللَّهُ ۚ أَنَّىٰ يُؤْفَكُونَ

The Jews say, "Ezra is the son of Allah"; and the Christians say, "The Messiah is the son of Allah." That is their statement from their mouths; they imitate the saying of those who disbelieved [before them]. May Allah destroy them; how are they deluded?

My coauthor writes that he doesn't know of any Jewish person who believes that Ezra is the son of God. He wonders why it is that the Quran states this. For context, Ezra is a prophet who memorized the Torah, went to sleep for 100 years, then woke up and wrote the entire Torah from memory. In the verse above, Allah is referring to those Jews who believed this miracle of his made him "A Son of God." Similarly, when Allah makes a similar statement referring to Christians—"[They] say the Messiah [Jesus] is the son of God"—Allah is referring to those who believe that (i.e., most practicing Christians). More specifically, He is pointing out that this belief is wrong. It doesn't matter if the believers of these claims are a minority group or a majority, or when they existed. Allah addresses these matters because He clearly does not take such claims lightly. That's why the Quran is best understood as a clarification of the previous scriptures and what transpired between or beyond their revelation.

Granted, some stories in the Quran end differently than stories in previous scriptures, but this is because, once again, the Quran is a clarification of those misinterpreted and misrepresented stories (such as Jesus dying on the cross, a widespread belief in Christianity yet openly rejected in the Quran). But the fact that Muslims and Christians cannot see eye to eye on the final moments of Jesus's life on this earth isn't grounds for us to demonize each other.

It's also instructive to look at how far Allah will go to achieve this clarification between the Quran and earlier scriptures. The Quran states that on the Day of Judgment, Allah will ask Jesus the following:

(Quran 5:116)

وَإِذْ قَالَ ٱللَّهُ يَـٰعِيسَى ٱبْنَ مَرْيَمَ ءَأَنتَ قُلْتَ لِلنَّاسِ ٱتَّخِذُونِى وَأُمِّىَ إِلَـٰهَيْنِ مِن دُونِ ٱللَّهِ ۖ قَالَ سُبْحَـٰنَكَ مَا يَكُونُ لِىَ أَنْ أَقُولَ مَا لَيْسَ لِى بِحَقٍّ ۚ إِن كُنتُ قُلْتُهُ فَقَدْ عَلِمْتَهُ ۚ تَعْلَمُ مَا فِى نَفْسِى وَلَآ أَعْلَمُ مَا فِى نَفْسِكَ ۚ إِنَّكَ أَنتَ عَلَّـٰمُ ٱلْغُيُوبِ

And [beware the Day] when Allah will say, "O Jesus, Son of Mary, did you say to the people, 'Take me and my mother as deities besides Allah?'" He will say, "Exalted, are You! It was not for me to say that to which I have no right. If I had said it, You would have known it. You know what is within me, and I do not know what is within Yourself. Indeed, it is You who is Knower of the unseen."

(Quran 5:117)

مَا قُلْتُ لَهُمْ إِلَّا مَآ أَمَرْتَنِى بِهِۦ أَنِ ٱعْبُدُوا۟ ٱللَّهَ رَبِّى وَرَبَّكُمْ ۚ وَكُنتُ عَلَيْهِمْ شَهِيدًا مَّا دُمْتُ فِيهِمْ ۖ فَلَمَّا تَوَفَّيْتَنِى كُنتَ أَنتَ ٱلرَّقِيبَ عَلَيْهِمْ ۚ وَأَنتَ عَلَىٰ كُلِّ شَىْءٍ شَهِيدٌ

I said not to them except what You commanded me—to worship Allah, my Lord, and your Lord. And I was a witness over them as long as I was among them; but when You took me up, You were the Observer over them, and You are, over all things, Witness.

The Quran states that Jesus will be put on the spot and questioned as to whether the claim to his being the son of God came from him or from his followers. Once this is clarified, Allah will then turn to those who made such a claim when they come forth for their judgment, and ask them to back up their words.

Nevertheless, Islam acknowledges the existence of other religions. And the fact that these other religions continued to exist in lands where Islam once ruled through the Caliphate is evidence that Muslims respected diversity throughout the ages. Hindus are still in India, despite the Islamic Mughal rule; Christians and Jews continue to reside in majority-Muslim countries or move there seeking employment. In other words, Judaism and Christianity managed to survive in countries where Islam blossomed and the Caliphate ruled; there was no campaign under Islam to extinguish whole religions from the planet as the Nazis did during World War II.

Islam doesn't see people of different faiths as enemies, and our differences don't have to be a barrier to coexistence. No one is a threat if everyone practices the core values of their faith.

The threat lies with those who wish to take away the rights of Muslims or anyone else because of their faith.

Lastly, when the Quran refers to "believers" and "disbelievers," it refers to potential paths a Muslim might follow in the world at large, not to a certain people or a default group of non-believers (i.e., all active followers of religions outside of Islam). The Quran does not write anyone off by default. In this world we all inhibit, while on our journey to the eternal world we are destined to reach, every human, Muslim or not, has the free will to decide their fate. I don't have the right to deem how anyone, including Bob, is seen in the sight of Allah. That right lies only with Allah and will be based on what Bob and others decide to do for themselves.

In the absence of this understanding, too many Muslims distance themselves from people of other faiths, or, worse, demonize and harm them. Too few are willing to open themselves up to other people of faith, even refusing to say hello to a fellow neighbor. In truth, many Muslims wonder how they will be received by the other—and so decline to interact at all. "What motive do they have to converse with me?" many wonder, thereby thinking for that person. This is all courtesy of the negative media coverage that makes Muslims think all non-Muslims are afraid of them. To many Muslims, avoiding their neighbors equals being respectful since they don't want to make them uncomfortable. The "othering" of Muslims of America has had a damaging impact, and expecting Muslims to try to find common ground or to work together with non-Muslims for the common good becomes even more difficult.

When random fears and unfounded suspicion prevent us from talking to each other, the negativity will continue to spiral—and the dangerous divisions continue. If Muslims want to see change and an end to the senseless violence and killings, if they want to work to uproot the generations of mutual hatred that have festered for too long and instead be good neighbors and good humans to one another, what we must do now is to create the resolve within each of us to walk down what will be a long road ahead. But that road exists—that's the good news.

CHAPTER 11

Preventing Prejudice that Isolates Muslims from the West

By Imam Azhar Subedar

The Islamophobia shared by so many Americans today has been nurtured not as a result of firsthand experiences with Muslims but by what I call the Islamophobia industry. This industry takes advantage of ignorance, misconstruing Shariah law to win points in a hate war they have manufactured to dehumanize "the other," namely, Muslims. The only way to stop it is when people like you, our readers, acquire the facts of Shariah and, with those facts, choose peace over misunderstanding. The rampant misconceptions about Islam have festered in our midst for far too long.

A few telling examples of the growth of this plague: In 2011, the Center for American Progress (CAP) published *Fear, Inc.: The Roots of the Islamophobia Network in America,* the goal being to identify and expose the organizations, scholars, pundits, and activists spreading misinformation and hateful propaganda about

American Muslims and Islam. The report found that between 2001 and 2009, seven charitable foundations provided $42.6 million to Islamophobia think tanks to support the spread of anti-Muslim rhetoric. To quote from that report: *"The efforts of a small cadre of funders and misinformation experts were amplified by an echo chamber of the religious right, conservative media, grassroots organizations, and politicians who sought to introduce a fringe perspective on American Muslims into the public discourse."*

Islamophobia today is a billion-dollar industry in North America, increasingly legitimized and normalized and leading to, among other things, a rise of hate crimes against Muslims across the nation and continent. According to one 2016 report cited on *Al Jazeera*, various groups spent more than $200 million promoting fear and hatred of Muslims in the U.S. between 2008 and 2013.

In June of 2017, ACT for America, the country's largest grassroots anti-Muslim organization, categorized by the Southern Poverty Law Center as an "extremist group," called for a nationwide "March Against Sharia." In a report published around that time, ACT for America was also singled out as one of 33 anti-Muslim groups with access to more than $204 million in revenue aimed at promoting legislation that targeted Muslims.

More recently, in 2021, 20-year-old Nathaniel Veltman deliberately slammed his pickup truck into a Muslim family waiting to cross the street in Canada, the place of my birth. That day, Salman Afzaal, 46; his wife Madiha, 44; his 77-year old mother; and their 15-year-old daughter Yumna were killed; his 9-year-old son was seriously injured. The incident continues to haunt me.

In today's America, where arguments about cancel culture and wokeness rage on, it often seems as if Muslims are the last minority group that it is okay to hate.

I've experienced this hatred myself. Several years ago, I was in a Dunkin' Donuts in Punta Gorda, Florida, on a bright and early Saturday morning. My kids were clamoring for doughnuts, and so, after morning prayer, I drove from the mosque to grab a fresh dozen. As I waited in line, I began to hear taunts of "Go back to your country!" coming from a person somewhere behind me. I didn't say anything in return. I didn't even dare to look back, as I didn't want to engage or enrage anyone. No one in that line spoke up for me. The person in front of me looked at that person, then at me, and continued to mind her business. Instead, the barista quickly made the rabble rouser his coffee, went up to him in the line and handed it to him, refusing to take a payment. The man left quietly. It seems he was a frequent customer.

I am sure that employee wanted to de-escalate the situation as quickly as possible. But I and many other Muslims across this nation have become numb to the reality that no one will speak out for our rights. And it is difficult for us to speak for ourselves if, seemingly, no one is ready to listen.

It's only when our children are mocked by teachers for wearing headscarves, or abused for praying in school or in public places, or when our places of worship are desecrated and our lives threatened that these kinds of slights, outright threats, and hate crimes get on the 10 o'clock local news. Beyond that, it feels as if we have to live with these daily humiliations and dangers.

One thing that would help is if more members of minority communities currently subjected to growing acts of hate, including Asian Americans, Blacks, Jews, and many others, took these moments of ignorance and used them to educate folks. When we do, change can happen, as was the case in Florida in December of 2022, when a teacher at Franklin Academy, a public charter school in Pembroke Pines, was filmed interrupting some Muslim students while they were in prayer. The video went viral, and the teacher was fired.

But that wasn't the end of the story. Afterward, Muslim community leaders and Muslim students in South Florida came together under the umbrella of the South Florida Muslim Federation to host a breakfast and discussion on cultural diversity for the school principals of the city of Pembroke Pines, including the mayor, the city manager, and its commissioners.

Writing people off is easy. Ruining someone's life and "canceling them" because of their ignorant or even hate-filled words or actions is all too common. Why not educate one another, reason with one another, and try to find common ground? We will all make more progress and create a culture of respect by teaching others.

I'm not saying it's easy. In November of 2017, I ordered a Lyft from my hotel to go to the Boonton, New Jersey, mosque where I was scheduled to deliver the Friday sermon. As I stepped into the car, the driver asked, point-blank: "You don't have a bomb strapped to you, do you?" Fearing for my safety, I began livestreaming my interaction with the driver on Facebook (without exposing his identity or his name) until he dropped me off. Afterward, Lyft contacted me and apologized. I made it clear to them that I didn't want the driver suspended, but educated along with their other drivers.

For too long, the world has been asking Muslims, "What are you hiding?" Today, I ask the Islamophobia industry and those who are consumed by it: "What are you undermining? Why? And what have you truly accomplished?" Is our world a safer place for it? I think not.

CHAPTER 12

Law Cannot Be Applied Selectively

By Imam Azhar Subedar

By now, you may have gathered that Shariah is frequently subject to misinterpretation. I don't have to look further than my coauthor to find an example. Before Bob and I even considered writing this book, the two of us had vigorously discussed whether Shariah law could coexist with man-made civil law in non-Muslim-majority countries. My coauthor concluded that this would be problematic, based, in part, on the verse below:

(Quran 4:92)

وَمَا كَانَ لِمُؤْمِنٍ أَن يَقْتُلَ مُؤْمِنًا إِلَّا خَطَئًا

And never is it for a believer to kill a believer except by mistake.

This basically states that a Muslim will not kill another Muslim—period. But in another verse, the second of the two, the statement is different:

(Quran 17:33)

وَ لَا تَقْتُلُوا۟ ٱلنَّفْسَ ٱلَّتِى حَرَّمَ ٱللَّهُ إِلَّا بِٱلْحَقِّ

And do not kill the soul which Allah has forbidden,
except by right.

Based on this verse, my coauthor wonders if Muslims are permitted, and indeed have a right, to kill non-Muslims. The answer is they don't, first and foremost because Muslims believe everyone and everything is the creation of Allah. Why, then, would Allah command Muslims to treat His creations (including Muslims and non-Muslims) differently? Moreover, why would He even create nonbelievers in the first place if he didn't want them to exist?

To further clarify, in the first verse, Allah makes it clear to a formerly tribal, warring people who have since accepted Islam that they are now part of the *ummah,* meaning that they are unified. Allah is saying that you can't ever kill your own people, even by mistake. And if someone does kill another Muslim by mistake, Allah has set forth a process for dealing with the matter—again, under the Caliphate. None of this implies that it's okay to take out one's anger on a non-Muslim, especially by killing them. Every individual's life is sanctified. Islam teaches that kindness, love, and preservation of life begins at home. To be true to others, we must first be true to ourselves.

These verses actually delegitimize ISIS, since the majority of their victims have been Muslims. A 2011 report by the U.S. government's

National Counterterrorism Center (NCTC) says: "In cases where the religious affiliation of terrorism casualties could be determined, Muslims suffered between 82% and 97% of terrorism-related fatalities over the past five years."

How could anyone killing Muslims—their own people—claim to stand for the cause of Islam?

The shooting in Christchurch in New Zealand in 2019, in which a terrorist killed a total of 51 worshippers at two separate mosques while livestreaming the entire bloody assault, illustrates how risky it can be to be Muslim today. Researchers at the University of Maryland's National Consortium for the Study of Terrorism and Responses to Terrorism (START) confirmed that Muslims are "absolutely" the most likely people to be victims of terrorist attacks worldwide, since the vast majority of terrorist attacks occur in Muslim-majority countries.

Based on my coauthor's interpretation of the second of the two verses above—"And do not kill the soul which Allah has forbidden, except by right"—if the 2 billion Muslims on this planet took up this command in the name of their faith (as my coauthor fears), chaos and strife would prevail, and no one outside the faith would survive. Yet the only time war is sanctioned in Islam is to put a stop to strife and chaos, never to initiate it.

For too long, Muslims, considered by so many to be "other," have been told to "go back to your country," as I was told that morning at Dunkin' Donuts. Yet despite having a wealth of Islamic countries to choose from, many of us opt to remain and contribute to the progress of this nation. Why? Because this is our home. Islamic and Western culture are intermingled within me; in addition to loving soccer (football), I am also a basketball fanatic. I love eating classic

American food such as burgers and ice cream, and these days, I dress mainly in Western garments, teaching the next generation of Muslims using lingo they'll understand to bring ancient texts into a modern context.

Despite the struggles all Muslims in the West have faced since 9/11, I continue to find Islam appealing and comfortable. I've also realized that I am not responsible for the actions of strangers who commit crimes in the name of Islam, just as all Jews and Christians and those of other religions are not responsible for crimes committed by individuals who share their faith, something my coauthor also acknowledges in these pages. I once felt the need to apologize for those who committed these acts; now I feel the burden of responsibility lies on the individuals alone. Rather than saying that I'm sorry for acts perpetrated by people in the name of what my faith is not, I'd rather spend my energy and time presenting my faith for *what it truly is.*

There is a vast difference between the ideology of extremists and Shariah. The former is a twisted perversion stamped with the word *Islam.* As for the latter, it is a divine teaching for its followers. And the only way we can defeat terrorism is to separate extremism from true Islam. I believe as strongly as ever that Shariah offers guidance and a perspective that people of all faiths can use to find solutions to some of our most pressing problems, especially now. Far from being a threat to the American way of life, I propose that non-Muslims think about looking at Shariah as a resource available to help improve their lives. That doesn't mean anyone has to adopt it. In this nation of ours, we have the freedom to choose—to believe or not to believe. But choosing not to believe in Shariah doesn't mean having the right to object to its presence in the life of others. Shariah has provided me with a foundation for my life, one that governs my actions and holds me accountable.

I say this to clarify the true nature of Shariah for non-Muslim readers and non-Muslims at large, many of whom still view Islam as a political movement with a dangerous agenda. This notion results in every act of extremism perpetrated by Muslims to be immediately classified as terrorism, defined by *Oxford Languages* as "the unlawful use of violence and intimidation, especially against civilians, <u>in the pursuit of political aims.</u>" Why is it that similar acts perpetrated by white supremacists are not always subjected to the same standard by the public?

By the *Oxford Languages* definition, *anyone* who threatens the peace of society and the lives of its people, regardless of their motives or goals, is a terrorist, including those who stormed our nation's Capitol and threatened our Congress with violence on January 6, 2021.

The day we successfully separate "religion" from the crimes of "terrorists," whoever they may be, is the day the world will win the so-called war on terror. That can only be accomplished by *restoring,* not *reforming,* the narrative of Islam, something all Muslims must work toward, starting with understanding the religion and living it for what it is. The Law of Allah is not subject to manipulation. That's why I believe that, just as Islam is compatible with Western civilization, Shariah can aid and assist in preventing the toppling of democracy.

As a Muslim, my Shariah orders me to obey the laws of the land where I live, as long as those laws do not infringe on my right to practice my faith. But if the time comes that my religious liberties are violated, and my government is unwilling to protect me, I will follow the instructions of my Shariah and make my home elsewhere, per the consensus of scholars based on the following Hadith:

"Emigration will not end until repentance ends, and repentance will not end until the sun rises from the west."
(Hadith, Abu Dawood 2479)

Which brings me around to the question of whether people of diverse beliefs and backgrounds can ever find commonality. Perhaps surprisingly, I've discovered the answer in the never-ending gun debate in our nation, one that predictably flares up after tragedies such as school shootings, which are becoming all too common.

In February of 2018, Darrell Scott visited the White House with other families and talked about the work he and his wife engaged in after their daughter was killed and their son gravely injured in the Columbine shooting:

"The focus must not be just on unity or diversity. Because if you focus too much on diversity, you create division. If you focus too much on unity, you'll create compromise. But if you focus on relatedness and how we can relate with one another, then you can celebrate the diversity, and you can see the unity take place. I'm all for diversity, I'm all for unity, but the focus really needs to be on how we can connect."

Another attendee, a high school junior named Ariana Klein who attended Stoneman Douglas high school where the Parkland school shooting occurred, added:

"And I just want to say that everybody right now is so stuck on what they believe that they're not even listening to what other people believe. We need to listen to the other points of view. We all need to realize that we all have different points of view and that . . . this solution is not going to be a singular thing. It's going to be multifaceted, and it's going to be created by a collection of different people working together. And we all have to realize that we all have our opinions, and together we're going to be able to work to a solution. And this is not just Parkland anymore; this is America. This is every student in every city, everywhere. It's everybody. It's not small. It's everything."

These statements poignantly articulate the desperate need for reason and connection in our nation, particularly between people who harbor hate toward "the other."

The necessity of finding common ground could be apparent to people of all religions and all walks of life, but ironically, religion remains the dividing issue and fundamental obstacle to long-term mutual understanding and acceptance. A devout Christian, in his response to our book, stated, "To me, and to most modern people, a religion is not worth bothering with if it is not true . . . why would any educated, intelligent person believe in the god(s) of any religion if the moral codes and concepts of the afterlife of such a religion were mere fiction?"

What may be your belief may not be mine and vice versa. I get it. However, to see one's faith as the only measure of universal truth and write off everyone else's beliefs as nontruths does not make humanity any less vulnerable to harm and danger.

I am comfortable in what I believe, and I do not see other people's beliefs as a threat to my own. Why not feel comfortable in your own skin first, and then be open to dialogue with others? Every conversation or engagement with folks from other faiths doesn't need to be an opportunity to proselytize or prove the superiority of one's own beliefs. We can all retain our different ideologies and still share thoughts on issues of common interest, especially when a mutual threat is presented. There does not need to be uniformity of ideology and theology to recognize the need for a movement that presents a united stance on humanitarian grounds. We can honor the validity of our own religion without condemning others or their beliefs. We need not see different theologies as a threat or the people who follow them as flawed. Also, when a faith and its people are labeled as evil or dangerous, I would hope that others who disagree with that faith would, on a humanitarian level, disagree just as strongly with the targeting of that faith and its people. Our call here is to our common humanity. There are concrete truths in this matter, irrespective of what one follows or lives by.

Let us all collectively bring justice back and uphold it as one body, for all people. Justice is the backbone of any healthy society. If a society is based on injustice, oppression, or inequality, or it oppresses minorities or the vulnerable, it cannot endure.

As for Islam, it is the same religion it was at its inception more than 1,400 years ago. It's the *people*—their understanding, their knowledge, and their practice of Islam—that has been polluted by misinformation, politics, and those who are trying to manipulate its words and injunctions for their own agendas. In the past, Islam was a macro solution meant to bring about peace between warring tribes and societies in conflict; today, Islam remains a possible solution to conflict, albeit on a more micro or individual basis. It is a source of solace and wisdom for people of all backgrounds, across all communities, who are searching to find meaning in life and a solution to their challenges.

Yet the effectiveness of Islam has also been impeded by the constant gridlock of so many ideologies, methodologies, interpretations, and sects, all convening on the doorstep of the faith to proclaim themselves its one true expression. Elements of the teachings of Islam today exist within various organizations and movements, all of them battling it out to prove their legitimacy and claim the right to speak for Islam as a whole. But each of them is missing the overarching theme. The essence of Islam is to be a good human being who lives a life of good morals and upright conduct and within the guidelines of Allah's teachings.

"Verily, I have only been sent to perfect righteous character."
(Hadith, Musnad Ahmad 8952)

To my mind, these words of Prophet Muhammad sum up 23 years of revelation and prophethood, simply and accurately. Based on this fundamental teaching alone, I would assume that every Muslim would realize the preeminent role character plays in defining a Muslim. Often we remember people less for what they said than for how they said it. Less for what they did than for how they did it. It is their kindness or their rudeness, their positivity or their negativity that live on in the minds of those who cross their path, even long after they're gone. A Muslim is only as good as their character, because their character is the measure of their commitment to the teachings of Islam.

As I stated earlier, all the laws, rules, obligations, and do's and don'ts in Islam revolve around one purpose: the perfection of moral conduct. Those who embrace a path of empathy and love for humanity; consideration and care for the creation at large; and reverence and respect for their Lord, Allah, are living and experiencing Islam and Shariah through their actions. It is only when we are able to see these laws in their correct context that we will be able to see Islam for what it truly is, lived out by Muslims across the globe throughout time. Islam is successful when it produces better human beings, not when one sect of the faith wins out over all others.

For the sake of perspective, in Islam's infancy, neither Sunni nor Shiite—the two most well-known sects of Islam (though there are plenty more)—existed. That's a testament to how far we've strayed from the faith's core message. It is no longer practical for Muslims to continue to defend a particular sect or branch of the faith or condemn those not aligned with their way. Instead, all Muslims must do the work of returning to the drawing board and refocusing on the practical life of Islam as outlined in Shariah. Further, all Muslims must consider the ramifications of remaining in thrall to their current ways while staying silent in the face of all that threatens Islam. In these troublesome times, continuing to push one's agenda or zealously claiming to represent the one true banner of Islam will only ensure the failure of all.

And to those who follow specific interpretations of the holy text made by various scholars of the past: *Stop overcomplicating Islam.* Islam was once attractive and notable because of its simplicity. Return to that simplicity and return yourselves to that beauty. While there may be varying interpretations of, say, where to place one's hand in prayer, that's not a reason to condemn or disassociate ourselves from those who practice differently.

For those who feel that their differences must remain a dividing factor within the collective Muslim body: In the Mosque of the Prophet in Madinah, two separate *Mihrabs* (prayer areas) still exist, even though only one is used at present. The purpose of having two separate prayer areas was to accommodate those who wished to conduct their late afternoon prayer at a different time; different schools of thought decree different prayer times. At one point in history, there were four separate praying stations in the Great Mosque of Makkah to accommodate people with different opinions on the time and method of praying. People may have differed in their interpretations of the Quran, but they still managed to gather under the same roof and coexist.

To be clear, I am not calling for an end to all sects in Islam. Nor am I suggesting that varying interpretations be wiped away for a homogenous whole. Neither strategy is possible. However, many among the new generation of Muslims seem to have little regard for which sect or school of thought they might follow. They want to be Muslim, and so do I.

That's why I'm calling for all Muslims across the world to move past the bitterness keeping us apart and join as brethren in faith. We must also put an end, here at home, to the growing extreme views on either end of our community as to who we see as Muslims and who we deem outside the faith. Cancel culture is ripe within our community, and a fixation on bringing a person down because they don't align with your views is an epidemic that will consume us all from within.

In 2019, during my first year of service as imam in Plano, Texas, one of the persons I met with over coffee to discuss a potential collaboration of interfaith work was a lead member of the American Jewish Committee (AJC) chapter of Dallas. The discussion was about his interest in my involvement with other Muslims in the metroplex who formed the local Muslim-Jewish Advisory Council (MJAC). As my faith teaches me, I was hospitable and respectful throughout our conversation. But I was not interested in what he proposed. Although I don't need to explain myself and what I did or did not do at this meeting, the backlash I received nationally immediately after posting the picture of us in the mosque rotunda was not only condemnatory but also portrayed me as a Zionist sympathizer and pro-Israeli Muslim. These are the types of extreme views that we gorilla-glue onto each other's back, thinking we are warriors of truth and not realizing that we are hurting the truth and those who are trying to propagate it. Ironically, six years later, this very post that remained in circulation within Muslim chat groups was used to bar me from a program at a mosque in Texas during Ramadan of 2025. I was literally in the airport parking lot when I was told that I had been canceled for the night. When you're fasting and hustling, trying to serve your community and your faith, an experience like this brings a very particular, and deep, kind of pain.

As Muslims, we are commanded to speak to everyone without preconceived notions. We engage with the hopes of conveying our message to them, just as they hope to convey their message to us. It's that simple. Speaking, last time I checked, isn't a crime.

In recent years, in the Muslim community in America, there has been disparagement of others within the faith in ways that I can't recall happening before. Not only one's views on the faith, but one's political views are seen as reasons for condemnation and rejection. In the recent presidential election of 2024, some in the Muslim community ostracized other Muslims who harbored resentment against the Republican candidate. The former group of Muslims deemed the latter to be "sellouts" to the Democratic party and to Biden's genocidal policies and support for Israel. They also claimed that the nominee for the Republican party was best suited to address and end the war in Gaza. Meanwhile, those who resented President Trump for his policies in his first term and feared a repeat in a second term categorized Muslims on the other side of the political spectrum as enemies of the Muslims of America. Sadly, what many on both sides failed to see was their own hypocrisy. For example, a group of Muslim community leaders gathered with President Trump onstage in Michigan and endorsed him for president. They have yet to be criticized (at the time of this writing) by the very Muslims who applauded and endorsed their move, even after Trump has greenlighted the rebombing of Gaza and threatened to take it over. Meanwhile, Mehdi Hasan, a reputable journalist who warned of the potential harm of a second Trump presidency and spoke in favor of Kamala Harris, trying to distance her potential presidency from the Biden administration's policies, continues to be canceled by the very same people.

All we are doing is hurting ourselves as Muslims. What we must do instead is sit down, take a breath, and meet with the brethren we disagree with. Smile, say salam, and discuss. Converse. Disagree, but remain respectful. For in the end, the judge is Allah, not ourselves. I'm calling for us to wake up and realize we are our own enemy before anyone else. Allah established our relationship with one another as *"Believers are plainly but each other's own brothers"* (Quran, 49:10). The mere duties that we have toward each other as believers should quell the ill will and bitterness that we harbor for one another. We must hold ourselves to this standard.

Beyond what we must do for one another within the faith, I also call for the end of the "othering" of those outside the faith. Every human is the creation of Allah, which means that every human deserves love and respect. Loving someone as Allah's creation does not necessarily mean accepting their ways, beliefs, or lifestyle. It means fulfilling the responsibility of one's existence on earth: taking care of our planet and its inhabitants the way Allah meant for us to do. To do that effectively, and to sustain the faith for generations to come, Muslims must return to the values embedded in their Shariah. Only then can we find common ground. Only then will our beliefs manifest through action and not words alone. Only then will society at large witness, value, and embrace our existence, whether or not they share our lifestyle. Because who would not be open to the values of stability, sanity, and preserving and protecting wealth, family, and property—in other words, that which is promised through Shariah?

Under Shariah law and its system of governance—and I'm talking about where it is practiced and upheld through and through, from scholars and judges to the governor and the Caliph—everyone is bound by roles, responsibilities, and restrictions. This includes those who adhere to Islam and those who happen to reside in a country under Shariah law but don't adhere to its tenets. The system is greater than any one person. No single individual can be the overriding and sole deciding force within that system, or the objectives of Shariah and the good of society as a whole will falter. Unfortunately, the current rise of authoritarianism across the world is testament to the fact that even human-made laws cannot guarantee unity among people.

CHAPTER 13

Coping with Destructive Forces

By Imam Azhar Subedar

After the October 7 attack in the Middle East, the actions of terrorists followed by the iron-fist "official" response to that attack stopped the progress of many interfaith relationships in its tracks, perhaps never to be resumed.

But if we end all dialogue and attempts at civility after every terror attack and military response to it, we will all have fallen victim to the terrorists. Let me be clear: The actions of Hamas on October 7 were actions of terror. There is never any justification for the killing of men, women, or children, nor for rape. It is wrong to claim that these actions were carried out and sanctioned by Islam. The Prophet Muhammad, in times of war, would impart instructions to his companions, which included some of the following:

- *"Do not kill any child, any woman, or any elderly or sick person."* (Hadith, Abu Dawood)

- *"Do not practice treachery or mutilation. Do not uproot or burn palms or cut down fruitful trees. Do not slaughter a sheep or a cow or a camel, except for food."* (Hadith, Al-Muwatta)

- *"Do not kill the monks in monasteries, and do not kill those sitting in places of worship."* (Hadith, Musnad Ahmad)

- *"Do not destroy the villages and towns, do not spoil the cultivated fields and gardens, and do not slaughter the cattle."* (Hadith, Bukhari)

If these are the guidelines given during war, how can the actions of Hamas be permitted outside of it?

As for Israel, deemed "the sole democracy in the Middle East," when Prime Minister Netanyahu declared war on Hamas and, by extension, Gaza, the country was lured into a second trap, thereby allowing the narrative to flip against the ones wronged and transforming them into the wrongdoers. The global protests in support of Palestine are a testament to how miserably this democracy failed to uphold its values, in part because its leader succumbed to his emotions just as the terrorists succumbed to theirs.

Netanyahu's declaration of war validates the right of Gaza to defend itself in Islam for all those who are in its path.

(Quran 22:39)

أُذِنَ لِلَّذِينَ يُقَاتَلُونَ بِأَنَّهُمْ ظُلِمُوا ۚ وَإِنَّ اللَّهَ عَلَىٰ نَصْرِهِمْ لَقَدِيرٌ

Permission [to fight] is given to those upon whom war is made because they are oppressed, and most surely Allah is well able to assist them;

Not only are they permitted, they are commanded by Allah to fight and defend their sovereignty.

(Quran 2:190)

وَقَـٰتِلُواْ فِى سَبِيلِ ٱللَّهِ ٱلَّذِينَ يُقَـٰتِلُونَكُمْ وَلَا تَعْتَدُوٓاْ ۚ إِنَّ ٱللَّهَ لَا يُحِبُّ ٱلْمُعْتَدِينَ

And fight in the way of Allah with those who fight with you but do not transgress. Indeed, Allah does not like transgressors.

Netanyahu's declaration of war also triggered the obligation of the surrounding nations to defend the people of Gaza or any human unable to defend themselves.

(Quran 4:75)

وَمَا لَكُمْ لَا تُقَـٰتِلُونَ فِى سَبِيلِ ٱللَّهِ وَٱلْمُسْتَضْعَفِينَ مِنَ ٱلرِّجَالِ وَٱلنِّسَآءِ وَٱلْوِلْدَٰنِ
ٱلَّذِينَ يَقُولُونَ رَبَّنَآ أَخْرِجْنَا مِنْ هَـٰذِهِ ٱلْقَرْيَةِ ٱلظَّالِمِ أَهْلُهَا وَٱجْعَل لَّنَا مِن لَّدُنكَ
وَلِيًّا وَٱجْعَل لَّنَا مِن لَّدُنكَ نَصِيرًا

And what is [the matter] with you that you fight not in the cause of Allah and [for] the oppressed among men, women, and children who say, "Our Lord, take us out of this city of oppressive people and appoint for us from Yourself a protector and appoint for us from Yourself a helper?"

All Palestinians have a duty to defend their land and people from the moment an invasion or attack is broadcast to the world as an act of war. Indeed, all the various faiths in Palestine must come together and defend themselves as one body despite the lack of resources and seeming imbalance of the two sides. That defense can stop only when the oppressor ceases its oppression.

All of this would have been preventable if the democratic nation of Israel had lived up to its professed ideals and values. Declaring war on an entire people—including women and children—because of the actions of a few is like blowing up an entire plane because there is one hijacker on board. As Israel continued bombing throughout Gaza, public opinion continued to harden against them, and by "them," I mean the government and military of Israel. I'll add that many Jews across the world have themselves demanded the removal of Netanyahu's government. At the time of this writing, the International Criminal Court has charged Netanyahu with war crimes, and many in Israel and well beyond believe this was the right thing to do. To me, this is proof that there is still common ground between Jews and Muslims and that dialogue is possible.

In the absence of dialogue, it's too easy to fixate on only one thing, whether those killed by Hamas or the innocent Palestinians whose lives were lost and properties leveled. But taking this kind of binary mindset can compromise anyone's ability to think straight, especially when it prevents us from speaking with one another. Worse, keeping the momentum of hate going requires an added level of demonization of the other, one that ultimately leads to moral failure.

Why is it so hard to see humans as humans? What crime justifies the killing of children in today's world? Why do people respond with concern and donations when their neighbors' homes are leveled by a hurricane, but with shocking equanimity when those same neighbors' lives are ruined by war? It's because of the words we cling to, words we use to validate our inhumane reactions. Words matter.

So what is the correct response to Hamas's terror? We must bring those who perpetrated these acts to justice, which means the criminals who committed the atrocities on October 7, not those they claim to represent. Hamas does not represent Islam, just as standing for Palestine does not mean support for Hamas.

Bob is passionate about the preservation of democracy in America and concerned about the forces massing against it. The fact is, under Netanyahu today, Israel's right-wing extremist government embodies my coauthor's fears. Meanwhile, up until October 7, Israelis themselves had been protesting continuously for 37 weeks to try to stop Netanyahu from overhauling the judiciary and thereby damaging the country's democracy. Add in Netanyahu and his party's often radical views, and it seems to me that a perfect storm is brewing.

During one phone call, I asked Bob why the Jewish community wasn't speaking out about the extreme right-wing pro-expansionist members of the Israeli government who are behind the killing of Palestinian Arabs. He responded by asking why Muslims were not speaking about the terrorist attackers on 9/11. His point was that they are doing what we did. In the meantime, no one is seeking to understand the reality on the other side beyond our long-held perceptions. That is why, in the midst of this all, we must keep talking.

Neither one of us could have foreseen how all Jews would end up bearing the blame for the events in Gaza and Israel. In a guest essay by James Kirchick in *The New York Times*, published on May 27, 2024, under the title "A Chill Has Fallen Over Jews in Publishing," Kirchick detailed the drawing up of a "blacklist" of Jewish writers who had not renounced Israel. As a Muslim, I reject the attempt by some to assign guilt and responsibility to my Jewish coauthor for decisions by the Israeli government. Yet the two of us stand on separate platforms regarding the aftermath of October 7: I see the Israeli government's reaction as atrocious; Bob sees it as self-defense. But we keep talking, attempting to relay our perspective so that we can come to see each other from the other person's point of view. We are both human.

Instead of talking through disagreement, it often feels easier to write off an entire people, particularly when we are among our own tribe. But the latter way sows division, while the former nurtures hope for a potential solution.

The October 7 attack has been the most contentious issue between Bob and me during all the years we have known each other. Each of us passionately believes that "the other" bears the greater moral responsibility for the tragedy that has unfolded. Yet we are still able to acknowledge our common humanity, primarily because we know and understand each other. This book was conceived long before October 7, but what happened between Bob and me further underscores the need for the book's message. The jury is out on whether understanding and dialogue or hate and revenge will ultimately triumph. Consider yourselves members of that jury.

CHAPTER 14

The Response That Cannot Go Unanswered

By Robert Gary

Imam Subedar acknowledges the horrors of the October 7 attack while failing to acknowledge that this was one of the greatest attacks on the Jewish people in generations. Hamas, it seems to me, was willing to violate all standards of war (not to mention humanity) to achieve a reaction, a goal, an advantage, however temporary. One example of that violation: Hamas fighters were given detailed instructions from an official handbook on how to invade civilian areas with the express purpose of kidnapping and torturing civilians. One section of the handbook, for example, instructed the invaders to kill the difficult ones and use the hostages as human shields. Their brutality mirrored the way ISIS videotaped beheadings of its hostages for worldwide distribution. Like a stone tossed into a pond, hate rippled out from the epicenter of the barbarism, engulfing everyone who identified with those innocent victims. Hamas knew that its actions would prompt a swift and strong response from Israel, one that would result in the deaths of many Palestinian civilians. Hamas showed that it was indifferent to those deaths when it used civilian sites such as hospitals for military purposes. In the final analysis, Hamas is the enemy of the people it claims to be fighting for.

This is why I object to my coauthor's description of the October 7 attackers as "the actions of terrorists" without acknowledging that this was a well-planned attack designed to destabilize Israel and its relations with its neighbors. I also object to his characterization of the Israel Defense Forces' response as a war upon the people of Gaza, which resulted in the intentional killing of children and the leveling of neighborhoods. To me, this was a response to an attack by Hamas, a terrorist organization, that had embedded itself within a civilian population. However, the entire point of this book is to show how important it is that, during moments of discord and friction, we don't revert to our talking points and engage in increasingly heated rhetoric but, rather, take a deep breath and de-escalate—even if such actions dismay those in our respective tribes. There are situations in which responding in kind may feel like the only option, but as we have seen again and again, it is also the least productive approach.

What if the default response was not to engage in more finger pointing but to genuinely attempt to find solutions? What if we attempted to learn from history instead of repeating it? One of the lessons learned from fighting the 20-year war in Afghanistan, for instance, is that you can't erase a culture by force. Another is that you cannot impose democracy on a resistant tribal culture, even with an investment of close to a trillion dollars. American values cannot and do not automatically supersede the values, practices, and traditions of other cultures. For sustainable change to happen, reform needs to come from within rather than being imposed by troops and bombs. Which brings me to my coauthor's suggestion that Islam must "restore" itself. For that to happen, it will also have to come from within—from Muslims and Muslim leadership themselves. I cannot repeat too often that when Muslims are the ones expressing hate, toward Jews or others, this hate must be loudly denounced by Muslims in the presence of other Muslims.

We non-Muslims have a part to play as well. We can attempt to understand Islam instead of condemning it or viewing it through the lens of Western values. The isolation and insularity experienced by so many of the country's 3.5 million American Muslims will continue as long as Islam continues to be (incorrectly) viewed as a form of terrorism, a perspective that also leads to hate crimes against Muslims.

As I've said, many non-Muslims (such as myself) have valid questions about a culture that appears to repress women (as do other cultures and religions), allows men to have up to four wives, and considers harsh penalties such as amputation to be a valid punishment for violating certain laws. But agreeing or disagreeing with the particulars of Islam, or of any religion, is not the point. The point is that the West cannot and should not aim to defeat Islam through hate, much less force. To defeat *true* terrorism, Muslims must be part of the solution. But that will only happen when Muslims openly address the question of why barbarism is being carried out under its banner—and call that barbarism out. To my mind, Islam has been too often silent on that issue.

One reason is that it is not clear who exactly speaks for Islam today. Since the abolishment of the Caliphate in 1924, no Islamic individual or nation has had the official authority to speak for the entire Muslim world. Of course, Judaism and Protestantism have no official leaders either. Despite that, these faiths condemned the acts of terrorism on 9/11. Given that all 19 of the hijackers were Sunni Muslims, the lack of an official condemnation from Sunni Muslims has understandably been interpreted as an endorsement of those attacks.

Like my coauthor, I believe that this leadership vacuum in Sunni Islam is a problem. As Imam Subedar has explained, each individual mosque is headed by an imam who is essentially free to guide his flock based on how he has been trained. In the United States, as we've said, many imams train at religious schools in Saudi Arabia, where they are indoctrinated in the extreme form of Islam known as Wahhabism. It's no surprise, then, that many of these imams did not condemn the 9/11 hijackers. While there is also no single leader in Judaism, as I've said, the fact that there are 2 billion Muslims and only 16 million Jews means that the question of who speaks for the Muslims is of vastly greater importance—at least for the Muslim community. Because unfortunately, the biggest megaphone for Islam still belongs to the likes of Al Qaeda, ISIS, and now Hamas, who claim they are carrying out the word of God, and whose every act of barbarism and violence continues to garner massive news coverage, which in turn stokes fear of Islam (and Muslims). And so the cycle continues, with new victims emerging all the time.

It's time to stop that cycle, the perpetuation of which only helps the extremists, whose end goal is to spark a global conflict between the Muslim and non-Muslim world. How can we do this? Not through the strength and stability of our political system, which many Americans tend to assume is one of our greatest weapons against international and homegrown terrorism. After all, when it comes to combating Islamic extremism, the West doesn't have a great track record. The astonishingly rapid collapse of the U.S.-backed democratic power structure in Afghanistan is evidence of that. The unknown implications of the collapse of Syria is another example. Instead, we must help Islamic societies become the best version of *themselves*. To do that, we in the West must focus on who we are and how we wish to live, on being *our* best version of ourselves. To my mind, that means living by the rule of law and seeking truth, regardless of what is at stake or where one prays or does not pray.

Personally, I am sick of the killing and the hatred and the superstition and ignorance. Ultimately, my objective is that my own people and Imam Subedar's people survive. Survival is not a foregone conclusion. We human beings must save each other from each other. Faith cannot replace science when it comes to global warming. Nor will God make peace with our enemies without our intervention. We alone have the power to stop the hatred. And what we *can* do is to turn down the temperature. That is the modest goal that Imam Subedar and I share. How we approach that goal, however, is unique to who we are and our life experiences. Imam Subedar's life is ordered through his religion. The beauty and complexity of his explanations and the intricacies of the rules and guardrails he has described are a majestic creation, and he has devoted his life to being the best he can be while living within that framework. Indeed, he believes that framework enables him to be the best he can be.

While I happen to be a relatively nonreligious person, what I do have is my affinity and love for the Jewish people and an ethical code instilled by my parents. As different as Imam Subedar and I are in appearance, background, religious philosophy, and everyday life experience, over the years that we've written this book, we've discovered that in many ways, we are also the same. Strip away the superficial differences and what both of us want is a world that cherishes humanity, whether that goal is achieved in the name and service of Allah or because it is simply the right thing to do. And still, pursuing our goal often feels like a lonely enterprise. Sometimes, on bad days, I fear that Imam Subedar and I have spent years crafting a message that no one will hear—or heed. What I am certain of is that Imam Subedar has found answers for himself, based in his faith and an education that empowers him to provide informed answers on the true message of Islam. I don't always fully accept or reject his learned interpretations, but what I know is that they are offered honestly.

Imam Subedar sees the message of Islam as one of hope, order, and peace. Given that view, it's no wonder that he is perplexed and distressed by the hate Islam can spark in non-Muslims. Any American Jew today will likely relate to my coauthor's legitimate concerns about Islamophobia. The United States, as we've said, is witnessing the growing strength of white supremacists, racists, Christian nationalists, and a populist authoritarian strain in American politics. In every country where fascist tendencies have appeared, the scapegoating of Jews as well as Muslims follows. Once again, politicians are talking about a Muslim ban and ready to revive accusations that state prosecutors are puppets of the "deep state" and controlled by (Jewish) billionaire George Soros. Evidence of racial and religious scapegoating is all around; it is a clear and present danger. Jews and Muslims must unite against this simmering hate. When we do, we will become a beacon for all people of good faith, of every religion, to stand with us. This book is meant to be a seed that nurtures that movement.

CHAPTER 15

A Policy of Hate and Division

By Robert Gary

There will always be purveyors of hate. The greatest danger arises when aspiring politicians and even governments seek to harness that hate for their own political gain. Authoritarian governments stay in power by setting people against each other, creating divisions that foster hate. America, too, is in the grip of artificially created culture wars. By stoking a fear of migrants, gays, transgender children, Blacks, Jews, and Muslims—or whoever is being "othered" at any given time—hate-mongers are not trying to protect the people so much as serve their own purposes. When it is said that "Jews control us" or that "Muslims seek to destroy our civilization," the immediate question must be: *Who is behind these messages and what purpose do they serve?*

One answer to that question is authoritarians, who play on our biases to separate us and weaken our common resolve. By pitting us against one another, they come one step closer to seizing control. Authoritarian governments have sanctioned many of the greatest abominations against humanity, including the murder of 6 million Jews by the Nazis during World War II; the genocide in Cambodia by the Khmer Rouge in the 1970s; and the Rwandan genocide in 1994. During most of these events, minority groups were targeted. The same thing can happen here. If an authoritarian government achieves control in the United States, it is the minorities who will be most at risk. Once power falls into the hands of dividers and haters, democracy and the rule of law may be lost.

That's why, like all vulnerable groups, religious minorities—including Muslims and Jews—must actively oppose attempts to manipulate their votes and their emotions. And it is also why, after the 2024 election, we *all* need to be on high alert. A few things to watch out for: efforts to concentrate power in the executive branch at the expense of the other branches of government; politically motivated prosecutions; the erosion of the rule of law; and misinformation knowingly circulated by the government. Truth should never be compromised for political advantage.

To my mind, the red flags signaling the rise of authoritarianism are, in fact, already waving. In a rational world, that should be enough to unite America's Muslims and Jews. One of the challenges of staying vigilant despite the red flags is that a number of America's Muslims were originally from countries headed up by long-standing authoritarian governments, and the people of these nations may be more accustomed to (and accepting of) a government controlling their destiny. Sadly, we don't live in a rational world. Too often, rather than improving our own and our neighbors' circumstances and the condition of the planet, we focus on our differences and demonize the other. This is our greatest vulnerability, and yet, when given the choice, we still frequently act against our own best interests.

That emboldens those who would silence journalists, whistleblowers, and political opponents. Equally concerning are the accusations and attacks on our courts that aim to portray them as little more than weaponized arms of a political party. These ideas are reinforced by hyper-partisan news outlets; censorship of books and attempts to control what our children learn; election interference; open threats of "vengeance" or "retribution"; and the demonization of some types of people as "poison" and "vermin." Muslims across the world have been vulnerable to unpredictable autocrats who could suspend their civil rights on a whim and even order internment. It is a question whether this threat has now come to America. Jews, too, cannot feel totally safe in what may be a new America. Jews may face roaming gangs of pardoned Oath Keepers and Proud Boys who will feel empowered to harass anyone who doesn't fit in with their white Christian view of the world. Waiting on the sidelines to see how they can take advantage of these historic events are right-wing Christian nationalists who are friends of neither the Muslims nor the Jews. To be clear, Christian nationalism is less about Christianity than it is about who should govern—despite the fact that they tend to frame issues in Biblical terms of good versus evil. The truth is, we should all fear a malicious government more than we do a Muslim who believes that polygamy is ethical.

As the saying goes, "The enemy of my enemy is my friend." The ultra right-wing coalition Netanyahu government and even many American Jews understandably approve of the Trump administration's unqualified support for Israel and "crackdown" on student support for Hamas. On the domestic front, these actions include the arrest of students, cancellation of student visas, withholding of funds from universities, and even the intimidation of attorneys with pro-Palestinian clients. It is impossible to be sure if these aggressive actions by the American government, ostensibly undertaken to protect American Jews, are well intentioned or a pretext to divide us. What we do know from the lesson of history is that diluting the rule of law, scapegoating, and tilting toward authoritarianism present a potential threat to the Jewish community. As Jews, we should not silently approve or stand by while the rights of the other are violated. If our government is engaged in actions that would be intolerable if directed at Jews, we should not look the other way because they are directed at Muslims.

Only by standing together can Muslims and Jews rebuff the growing threat of hate in America. I would encourage the leadership of the American Jewish community to continue to reach out to their Muslim counterparts. Rabbis and imams should regularly attend one another's mosques and synagogues as guests, and explicitly and loudly condemn hatred. That is one way to keep moving forward toward peace and coexistence, despite our very real differences.

CHAPTER 16

A Friendship Put to the Test in Real Time

By Robert Gary

A few days after October 7, Imam Subedar coauthored an opinion piece for *The Palm Beach Post* expressing his views on the Hamas attack. His perspective, understandably, was that of an American Muslim and a supporter of the cause of the Palestinians. After it was published, he sent me the article, and I circulated it among my friends. In it, he acknowledged the Israeli civilians who were "killed, injured, or taken by force," as well as the "innocent Palestinians . . . who have been killed . . . and whose lives are capsized." He wrote: "Violence will at the most always be met with violence, whether one starts the video when Hamas strikes at Israel or we start the video when Israel strikes at Hamas . . . ." For many Jews I know, the suggestion of moral equivalency between Hamas's attack and Israel's response felt deeply offensive, particularly when children were still being held hostage and the blood of the slaughtered had barely dried. Meanwhile, the reaction from some other imams to my coauthor's article was that it was too conciliatory.

Typically, the first reaction to an attack on one's tribe is to rally to the support of that tribe and to condemn "the other." And that was my reaction as well. In Jewish circles, Hamas is associated with the language of its charter, which states: "Israel will exist and will continue to exist until Islam will obliterate it, just as it obliterated others before it." The charter also states, in Article 6, that Hamas seeks to raise the banner of Allah over every inch of Palestine, and that this goal is rooted in the Quran.

To most Jews (and most human beings), negotiating with a party that is calling for your destruction is not possible. It turned out that Imam Subedar was not familiar with Hamas's charter and its call for the elimination of Israel, which raised the question of what other information might be missing from our conversations. When I brought it to his attention, I expected him to condemn the document and Hamas along with it. That is not the response I got. What he told me is that he "did not care" about the charter. What he cared about, he said, were "the values of Shariah, which is from Allah, and not the Hamas Charter, which is from a fringe group." In his view, the current problems in the Middle East stemmed from "the occupation, illegal settlements, and inhumane treatment of Palestinians, over the course of many decades."

After Imam Subedar's post–October 7 Op-Ed, a college administrator I respected and to whom I had sent the article told me that Imam Subedar's views reflected his own. My first impulse was to sever all ties with this person; I told myself that he had revealed something true about himself that was unacceptable to me as a Jew. Obviously, this reaction was contrary to the approach that Imam

Subedar and I advocate in this book. In the heat and angst of the conflict in the Middle East, I concede that our goal of engaging in a dialogue and establishing an understanding based on shared values is sometimes more easily said than done.

But as the days passed and Imam Subedar and I kept talking, I realized that I had no wish to cut ties with either my coauthor or my other associate. Despite everything, I still believe that human contact and understanding is the antidote to blind hate. Imam Subedar and I had built an understanding and a relationship that was able to survive the strain between our tribes. We valued each other as people, and so neither he nor I ultimately allowed the actions of others to destroy our relationship. Doing so would have played right into the hands of Hamas, whose attack is a living example of why dialogue is more essential than ever. The objective of Hamas is to sow regional conflict and disharmony—specifically, to disrupt the ongoing efforts of Arabs and Jews (i.e., Saudis and Israelis) to normalize their relations. The results, as predictable as they may have been, are horrific: innocent civilian hostages held in brutal condition, a massive ground invasion of Gaza by the Israel Defense Forces, further pain and hostility, and the deaths of tens of thousands of innocent people. Where this will end remains to be seen.

For example, what could have been more unthinkable than the suggestion by an American President that Palestininas be resettled from Gaza and that Gaza be developed as a luxury resort? This suggestion was particularly surprising in light of the support given by the American Muslim community to President Trump, who campaigned in Muslim communities on the promise of bringing peace to Gaza. The Muslim community rejected Joe Biden and his replacement, Kamala Harris, because they blamed "Genocide Joe" and all associated with him for America's failure to rein in the Israel Defense Forces. However, it was reported in *The New York Times* on March 18, 2025, that "Israel's hand in the talks has been strengthened in recent weeks by backing from the Trump administration, which has delivered more weapons to the country. The White House press secretary, Karoline Leavitt, said Israel had consulted the White House before launching the strikes." What will the Muslim response to President Trump be? As a Jew and an American, I am conflicted between the desire to see, at all costs, the hostages returned to Israel, Hamas defeated and expunged from Gaza, and the norms and guardrails that have safeguarded American democracy not cast aside for the sake of expediency.

For there to be any meaningful dialogue, both Muslims and Jews must find a way to consider the same set of critical facts. Without my ongoing exchanges with Imam Subedar, I would never have known that he was unaware of its charter, which I consider to be the single most important fact about Hamas. Only through conversation can both sides be certain that all the necessary information is known to all. That said, there may obviously be a disagreement as to what information is viewed by each as important or critical.

Along with the absence of critical information, harboring false information is equally destructive. Once lies are released into the ether, the cascade of false information too often achieves the desired effect—reaping alienation and hostility—even when correct information replaces it.

The Jewish people are well aware of what can happen when a lie is allowed to take hold. Hitler falsely blamed the Jews for Germany's loss in World War I, then used that lie to achieve political power and orchestrate the Holocaust. In America today, giving credence to the belief that the results of the 2020 presidential election were invalid has become a litmus test for Republican loyalty. History shows that false narratives can keep fury and hatred simmering for years.

Of course, for every individual (and tribe member), there are certain fundamental tenets that feel virtually unassailable. Abandoning those tenets, regardless of their veracity, can be tantamount to relinquishing membership in your tribe. What's important is to identify these deeply held tenets and subject them to honest dialogue. Only then can conversations with other tribes continue to move toward mutual understanding anchored in a shared reality.

In many respects, this book is an attempt to identify the Muslim narrative in order to help create better understanding between Muslims and non-Muslims and pave the way for meaningful dialogue. This is of course complicated by the reality that there is no one single Muslim narrative. Yet in the wake of the October 7 attacks on Israel, I must admit that I still sometimes find it difficult to talk with anyone outside of my tribe, my coauthor included, about what has transpired. Maybe that is because "others" don't share the narrative that is central to my identity—to my tribe. For instance, we as Jews have a commitment to humane behavior that stems, in part, from the centuries of persecution we have endured. As a result of this narrative, it will take a mountain of evidence for me to accept that my fellow Jews in Israel are intentionally inflicting unnecessary pain on the Palestinians out of malice, or that Israel is not harsher on the Palestinians than it needs to be for its own security. But a willingness to identify these tribal truths and narratives opens up the possibility that they will be abandoned if the evidence against them is solid and convincing.

It will take a few brave souls to breach the current barriers to true dialogue. I believe Imam Subedar is a man willing to take such risks. I am not always sure that I am.

CHAPTER 17

Exploring Solutions to Extremism

By Robert Gary

As Imam Subedar has explained, Islam is not monolithic; like every religion, it has its own internal struggles. He would agree that none of us has to accept the beliefs of others. We do, however, need to make the effort to understand religious practices that are different from our own rather than condemn them. Because of Imam Subedar's efforts to provide insights into the true nature of Islam, I've attempted to put my own skepticism of that faith aside. I'd always started from the premise that Islam was violent or, at least, problematic. Imam Subedar's arguments suggest to me that other interpretations are possible. I do fear that many Muslims are learning about their faith from extremist imams trained in Saudi Arabia by Wahhabis. And that, after reading the Quran without guidance from a scholar such as Imam Subedar, they try to put its sometimes harsh-seeming commands into practice. Religion is unique in that it doesn't require verifiable evidence. In the Abrahamic monotheistic faiths, the divine being communicates either through a sacred text and/or a spiritual leader. These sources, together with a personal relationship with God, are more powerful to the faithful than any scientific proof could be.

It follows, then, that if these beliefs are beyond question and are not subject to change, there is little to be done when some of them conflict with other groups or certain cultural norms. Our goal is to bring about tolerance through understanding despite those conflicts.

It is a fact that Islam remains "foreign" to most Americans, who know little of its theology and how it is practiced. That is one reason I have traveled the world to meet Muslims in their native lands of Egypt, United Arab Emirates, Bahrain, Qatar, Oman, Iran, Morocco, India, Israel and the West Bank, Jordan, Turkey, and beyond. Wherever I have gone, I have found the people I encountered to be gracious and amiable, living their lives just as the rest of the world does. Meanwhile, ignorance of Islam is widespread, and I witnessed it firsthand during a visit to the magnificent Sheikh Zayed Grand Mosque in Abu Dhabi. There is an area in that mosque where, in preparation for prayer, observant Muslims wash their feet. As I wandered through, awestruck by its beauty, I approached this area and found it being used as a urinal by a group of male tourists. Presumably, they knew nothing about Islam nor the practice of cleansing oneself before prayer and had mistaken this segregated area for a men's room, a mistake that could have led to violence. This defilement, however unintentional, could have been avoided if they had possessed even a basic familiarity with Islam and the concept of Muslims purifying themselves before prayer.

In that same mosque, I had the good fortune to meet with the English-speaking imam, and we had a thoughtful and balanced conversation about the Quran and Islam. Afterward, he got up, walked over, kissed me on the head, and said, "You're the most reasonable Jew I have ever met."

Over the years I have pondered this "compliment" and concluded that many Muslims' view of non-Muslims (and particularly of Jews) can be as closed-minded as most Americans' views of Muslims. And no wonder. As a not particularly observant Jew, I am aware of what some of the prayers and stories in our prayer books and services might sound like to non-Jews. I vividly recall sitting in my synagogue in Lorain, Ohio, years ago during the holiday of Passover, reading prayers about God slaying the firstborn sons of Egyptians. Next to me was a young Palestinian man, Faris Asad, who was my guest that evening. I recall thinking that the words he was hearing must have sounded barbaric. (Incidentally, Faris Asad went on to become the Consul General of the U.S. Consulate in Jeddah, Saudi Arabia.)

Ironically, it took writing this book for me to realize that my own Islamophobia was so ingrained in my psyche that I registered it as a truth rather than a prejudice. Because I was too intellectually lazy to push beyond what I thought I knew into what I truly did *not* know, my fear of Muslims flourished unabated. One example I look back on with chagrin: In 2011, as the only non-Muslim in my insular island community who had actually read the Quran, I was invited by my friend, Ruthie Maass, to speak about Islam to her book club. Ruthie is a rare jewel of a person who is intellectually curious and radiates an energy capable of lighting up the dark spaces we all possess. I reviewed for the assembled women the many violent and anti-Semitic passages in the Quran and patiently explained that since the Quran was Allah speaking, a Muslim was not free to ignore these passages and still call themselves a Muslim. What I didn't realize at the time was my own hypocrisy. As a Jew, I knew

I was free to take or leave the more extreme and violent passages of the Hebrew Bible and that doing so would not disqualify me as a Jew. Similarly, I took for granted that my Christian acquaintances and friends could continue being Christians whether or not they ignored some of the more antisocial and violent passages from the pages of their Bible. Yet I did not extend the same license to Muslims in terms of their ability to decline to "smite the infidel wherever you find them" and still be a Muslim in good standing. I merely read the Quran (in translation) in full (which is more than I ever read of the Jewish or the Christian Bible), listened to the daily barrage of "Islamic"-inspired atrocities being broadcast in the news, and decided not to give my Muslim neighbors the benefit of the doubt. It was Ruthie who, during that book session, gently pointed out my hypocrisy, noting that every religious text contains violent passages that are not followed literally. *Why would Islam be different?* she asked. And still, I stuck to my guns, smugly explaining that Islam was different because the Quran was considered to be the "actual" word of God and still is to this day.

I have thought back to Ruthie's challenge many times since then. Thanks in large part to my friend and coauthor Imam Subedar, my perspective has evolved. For one thing, he has written this book despite the fact that it could pose real danger for him and his family, and I admire him for his courage. Recently, we were discussing this danger, and I said, half-jokingly, "You can always come live in my basement, but I don't have a basement." His response was, "Well, in that case, you may have to build one." As I witness his strength, integrity, and good humor, I know there is hope for us all.

I share these anecdotes because to me, they accentuate the need for this book. I am grateful, too, for my coauthor, who offers a bridge to understanding. He also makes the point that Islam and terrorism are not synonymous. Unfortunately, the actions of a few have created a backlash against all Muslims. If *I Am the Other* pushes just one reader to see that not all of our Muslim neighbors are potential recruits for ISIS, the book will have been a success.

Of course, certain stark cultural differences between Islam and the West remain, differences brought into sharp relief by Imam Subedar's candid explanation of Sharia and some of its controversial tenets, particularly regarding women and marriage. His words are a testament to his honesty and his unwavering goal of providing insight into the minds of practicing Muslims, even if those insights make non-Muslim readers uncomfortable. Imam Subedar also writes proudly of the Caliphate, considered one of the golden eras of Islamic history, when science and learning flourished. One of the greatest assaults on Muslims has been the tarnishing of this heritage, some of it done by Muslims (or those who declare themselves to be Muslims). For 1,200 years, until 1924, the Islamic State was led, at least technically, by a Caliph. Then, in 2014, Abu Bakr al-Baghdadi, the leader of ISIS, claimed to be forming a modern Caliphate from the Great Mosque of al-Nuri in Mosul and named himself the new Caliph.

The ISIS sham of a Caliphate lasted only three years (roughly between 2014 and 2017), until the territory ISIS held was liberated by the U.S. army and the terrorists were driven out. Yet the damage to Islam's proud history was already done, given that the term *Caliphate* is now associated with a terrorist state that executed and beheaded "infidels" to further their goal of installing their version of Islam by force. For non-Muslims, the Caliphate and ISIS are now inextricably linked.

Take the example of the 2020 Netflix series *Caliphate*, which focuses on the horrific treatment of women under the new ISIS regime. As I watched the series, I thought about how offended I'd be if there were a similar Netflix series depicting Jews plotting to take over the world, as is falsely depicted in the infamous (and untrue) anti-Semitic screed *The Protocols of the Elders of Zion*. The latter was published in 1905 but has since been translated into many languages. This fabricated tale of powerful Jews plotting to control the world has been a bestseller in Egypt and other parts of the Muslim world and is accepted by many as authentic. The difference is, if Netflix decided to produce a series based on *The Protocols of the Elders of Zion*, there would likely be an outcry that would quickly result in boycotts and the show being canceled after an episode or two. I expect and hope this would most likely still be the case, even though at the time of this writing, the demonization of Jews is moving frighteningly into the mainstream. However, there was no such outcry when *Caliphate* aired because most people considered it to be accurate.

To be clear, I am not suggesting that we ban TV shows that portray ISIS (or any group) as violent extremists. My point is that the bias against Muslims in American popular culture serves to isolate them and make them targets of derision and prejudice. Islam is clearly different from Judaism and Christianity. Yet it is also distorted for reasons that lie beneath the surface. The resulting isolation makes it easier for Muslims to turn away from the mainstream, and it can become a source of radicalization, particularly for alienated young Muslims who see themselves as having a target on their backs for merely practicing their faith.

One of the goals of Al Qaeda, ISIS, Hamas, and the like is to create conflict between Muslims and the non-Muslim world. Our media and entertainment industries unintentionally further that goal. *I Am the Other* is our attempt to shed light, not pour gasoline, on the problem of extremism while showing the "real" Islam, not the violent, Islamophobic versions that the media and entertainment industries and extremists themselves would have us believe.

Imam Subedar's frank discussion of what life has been like for Muslims living in the U.S. after 9/11 is a potent reminder that moderates of all stripes need to stand together against the common threat posed by the most extreme and intolerant members of any group. In today's world, the truth often seems to be a choice we make based on what fits our personal narrative. And when the truth is twisted to what is convenient or politically expedient, the effects are corrosive to society and often threatening to its people. Authoritarians want their own truth, and when they achieve it, the consequences can be deadly. As early as February of 1933, an article was published in a Nazi publication, the *Völkischer Beobachter,* urging Germany to get rid of its "Jewish vermin." For Jews, anyone who seeks to deny the mass murder of 6 million feels like an existential threat to our existence. For the same reason, Jews must not foster the lie that all Muslims are extremists seeking to undermine Western civilization.

Nor should we fall victim to the trap that there are no shades of gray in even the most extreme situations. We all want the lines dividing right from wrong, and moral from immoral, to be bright and clear. Most important, we want our heroes and villains to be easily discernible. Al Qaeda was the villain on 9/11, when all Americans were understandably shocked and appalled by the unprovoked attack on the World Trade Center. However, what of the American government telling people in New York the air was safe to breathe before the Environmental Protection Agency had all the facts? Or that the White House may have had a hand in toning down statements regarding the potential risks from exposure to the dust from 9/11? These concerns are documented in the EPA Inspector General's highly critical 2003 report about 9/11 and the agency. EPA Administrator Christine Todd Whitman assured the public that airborne contaminants were not a concern, when testing revealed that asbestos levels at the site were double or triple the level considered dangerous by the EPA. This false information caused direct harm to me, my family, and many others. Yet all of our collective anger continues to be directed at Islam and its adherents long after 9/11, while the harm caused by our government is barely a footnote. One act does not excuse the other, but it illustrates how it is human nature to blame the other while dismissing our own failings as insignificant.

Imam Subedar and I strive to speak the truth to each other, and in *I Am the Other*, we have aimed to create a safe space in which to speak those truths. Being a truth seeker requires seeking out the facts and accepting them regardless of the consequences. That is what we have tried our utmost to do.

CHAPTER 18
Lies and Conspiracy Theories

By Robert Gary

I t is undeniable that lies and conspiracy theories have power.

Shortly before the solar eclipse in early April of 2024, I got a call from Imam Subedar, who told me that the Muslim world was buzzing with a story that sounded crazy to my ears. Apparently, five red heifers were donated by an evangelical farmer from Texas and sent to Israel. The most unblemished heifer, he explained, would be sacrificed some time after the solar eclipse, then, afterward, the Al-Aqsa Mosque in Jerusalem would be demolished by Israelis. Imam Subedar said that rumors were circulating in the Muslim world that after the mosque was destroyed, the Third Temple of Jerusalem (thought to be the site where Jews worshiped in ancient Israel) would be rebuilt on that very spot.

The Al-Aqsa Mosque, located in the Old City, was the second Islamic place of worship and is mentioned in the Quran as being "holy." Muhammed directed his followers to face toward this mosque during prayer, until Allah changed the direction, making Mecca the focal point. A few hundred yards from the Mosque is the

Dome of the Rock, where, according to Jewish tradition, Abraham bound Issac for sacrifice and where the Temple of Jerusalem once stood. That site is holy for Muslims as well: The Dome of the Rock is where Muhammed is believed to have risen to heaven.

These sites have long been a source of great friction between Jews and Muslims, and the destruction of this mosque by Israel would undoubtedly spark waves of violence between Muslims and Jews all over the world. Indeed, as Imam Subedar further explained to me, this alleged plan to destroy the Al-Aqsa Mosque may have been what prompted Hamas to attack Israel on October 7, 2023.

My first response to his story, as I have said, was to write it off as insane. But when I began searching online, I saw that news items about this supposedly forthcoming event were everywhere (except the news sources I typically frequented). After our call, I promptly emailed articles I'd found to Rabbi Mark Winer, a recognized interfaith activist and scholar who had been appointed by Queen Elizabeth as a Member of the Order of the British Empire. A few minutes later, he called me back to say that he was aware of these stories but, like me, thought they were nuts. He went on to explain that the legend of the red heifer originated with the Jews and was linked to the rebuilding of the Third Temple (the ashes of a red heifer were apparently a crucial element in restoring Biblical purity and thus allowing for the rebuilding.) This, too, Rabbi Winer described as "nuts," just like the Muslim conspiracy theories that were swirling around regarding the impending destruction of the Al-Aqsa Mosque. Whether the red heifers were actually in Israel or not, what we know for certain is that the mosque was not attacked and is still standing after the eclipse.

Spreading lies for political purposes is nothing new, be it Islamophobes branding the entire Muslim American community as terrorists or Al Qaeda and ISIS asserting that their barbaric violence is authorized by the Quran.

Muslims and Jews alike should be alarmed when *any* community is targeted for political purposes. During the 2024 presidential election, a rumor began circulating that Haitian immigrants, living legally in Springfield, Ohio, were eating the pet cats and dogs of their neighbors. When someone uses their access to traditional media or the Internet to undermine trust and demonize segments of the population for political purposes, you can be sure that democracy itself is under attack. That's why I decided to drive the three hours from my home in Sandusky, Ohio, to Springfield in order to visit the Rose Goute Creole Restaurant, which is owned and run by a Haitian woman who had legally relocated to this Ohio town. What I found when I arrived was a no-frills restaurant whose customers were largely Hatians. The women behind the counter spoke no English, but luckily, the menu had pictures. I pointed to the roasted goat but was actually served deep-fried chicken.

After a leisurely lunch, I proceeded to downtown Springfield, which was empty except for one young man with an elaborate camera setup who was photographing City Hall. I strolled over, engaged him in conversation, and expressed my concern over the false stories that were circulating about his town—that Haitians there were eating the dogs and cats. To my surprise, he responded that the stories were true, citing a social media influencer he trusted. Scapegoating has been used throughout history and is used today to disenfranchise Muslims, Jews, and, now, Haitians. So yes, I care that Trump and Vance spread the lie that Hatiatians are eating people's pets in Springfield, Ohio.

The Internet, social media, and artificial intelligence are making it all too easy to perpetuate lies like this one. In the time it takes to make lunch, it's possible to influence millions of people with toxic disinformation. Yet, incredibly enough, there is no universally trusted resource where people can go to help separate fact from fiction.

In an attempt to fill this gap, Imam Subedar and I have a proposal. We propose a nonprofit fact-finding body made up of highly respected individuals from diverse faiths, cultures, and backgrounds to analyze information and investigate conspiracy theories and rumors that impact Muslim-Jewish relations in the Middle East and beyond. The goal: to provide support for accurate statements and to debunk lies, propaganda, and misinformation before more wars are started and lives lost.

This group would have a multinational board composed of those who have earned a reputation for honesty, integrity, and, most critically, an unrestrained passion for the truth. These individuals might come from academia, the business world, or other sectors. The only criterion is a willingness to serve without compensation or political agendas. Their only mandate is to seek the facts and serve the truth.

We would seek funding from private sources or foundations that would agree not to interfere with the independence of the mission. Much of the work could be done remotely, but the board would meet in person at rotating locations to create the necessary trust and harmony to make the project work.

We envision prioritizing issues for review that, if left unchecked, could exacerbate biases or lead to open hostility, violence, or even armed conflict between Jews and Muslims.

The board would prepare an unbiased report on the issue, providing supporting source material for the conflicting views and the findings. In the Wild West that is cyberspace, the media has been polarized and politicized and, perhaps, intimidated, and even longtime consumers of legacy news outlets no longer trust their preferred newspapers. If we lose the ability to agree on what is true, extremism and hate win and democracy loses.

Imam Subedar and I have some other ideas, too, including what we are calling a blueprint for civility and understanding. Think of it as a set of rules for human interaction that will help lead the world away from the abyss we seem to be hurtling toward. We hope that you, our readers, will consider these and make civility, not suspicion, the starting point when encountering people from different cultures and religions. We have also proposed some simple guidelines for building bridges between people. Too often, the alternative is to condemn the other based solely on appearance or what you think you know about who they are. All we ask is that the benefit of the doubt be given to the stranger and that our rules be applied if they fit the situation.

CHAPTER 19

A Proposed Blueprint for Civility and Understanding

By Robert Gary and Imam Azhar Subedar

- Do not assign collective guilt to a whole group because of the actions of a few.
- Do not personalize disagreements, whether they arise from politics, policy, or tribal loyalties.
- Take the time to learn the history behind any conflict.
- Throw out your past assumptions when you're approaching new situations and groups.
- When you encounter unfamiliar opinions and viewpoints, research their credibility (or the credibility of their messenger) before you embrace them.
- Be aware of your own biases and prejudices. We all have them.
- Pause before you automatically reject information that disproves your viewpoint.

- Read a variety of news sources, not just those that provide support for your views.

- Develop personal relationships with people who hold opposing views and endeavor to have some honest conversations with them.

- Do not assume someone you disagree with is considering the same "truths" that you are.

- If possible, determine what "facts" you hold in common and which are in opposition.

- Agree to determine which information is most likely accurate in an objective fashion, say, by asking for sources to determine if they are credible. If the source is an organization with an obvious bias or an individual with an axe to grind, share what you have found. You may be surprised to find that reasonable and informed discussions can lead to a reasonable and informed result.

- Take the time to understand the nature of, and reasons for, the other person's values.

- Treat the values of "the other" with respect and demonstrate appreciation. Even if you don't share those values, it doesn't mean that they are wrong and you are right. Remind yourself that shades of gray exist, and in that area of ambiguity may lie the solution for a compromise.

- Seek to identify and eliminate societal influences that perpetuate division and hostility. (Classic examples are the simple narratives of Jewish oppressors versus the oppressed Palestinians; Arab versus Jew; and the simplistic message that Muslims seek world domination through the sword.)

- Whatever the issue, take the long view. Consider whether short-term gains would justify the potential loss of the freedoms provided by democracy.

- Prioritize finding a path forward that minimizes the loss of life and eliminates the threat of future violence.

It would be naive and simplistic to suggest that following these guidelines will make a difference in a global way. That's because in most instances, parties in conflict are not motivated to understand and coexist with their opponents but would rather win (and, if necessary, inflict pain and retribution on those who stand in the way of their desires). But progress *can* be found in small steps, starting with individual conversations that build trust rather than hostility. One example that comes to mind was a gathering that took place in January of 2017, before a packed audience at a mosque in Longwood, Florida. Imam Subedar and a local pastor had just finished a talk on opening channels of communication between Muslims and non-Muslims. Afterward, everyone mingled, getting to know the people outside of their faith community. That's when Imam Subedar noticed a tall, husky man in overalls, looking none too friendly, making a beeline for him. But instead of the expected confrontation, the man stuck out his hand and introduced himself, warmly saying, "Thanks for doing this. Every night, I go to sleep with my gun by my side 'cause I feared you people would come and kill my family. Now that I know you are not, I can sleep peacefully."

Another conversation worth mentioning is one that Bob Gary had on a plane, in April of 2024. His seat neighbor, a man who introduced himself as Tony, saw him working on this book and asked what he was doing. When Bob explained, Tony asked which side he was on—that of the Muslims or the Jews.

Bob explained that the book didn't take sides but tried to provide information so that whatever position readers ended up taking, it would be based on information. Tony promptly responded: "I know all I need to know, and the Muslims are a problem."

When Bob asked what Tony knew about Islam, he replied that his knowledge was pretty much limited to the fact that Muslims were responsible for 9/11. The two then proceeded to have an engaging conversation about the book, with Tony insisting that it was imperative to take a side and Bob pushing back that whatever side someone takes, it should not be based on emotion but credible facts that allow for informed judgments. As the plane landed, Tony said, "This is the most interesting conversation I have ever had on a plane."

These are only two isolated conversations, but to our mind, they open a world of possibility. When talking to anyone who seems "other," if the default could be changed from defensive and hostile to open and cautiously receptive, the positive outcomes the two of us experienced in our two encounters could be multiplied by tens of thousands. You, too, can choose to be part of the solution by having these reasoned conversations. They are a small but effective way to stave off hate. Haters tend to hate in groups, often in chat rooms and on social media platforms, or at rallies that celebrate their common bond. It's a team sport. The only way to defeat hate is with reasoned, respectful conversations that lead to knowledge and understanding.

The more time you spend interacting with the object of your hate, the greater the chances that empathy will prevail. As your authors, we hope you have observed the potentially curative nature of open conversation, because it's conversation that allowed the two of us to continue our work, despite a war that nearly divided us.

We need to amplify the voices of reason and understanding, voices that are too often drowned out in a world consumed with conflict. If we continue to cling to our respective tribes, consciously or unconsciously excluding everyone we perceive as different, chaos is the inevitable result. Instead, we must recognize and celebrate our differences as part of the human condition. This is a reciprocal obligation. Muslims must not demonize and attack Jews because of their religion, nor should Jews condemn Muslims for their faith. When two peoples are contesting the rights to the same land, conflict is inevitable, but does this conflict necessarily have to extend well beyond the area in dispute to every Muslim and Jew? We say no.

Shariah law may feel "different" to many non-Muslim readers. Yet those in the West can coexist with any fellow citizen who respects and follows the laws of their home country, even as they are guided and inspired by Sharia (or the teachings of any faith). The challenge is not to eliminate our differences but to understand and respect them and still remain neighbors.

If you've read this far and gained increased understanding and tolerance, know that you are making that reality possible. As a Muslim and a Jew, we choose for our final words in this book some of the first official words of the newly elected Pope Leo XIV: "God loves everyone; evil will not prevail"—a message that unites Christians, Muslims, and Jews.

Glossary

Allah

Allah = One God

Muslims believe in one God. The word *Allah* is not a name. It is the Arabic word for "God."

Athar

An athar is the word of a companion of the Prophet Muhammad, and not the word of Muhammad himself.

Fatwa

A fatwa refers to a prescription made by a qualified individual—i.e., a qualified mufti—under the framework of Islamic law. When written by a mufti, a fatwa is meant to address a predicament or situation that has no clear prescription or explanation in the Quran or Hadith. A mufti will use their understanding of the religion from these two sources while also considering current matters of the day, thereby providing context and a path forward for the one seeking clarity. A fatwa is not legally binding to the one to whom it is prescribed, and it doesn't apply to all Muslims. Furthermore, anyone who doesn't fit the description of a mufti isn't allowed to give a fatwa. If someone who isn't qualified, like Osama bin Laden or Abu Bakr al-Baghdadi, claims to give a fatwa, then under

Shariah, their word should rightly be seen as their opinion rather than fatwa.

Hadith

Hadith is a compilation of the words and actions of Muhammad (*peace be upon him*), often used as a resource.

Contrary to what some may assume, the Quran isn't a compilation of Prophet Muhammad's words or actions, nor is it the story of his life. The correct term for the writings that comprise the Prophet Muhammad's words and actions is *Hadith*, an Arabic word meaning "conversation" or "speech." The Hadith includes descriptions taken from eyewitnesses—people known as the companions of Muhammad, who relayed the lifestyle, practices, and actions of the Prophet Muhammad, in addition to his words. Unlike the disciples of Jesus, these companions are anyone who lived during the time of Muhammad and saw him in person, had faith in his message, and died a Muslim. From amongst the 100,000-plus companions, a select number noted Muhammad's life, words, and ways, then passed these on to others, who then did the same. Even when the first few generations beyond the companions of Muhammad were gone, a Hadith could still be traced back to the original companion who transmitted it, via a process of documentation known as a "chain of narrators." Specifically, each Hadith has a chain of custody starting from the author who compiled it all the way back to the original companion who transmitted what they learned directly from the Prophet Muhammad and everyone who narrated it in between. Collectively, they form that chain of narrators.

When a reference is made in this book to a Hadith, it will be labeled with the book name followed by the Hadith number. For example:

(*Hadith, Bukhari 1*). In the Sunni Muslim world, Bukhari is widely considered to be the most authentic compilation of the six canonical books of Hadith available, primarily because of the strength of the chain of narrators (i.e., people who transmitted its narrations). Named after the Persian scholar Muḥammad ibn Ismail al-Bukhari (810–870), widely known as Imam Bukhari, this book is notable not only for its intellectual integrity, but for the authenticity of its transmitters, who were committed to preserving and transmitting Muhammad's words correctly, and who practiced what they preached.

Other books from the six canonical or well-known books of Hadith include Muslim, named after the Persian scholar Muslim ibn al-Hajjaj (815–875), and Tirmidhi, collected by Al-Tirmidhi.

Aside from the six, there are more than 40 other major books of Hadith. All in all, more than 140,000 Hadith are preserved between their covers.

Halakhah

The Jewish term Halakhah means "the way we walk" on this earth (implying the proper way to conduct our lives via Halakhah—the legal system that governs our actions).

Imam

Imam is the title for an Islamic spiritual leader of a community or society, often—and preferably—a scholar of the faith. This term is commonly used by Sunnis to describe the person who simply leads prayers in the mosque, while Shiites reserve this title for those whom they hold in high esteem in the faith, whether imams or clerics.

Islamophobia

Irrational fear of, aversion to, or discrimination against Islam or people who practice Islam.

Mufti

Mufti is the title for someone who has not only obtained a formal degree to become a scholar of Islam (i.e., one who has mastered the 15 essential sciences to correctly understand the Quran and Hadith in their true framework), but who has also studied a few more years beyond that to direct the course of modern-day Islamic jurisprudence, including with the ability to write fatwas.

Prophet/Messenger

In Islam, a prophet is someone selected by Allah to uphold and propagate the religion or a new message. Prophets include John (Yahya), Jonah (Yunus), and Jacob (Yaqoob). A messenger, on the other hand, is someone Allah has sent with a new divine revelation, such as Jesus (Isa), Moses (Musa), and Muhammad (peace be upon all of them). Muslims are instructed to revere and respect all of these prophets and messengers, including when simply reciting their names. That's why, when a Muslim utters or reads the name of any prophet or messenger, and they believe in all of them as they are instructed to, they say, *"Peace be upon him,"* out of honor, admiration, and respect.

Quran

Quran = Holy Book

To Muslims, the Quran is the direct word of Allah. It was revealed over the course of 23 years via the angel Gabriel to the Prophet Muhammad (*peace be upon him*), who was assigned by Allah to be the final prophet sent on this earth. The Quran is a continuation of the books containing God's word—i.e., the Zabur (Book of Psalms), the Tawrat (Torah), and the Injil (the revelation given to Jesus by Allah, the Gospel of Jesus, part of today's Christian Bible). It contains stories of the previous prophets, injunctions of morality, commandments for living daily life, and information on future events.

The Quran is recited by believers as an act of worship both inside and outside of the prescribed prayers, which happen five times a day. The Quran itself is divided into 114 *surahs*, or chapters, which are further divided into verses—over 6,000 of them. When reference is made to particular passages in the Quran, it will be set in parentheses. For example, (19:20) refers to chapter 19, verse 20— in both the Arabic and English versions of the Quran.

Radical Islamist/Islamic Extremist

Someone who takes the name of Islam to validate their terrorizing actions or sentiments.

It may surprise many to learn that a person cannot be both a Muslim and an extremist. That's because the two terms contradict each other. Islam is a path of moderation. Extremism in the faith is shunned in Islam. Today, however, the terms *"radical Islamist"* and *"Islamic extremist"* are commonly used to describe an individual who harbors extremist beliefs and exhibits radical behaviors, then justifies those beliefs and behaviors by associating them with the Islamic religion. In doing so, they are expressing their ignorance of Islam's true nature and taking the Quran out of context.

Shariah

In Arabic, Shariah originates from the root ش ر ع , which literally means "to begin" / "to set about" / "to enter upon." Another meaning is "to explain." More specifically, Shariah is defined as "a path, explained by God (Allah) to its followers (Muslims), that leads one to a successful life in this world and the Hereafter, also known as the laws that guide a Muslim's life—Islam." Basically, Shariah is divine legislation, and Islam is the practice of it. Faith/belief (*imaan*) is required for the acceptance of those actions by Allah.

Sunnah

The practices and lifestyle of Muhammad, passed down by Muhammad's companions, are known as the *sunnah*. For any Muslim to live a complete Islamic life, they must strive to live their life in accordance with the sunnah, from how they eat and sleep to how they conduct themselves throughout their lives.

TaNaKh

The TaNaKh is the Jewish Scriptures comprising the books of law, the prophetic books, and the collected writings. The Torah is the first five books of the Hebrew Bible, while the TaNaKh is the whole Hebrew Bible.

We invite you to visit iamtheother.org to explore our journey through photographs, find the appendix related to the references made within this book, and much more.

Appreciation

We want to extend a heartfelt thank you to everyone who took the time to read this book, including you. We would also like to recognize, beyond thanking, some of the many folks who read this book when it was still in manuscript form. These individuals are as follows:

Rabbi Peter Kasdan

(Bob): I want to thank my friend and tennis partner, Rabbi Emeritus Peter Kasdan, for his insightful comments on our book. Rabbi Kasdan was Rabbi of Temple Emanu-El in Livingston, New Jersey, for 30 years. He was President of the Scholarship Fund for Ethiopian Jews and the Rabbinic Advisor of the Jewish Genetic Disease Consortium. He has received numerous awards, including the Union of Reform Judaism Distinguished Service Award and the Central Conference of American Rabbis' Rabbi Samuel Cook Award for Lifetime Service to Youth Work. He captured our book's essence when he wrote, "Millions of people need to read this book if we are to make this country a better, more accepting, and less rejecting place."

Fisal Khan

(Azhar): I want to extend my gratitude to someone I am proud to call my uncle, Fisal Khan. He recently retired as a teacher in British Columbia, where he taught history and social studies for 18 years. A graduate in International Studies from York University, he completed a master's degree at the University of Toronto and a B.Ed. in Education. He also spent four years in a Ph.D. program specializing in American foreign policy. His passion is to write and understand the changing dynamics of our global system and the United States' role in it. He took the time to read the book and provide us with his honest feedback. He said, "The journey through life, whether it is embracing faith or secularism, is a complex one and a brave endeavor. Both Azhar and Robert have risen to the challenge and provided us with a rich and detailed tapestry of their knowledge that is also very relevant today."

In addition to Rabbi Kasdan and Professor Khan, various religious leaders, including several Islamic scholars, imams, and rabbis, have reviewed the book to assure religious integrity. While respecting their privacy, we acknowledge their contribution.

Epilogue

Just before publication, Israel deployed 200-plus planes to destroy Iran's nuclear program. Iran responded with missile strikes. It is only too clear that the Middle East experiences events of potentially worldwide significance almost daily. Our book is intended not as a chronicle of these events but as a framework or an example of how dialogue can and must be sustained between Muslims and Jews. This need for continued dialogue is all the greater during times of escalated conflict.

Our collective responsibility is to provide the seeds of rationality, and those of us who are not in the heat of battle may be in the best position to do so. In speaking to one another and seeking ways to end the killing and oppression, we are not supporting "the other side" but expressing our love for our people. When individual human beings initiate—and maintain—open conversations across a divide, no matter the changing circumstances, they are engaging in one-on-one diplomacy.

Acknowledgments

My brother once advised me to focus on what I want to accomplish in life. He told me that some people are so motivated by whatever cause is important to them that they will sacrifice everything to achieve it. What life has taught me, however, is that the ultimate sacrifice is often made by those surrounding that individual—the people who voluntarily sacrifice themselves and their time to help the individual achieve their goals.

Over the years my coauthor and I took to write this book, my family was there for me as I fought my personal battles to bring this project to completion. I am deeply grateful for their allowing and encouraging me to pursue my passion.

I also extend heartfelt gratitude to all those who took precious time to read this book and provide valuable feedback. These readers include Muslims, non-Muslims, imams, and rabbis, and their constructive criticism and comments were invaluable. I am also grateful to those who contribute to the O'People Foundation, helping me defray the costs associated with writing this book.

Lastly, Michelle, Paula, and Marli, our prominent editors, spent countless hours imparting valuable gems and asking us tough questions, going far beyond their task to edit this book. The book is where it is because of each of you. Thank you.

—*Azhar Subedar*

During the multiple years the book has been in process, my wife, Karen, indulged my long hours in front of the computer, my friends agreed to read selected passages, and various rabbis and Jewish community leaders provided insight into Jewish issues and even my role in this project as a secular Jew. In particular, I thank DJ Young for his much-needed insight into the Christian community, and my grandson, Andrew, for his indispensable contribution to the cover design.

It is our editors, however, whom I single out for my deepest thanks. Our first editor, Michelle Levy, began the process of converting random snippets into the beginnings of a book. After that, our brilliant and thoughtful editor Paula Derrow took our hand and skillfully led us step by step, topic by topic, rewrite by rewrite. Quite simply, there would be no book without Paula. I can't count the number of times I said to Imam Subedar, "She is so good." Paula, your imprint is on every page, and I am grateful we found you. Marli Higa was the last to join the team, but she exceeded our already high expectations.

—Bob Gary

About the Authors

Robert (Bob) Gary served as a state and federal prosecutor, a Special Assistant to the Governor of Ohio, and a trial attorney. During his 13-year career in the U.S. criminal justice system, he prosecuted murderers and rapists at the local level; at the federal level, he worked in the U.S. Department of Justice as a federal prosecutor in charge of major investigations and prosecutions of Mafia figures and corrupt labor leaders. Gary also directed a state agency that formulated policies designed to combat organized crime and provided special assistance to the governor of Ohio on criminal justice issues. He is deeply interested in American politics and is a passionate advocate for democracy and the rule of law.

Azhar Subedar is an Islamic scholar with a master's degree in Islamic Sciences and Arabic Literature from the Institute of Islamic Education and over two decades of experience in leading Muslim communities in America. He is also passionate about engaging and teaching non-Muslims, whether religious leaders of different faiths or elected officials. He has been invited by both Republicans and Democrats to lead prayers at significant political events.